THE
VOCATIONAL-GUIDANCE MOVEMENT

ITS PROBLEMS AND POSSIBILITIES

BY

JOHN M. BREWER

HEAD OF THE DEPARTMENT OF PSYCHOLOGY AND EDUCATION
LOS ANGELES STATE NORMAL SCHOOL
FORMERLY INSTRUCTOR IN EDUCATION, HARVARD UNIVERSITY
AUTHOR OF "ORAL ENGLISH"
AUTHOR, WITH ROY WILLMARTH KELLY, OF
"A SELECTED CRITICAL BIBLIOGRAPHY OF VOCATIONAL GUIDANCE"

New York
THE MACMILLAN COMPANY
1925

Norwood Press
J. S. Cushing Co. — Berwick & Smith Co.
Norwood, Mass., U.S.A.

To

E. G. B.

PREFACE

VOCATIONAL guidance is bound up first of all with educational problems, and second with economic and social questions. On this account the reader must not expect a book on the subject to offer anything like a complete program or solution of the problem. The breadth of the field considered in this book, however, should prove a distinct advantage to those readers who are willing to set aside the desire for short cuts and to work out thoughtful proposals for bettering hopeful but inadequate pioneering on the one hand and complete neglect on the other.

If the movement for vocational guidance has so far proved but one thing, it is that the indefinite education for the vague thing called "complete living" or "physical, mental, and moral development" must give way to a well-considered aiming at specific needs — needs such as those represented by the individual's right, duty, and desire to fulfill family relationships, to vote intelligently, to maintain a good standard of living, and to coöperate in all phases of endeavor for human good. These specialized trainings are by no means narrow; it is the indefinite education which has been narrow.

Vocational guidance must be considered as different from vocational education; the latter is concerned with but one of the steps in adequate guidance, but its advocates have too often neglected the other steps in the complete series. This complete series, so far as the individual is concerned, may be stated as follows: (1) Laying a broad foundation of useful experiences; (2) Studying occupational opportunities; (3) Choosing an occupation; (4) Preparing for the occupation; (5) Entering upon work; (6) Securing promotions and making readjustments.

As a civic force, vocational guidance is concerned with increasing the knowledge of occupational problems, as a necessary basis for their coöperative solution. As a moral force, the counselor must inculcate not only the personal virtues needed in the successful pursuit of one's calling, but also the social helpfulness based on the understanding that the coöperative opportunities are greater than the competitive, and on the theory of society, "We are members one of another." As an agent of culture, vocational guidance seeks for harmonious and refined living in street, store, factory, shop, farm, and mine, as well as in the literary society and at the fireside.

This book is offered as a contribution to the preparation for the task ahead of us: it is the hope of the writer that it may become a part of the literature of the reconstruction.

I thank Professor Paul H. Hanus for his guidance and criticism during the course of the investigation, and the other members of the Division of Education of Harvard University for occasional assistance and suggestion.

Mr. Meyer Bloomfield gave me the benefit of his wide experience in the movement. Mr. Frederick J. Allen read the manuscript and offered valuable help. Miss Susan J. Ginn gave information relative to the work in Boston. Counselors in various parts of the country contributed by detailed replies to my requests for further enlightenment about their work. Edith Gaddis Brewer assisted throughout the study.

Economy in publication has been aided by an abbreviation of the footnotes. In all cases the proper names refer directly to the Bibliography, Appendix II. Three books to which constant reference is made in the text and the footnotes are as follows: Bloomfield's *Youth, School, and Vocation* and *Readings in Vocational Guidance;* and Davis' *Vocational and Moral Guidance.*

JOHN M. BREWER.

Los Angeles,
California.

CONTENTS

CHAPTER   PAGE
   I THE PROBLEMS OF VOCATIONAL GUIDANCE   .   .   1
  II BEGINNINGS IN VOCATIONAL GUIDANCE .   .   .   20
 III VOCATIONAL GUIDANCE THROUGH EDUCATIONAL
        GUIDANCE   53
  IV VOCATIONAL COUNSELING AND THE WORK OF THE
        COUNSELOR   97
   V PSEUDO-GUIDANCE   143
  VI THE YOUNG WORKER   178
 VII THE PROBLEMS OF EMPLOYMENT   199
VIII A PROGRAM FOR VOCATIONAL GUIDANCE   .   . 227

APPENDICES
   I GLOSSARY OF TERMS   289
  II BIBLIOGRAPHY 292
 III PROBLEMS AND QUESTIONS   310

INDEX OF NAMES   325
INDEX OF SUBJECTS 328

xi

THE VOCATIONAL-GUIDANCE MOVEMENT

CHAPTER I

THE PROBLEMS OF VOCATIONAL GUIDANCE

THE purpose of this book is to make clear the problems with which the vocational-guidance movement deals; to examine and evaluate the attempts so far made to solve these problems in schools and in occupations; and to propose plans, in the light of what has already been accomplished, for the further progress of the movement. The purpose of this chapter is to scrutinize the definitions and assumptions which underlie vocational guidance as its activities are carried on to-day.

What is Vocational Guidance? — The common meaning of the two words in the phrase vocational guidance suggests that we are concerned with helping persons to choose, prepare for, enter into, and make progress in occupations. Such activities as the following, then, would be considered as exemplifying vocational guidance: giving information about commerce and industry, in order to help in the choice of an occupation or a job;

giving opportunity to discover talents, with the vocational choice in mind; advising pupils to enter this or that school, for the purpose of discovering their talents or preparing for an occupation; advising in regard to promotion, change of job, after-education, or advanced study; supervising the entrance into or progress in particular positions or chosen occupations.

We shall assume that the rendering of such help to young people fairly represents vocational guidance, and shall proceed to a study of the problems involved in the process.

The Importance of Vocational Guidance: One's Occupation as the Center of his Interest. — " For the great masses of men, life is organized around work," [1] and this is the reason why it is important that every child have adequate vocational guidance. Eliot shows " the value during education of the life-career motive." [2] He calls attention to the success with which the career motive is used in the professional schools, and in the lower schools wherever tried. He points out that there need be no danger of appealing too early to the career motive, since the child's interests may be kept broad, and since he may be left free to change his plans at any time, without serious difficulty.

The love that young children have for playing occupations, the interest shown by pupils in those studies which they think are " practical," and the activity manifested

---

[1] See bibliography, Appendix II, Greany, Bloomfield's *Readings*, p. 268.
[2] Bloomfield's *Readings*, pp. 1-12.

by children in making things, all indicate that if the adolescent boy or girl can be induced to select from five to ten occupations for consideration and study, his school work can be made to improve, his interest in observing the life about him increased, and his moral purposes deepened. Future family duties, possible activities of citizenship, moral and spiritual responsibilities, which still seem remote and hypothetical to the young mind — at least so far as the current modes of presenting these duties go — seem vague beside the effectiveness of the vocational appeal.

The Bearing of the Vocation on Life. — Not only is the vocational appeal an insistent and obvious one; it frequently enforces the other duties of life. Thus, the logic in the title of a publication in this field, *Vocational and Moral Guidance*, is that there can be no true success in the vocation without sound morals.[1]

Further, vocational guidance inculcates ideals of citizenship. Not only should the pupil be shown the economic values to the community in the kinds of work he is considering; he should also see how dependent he and his business or employment will be upon good government, just taxation, equal opportunity before the law, publicity in civic affairs, trustworthy sources of information, adequate recreational facilities, and a rectification

---

[1] Jesse B. Davis in this book cites the case of a boy who had all the mental and physical qualifications for a certain occupation, but failed through an uncontrolled temper (p. 87). Every counselor, as well as every enlightened employer, knows that certain qualities such as kindness, courtesy, and willingness to be of service are indispensable.

of economic injustices.   The boy with a career in mind is in a better position to study these things effectively.

The wise settlement of the question of vocation sets free other life interests, which then gain direction and impulse, and are allowed to proceed toward a well-rounded development.   If the question of occupation is unwisely settled, or left overlong unsettled, there may develop distrust, pessimism, and temptation, and finally immorality and bad citizenship.

The Need for Vocational Guidance is Obvious. — The writings on vocational guidance contain adequate discussions of the need for the work, and we shall say little on this topic here.   Bloomfield [1] justifies his term " vocational anarchy," and both he and Philip Davis show how the suggestions of the street now determine occupations for the young people.[2]   Such good studies of the need have been made that no student of the problem fails to see it as an urgent demand.[3]   Yet the public mind moves slowly, and the education of community opinion needs to be extended greatly.

The amount and character of the false guidance which goes on is proof enough that the schools and other educational agencies should take up the work.   Worse than quack medicines, because they poison the mind rather than the body, these attempts to give advice, and to charge money for it, are crying aloud to young

---

[1] *Youth*, etc., pp. 3–5.   [2] *Streetland*, Chs. 6 and 7.
[3] For a summary of the arguments on need, *see* Woods, in Bloomfield's *Readings*, pp. 30–31.

people just at the age when their desires for experimentation and self-discovery are greatest. In a prominent statistical annual, issued by a New York newspaper, and frequently used by high-school debaters, there are several advertisements which should cause concern to those interested in vocational guidance. One is headed, " strengthen your will " ; another offers to tell how to master others and make them do as you wish; another offers to read your life; three to teach hypnotism; another to build your memory so that it will never fail.

We have pointed out above that happiness, good citizenship, morality, and social usefulness are frequently bound up with the choice of a vocation. Such a momentous choice can no longer be left to chance.

What Vocational Guidance is not.   Attempts to Limit the Field. — No one step or operation in the systematic process of advising a person about his vocation can be singled out and labeled vocational guidance. We shall not quarrel with an attempt to discover which step is the most important, but we shall take exception to certain prevalent assumptions that the field is limited to any one act or any one period of the child's life. If the ordinary meanings of English words are to hold good here, no single step can be called " the heart of vocational guidance."

Placement Alone is not Adequate Vocational Guidance. — In the introductory statement of a recent article we find this sentence:

Indeed the act of placing a boy or girl in that job which will be suited to his or her abilities, future welfare, health, and happiness, might almost be offered as a definition of vocational guidance.[1]

Perhaps the "almost" should save the statement from challenge, but the definition is a prevalent one, and there are many so-called "vocational-guidance" officers, both in school departments and in other institutions, whose whole time is taken up with placement and the investigations necessary thereto.

We shall discuss in a later chapter the appropriate subordination of placement to other activities of vocational guidance (Chap. IV); our aim here is merely to point out that we cannot accept the statement that placement is almost the whole of guidance. Obvious needs, trustworthy experience, and good practice, as we shall see, as well as the meaning of words, prevent such a restricted definition.[2]

---

[1] Odencrantz, p. 169. Aside from the present issue on definition, one may fairly ask, Is there any one job which will satisfy these tests?

[2] The breadth of the field is shown by this extract from Bloomfield, *Youth, School, and Vocation* :

To some people, indeed, the placement features of vocational guidance are alone practical, while the efforts looking to a reorganization of school and vocational opportunity in terms of career-values, which may be said to be the mainspring of the vocational-guidance movement, appear to them as a commendable though rather remote ideal.

The truth is, however, that vocational guidance does concern itself with all the problems of work-getting, with helping children to a start in life in a way less wasteful than the present, and with active supervision of youth's vocational skirmishes (p. 158).

Guidance is not a Temporary Act. — One writer remarks:

Since vocational guidance has to do with the "start in life," and since it necessitates an articulation between the school and occupations, the time at which it may be exercised most intelligently is that at which the pupil leaves school.[1]

It is true that the writer of the foregoing quotation goes on to show that for some pupils he plans guidance before that time, and guidance after leaving for most of them. But does not the statement as it stands have the effect — unintentionally, no doubt — of limiting the application of vocational guidance to one period and one activity? A Cambridge lumber company uses in its advertising placards the expression, "Sudden Service." Such service may be rendered by a lumber company; can it be profitably rendered by a vocational counselor? Patent considerations point to the answer: If the program of vocational guidance is to be adequate to the great task with which it deals, it must provide for a study of the successes of the child during the years before he can possibly go to work. No other plan could yield the data necessary for guidance.

Further, the *school-leaving* time, with its atmosphere disturbed by many influences, is hardly the psychological

---

[1] Leavitt, Frank M., *The School Phases of Vocational Guidance*, p. 688. That the writer has a broad conception of the duty of vocational guidance is shown in his address at the Richmond Convention, as president of the National Vocational-Guidance Association, which see. See also his article in *The American Journal of Sociology.*

moment to apply systematic vocational guidance, even if it were possible to confine it to one period. Due to the very nature and complexity of the problems involved, vocational guidance cannot be satisfactory without a program which follows the development of the individual over a number of years.

Vocational Guidance is not merely "Practical" or "Idealistic." — In the article last quoted, the statement is made:

In developing a program for vocational guidance, therefore, we must distinguish clearly between the immediate and the ultimate purpose, and must realize that the "next step" is the most important consideration (p. 687).

No doubt this is just half the truth, and perhaps not the fundamental half. In counseling an individual child we could hardly say that the next step is a consideration more important than his ultimate goal. Such a policy would savor too strongly of the vaudeville song, "I don't know where I'm going, but I'm on my way !" We may fairly ask, Can the vocational-guidance movement, any more than an individual, afford to take next steps without first attempting to ascertain in what direction these steps lead? The two ideals must be irrevocably bound together. We do not need to slight the importance of one in holding in mind the other.

But it may be said that economic conditions make it impossible for the teacher to widen vocational opportunity, and that therefore he should concern himself rather with meeting practical situations as they exist to-day. It is said in the same article:

It is futile to talk about the value of the life-career motive in the guidance of this group, for most will have to be contented with "jobs" for many years, and perhaps may never enter upon a genuine "career" or "vocation." (The group referred to is "The group which leaves school at the termination of the compulsory age limit with about an eighth-grade training.") [P. 689.]

Undoubtedly school people need to pay more attention to practical aims and to practical education. At the same time, however, they need to add their influence to the forces working for civic, social, and political betterment. The child must not be set into a place and left to do all the conforming; he must be taught to apply his control to the forces which seem to hem him in. In order to show him how to do this, the teacher himself must participate in the control. In the words of Devine:

The omnipresent local social economist is the school. The assumption of social responsibility for poverty, disease, and crime clearly involves the transformation of the school. . . .

The social economist holds that the prevention of poverty, disease, and crime is the first, elementary, fundamental obligation of the public school system.[1]

Vocational Guidance must not Restrict Opportunity. — Closely related to the foregoing discussion is the question: Does vocational guidance aim to widen the opportunity for the " common people," or to restrict

[1] Quoted by President Leavitt, *Nat. Voc. Guidance Assn.*, 1914, p. 5.

it? For the query is frequently raised: After all, can there be a wide freedom of choice, at least for the greater number of children? According to Schneider [1] the number of " energizing " jobs is decreasing; how then, it is asked, can we be so shortsighted as to make more skilled workers? Shall we not, if we cling to democratic ideals, educate children for work they can never find? What guidance can we give those manifestly destined for the unskilled occupations? What shall we do — indeed, what can we do — for the child who leaves school to begin work at the end of the sixth or seventh grade? What shall we do with the boy with extravagant ambitions? Thus Sears expresses concern that some seventh and eighth grade boys had not yet decided upon an occupation:

Little can be said as to the meaning of this, but if it really means that that per cent [ten per cent] of boys are not pre-disposed toward some calling, then perhaps ",nurture" in place of "nature" must constitute itself the sole guide in the matter, and in the light of the industrial demand for workers, and its best judgment of child nature, train these boys to become responsible members of the community (p. 752).

and again:

The boys are to too large an extent aiming at something they can never reach. The function of the schools is first to rationalize those aspirations, and then to carry forward the present plans for occupational training suggested above, which the writer has observed in successful operation in at

[1] *Education for Industrial Workers*, pp. 9–11.

least one large vocational school in the city (Oakland). [P. 756.]

We shall deal with these issues later (Chap. V). For the present, however, we may note one or two objections, and indicate possible alternatives. First, there is no reason why seventh and eighth grade boys and girls should be required to decide on their occupations. Second, the school must avoid interfering with the plans of individuals, and must confine its efforts to other channels. Third, guidance cannot pass into prophecy — out of twenty would-be lawyers it will be impossible to tell which are the two or three who will reach the goal. Finally, there are other ways in which these problems may be attacked: we may take our part in a campaign to improve the tasks and the recreational opportunities of the unskilled; we may instruct the children about the character of the problems ahead of them if they choose difficult roads; and we may make it easier for the child to change his aim when necessary, without any loss of self-respect.

If vocational guidance is to serve a state committed to democratic principles, it cannot proceed otherwise than through striving for open opportunity based on breadth of vocational intelligence.

Vocational Guidance does not Mean Classifying Children and Prescribing Occupations. — There is no authority in definition, theory, or practice for prescribing vocations or classifying children; for neither activity is there any right or possibility. In spite of the confident attempts to classify, psychological analyses have not yet reached trustworthy results.[1] Vocational guidance does not mean that older people will impose ideas upon the children; the business of the teacher is rather to provide the environment in which each child will make for himself the series of choices which will determine his course of life.

Summary. — Turning again to the definition we have assumed, — that vocational guidance is concerned with helping persons choose, prepare for, enter into, and make progress in occupations — we are now able to compare the details of this statement with those activities which we have said vocational guidance is not. In brief, help in taking any single one of these steps in vocational progress, taken by itself, cannot be claimed to be the sum and substance of vocational guidance; and further, the guidance given the child must be both practical and idealistic, continued long enough to be based upon accurate knowledge of the child, aimed at broadening his opportunity, and free from classification and prescription.

What is Educational Guidance? — Conscious effort to assist in the intellectual growth of an individual is educational guidance. The following acts will serve as examples: telling about the arithmetic needed in a certain trade; aiding in the choice of a course or a school;

[1] There are types of thinking, but we cannot say that there are types of mind. Vocational guidance cannot afford to wait on psychology, though it may use whatever constructive results are offered. The danger with using the theory that there are types of children we shall discuss in Chapter V.

helping in plans to return to school; advising one to broaden his curriculum by studying music; advising a worker to transfer to another department in order to learn a new kind of work; telling how to play a game. Anything which has to do with instruction or with learning may come under the term educational guidance.

Most educational guidance is also vocational guidance. But when it has to do strictly with social, civic, recreational, and moral affairs, though it may bear indirectly on the occupation, it cannot be called vocational guidance in the strict sense of the term. For example, advising a child to study Latin merely to broaden his outlook is educational but not vocational guidance. On the other hand, helping a boy to secure a promotion in his occupation is an act of vocational but not of educational guidance.

The distinction depends on the purpose involved: whether to improve the child's vocational chances, or to advance his education.

The chief educational guidance needed at the present time, and the chief way it can serve the vocation of the child, is advice about, and improvement of, his schooling. It is for this reason that Bloomfield speaks of educational guidance as the first step in vocational guidance, and says further:

The question of choice of a life-work involves quite as much selecting the right kind of further schooling as the right vocation.[1]

1 *Youth*, etc., p. 28.

How Vocational Education Helps Guidance. The Prevocational Idea. — In this choice of further schooling vocational guidance is no longer dependent on mere advice; vocational education has provided for experimentation and actual preparation. Experimentation comes through the prevocational school (see Glossary, App. I), in which the child is successively allowed to participate in several kinds of mental and manual activities, for the purpose of self-discovery. There is no purpose to favor the manual studies, but only to provide *both* manual and academic studies, in order that broad activity, correlation between theory and practice, extended vision, and more intelligent choice may result. The following statement of aims is significant:

The advocates of early vocational education have no fear that their propaganda will endanger liberal education. On the contrary, they hold that the reorganization of education on a vocational basis will give motive for extended education and thus provide time and opportunity for liberal culture. They advocate the education of the individual along the lines of his greatest endowment and as broadly as possible. The antiquated liberal plan assumed that those who found books too much for them would drift into the ranks of the manual workers and get on as best they could there. In abandoning this view it is not necessary to go to the opposite extreme, namely, that pupils should be tested and all who prove to be skillful with their hands be trained for the trades and those who show no aptitude for handiwork be left to drift into the professions. The one test is no more decisive than the other. Of the two, however, the second is less fraught with danger, for in the shop as well as in the classroom there is opportunity to discover pupils who are fitted to deal with theories and general application of ideas.[1]

Vocational Training. — The second service rendered by vocational education is the actual training given those who have decided on their occupations. This training may be given in a trade school, a coöperative or part-time school, a commercial or technical day or night high school, or a college or professional school; however rendered it is a significant aid to efficient vocational guidance.

Our study has so far considered the general problem with which vocational guidance deals, the importance of the work, the false assumptions, and the relationship of vocational to educational guidance and vocational education. We shall next attempt to analyze the problem — to state the main questions with which vocational guidance, in school and in the occupations, is concerned.

The School Problems of Vocational Guidance. — The following lists of questions indicate three things: (1) the extent and importance of the field; (2) the problems with which present efforts to furnish vocational help are concerned; (3) the topics with which this book will deal. The questions in this section will furnish the basis for the study in the next four chapters.

GUIDANCE PROBLEMS IN THE SCHOOL

1. What can be done to give children vocational outlook, insight, and purpose — to widen each child's " vocational horizon "?

[1] Van Sickle.

(a) What can be done to counteract the restricted viewpoint of the child's immediate experience?

(b) How can we best lead the child to see the value of more education? How can we rouse him to the need for mental and moral preparedness?

2. How can the individual discover his talents?

(a) How can we help him to self-discovery?

(b) What school plans and program of studies will aid?

(c) How can the present studies be made to yield more vocational stimulus and guidance?

(d) Are there any tests which will help?

(e) What indirect methods of guidance are there? Student government? Play, and games? Athletics? Scouting? Clubs, societies, and other activities? Visits to stores and factories? After-school and vacation employment?

3. How may a person prepare for his occupation?

(a) What are the available methods, with the advantages and disadvantages of each? What are the aims, practices, and results of each?

(b) What studies or continuation courses can be offered to working people?

4. How shall we obtain and use occupational information?

(a) How may we survey the vocational opportunities before the children of any given community?

(b) How may we best classify vocational information?

(c) How may we present this information to the children? What courses on vocations should the school give? How should these courses be managed? What printed matter should be used?

5. What are some of the methods appropriate in guidance?

(a) What shall be the point of view and method of the teacher, in reference to the occupational futures of the children?

(b) How may the school aid the young person in securing employment?

(c) What plans for follow-up investigation and advice shall be adopted? Should school authorities supervise the employment of minors up to the age of 18? Up to the age of 21?

(d) How may the school best coöperate with the employers of labor? With organizations of workers? With civic and philanthropic associations? With parents?

(e) What should be the function of a central vocational bureau, and of an expert counselor?

(f) How shall we go about interviewing and advising the individual child? What shall be the manner of our approach? What shall be the extent and limitations set upon our active guidance?

6. What may be learned from actual accomplishments, in this country and abroad?

7. How may a principal or superintendent inaugurate a plan for vocational guidance?

The Occupational Problems of Vocational Guidance. — Many of the questions in the preceding list relate to the occupation as well as the school. Following are some additional topics which concern commerce and industry more directly. Consideration of these problems will appear also in some of the early chapters of this book, and especially in Chapters VI and VII.

GUIDANCE PROBLEMS IN OCCUPATIONS

1. How is the transition from school to work made, and how may it be improved?

(a) Why do children leave school early? Are the reasons good ones? What is the remedy?

(b) Is the work of children under sixteen needed to carry on American industries?

(c) What kind of work do young children do?

C

(d) Why is supervision needed? How are children misguided, kept in ignorance, or exploited?

(e) How do children secure employment? How may improved methods be inaugurated?

2. Shall there be vocational guidance for those destined to enter the unskilled occupations? Do they need any guidance?

(a) Can we be sure which children are so destined? Can destiny be changed?

(b) What would be the economic effect of educating each child to his fullest ability? Is there danger of over-education?

(c) What effect on vocational guidance arises out of the increase in the number of the unskilled workers?

3. What are the opportunities for promotion and career in each job?

(a) How may we know them in advance? How can we catalogue or write the specifications of an occupation or a job?

(b) What are employers, employment managers, or other executives doing for vocational guidance, and how may their activities be extended?

(c) What may be done about blind-alley jobs? How can the blind alley be opened and made to lead to something worth while?

4. What should we do about the changing from job to job? Is this changing educative? How may it be properly supervised? What shall be done about misfits and re-adjustments?

5. What have overwork, misemployment, unemployment, and poverty among workers to do with vocational guidance? What has the vocational counselor to do with them?

6. Are social service (welfare work) and scientific management for the benefit of the workers or for profit or for both? What may be done to improve the aims and methods of such work? How can it be made less paternalistic?

7. What plans are being followed, or may be followed, to aid the unskilled worker, both to improve his earning ability, and to develop helpful recreational interests?

8. What occupations are likely to have increased demands for workers? Which are likely to diminish in their demands?

9. Which occupations are economically and socially advantageous, to the workers and to the community? Which are the reverse? What should the vocational-guidance movement do about such occupations?

CHAPTER II

Beginnings in Vocational Guidance

The field of vocational guidance is so wide, its activities so varied, and its development so recent, that no study can include all the present plans in one comprehensive survey. Many schools have for years done vocational counseling, but have received new stimulus and aid from the interest developed by Frank Parsons less than ten years ago. Our purpose in this chapter is to present and criticize certain typical plans actually in operation at the present time. This examination will form the basis both for a program of practices which have been tried and found helpful, and for a possible statement of what remains still to be accomplished. It is not claimed that the plans here examined are the best that can be found, but that they fairly represent the vocational-guidance movement as it expresses itself to-day.

Early Recognition of the Importance of Guidance. — It is as difficult to trace the beginnings of vocational guidance as to trace the discovery of the use of steam. Who did the most, — the man who saw the need, the one who told the world about it, or the one who took the first step toward the solution of the problem? Many persons have appreciated the need of vocational guidance through reading Plato's *Republic*, and yet have done nothing to work out any plan. In 1670, Pascal stated the importance of a wise choice of occupation. The introductory statement of a vocational-guidance document published in England in 1747 is placed at the beginning of Bloomfield's book, *Readings in Vocational Guidance*. In 1795 Henry MacKenzie wrote:

Indeed, the education of your youth is every way preposterous; you waste at school years in improving talents, without having ever discovered them; one promiscuous line of instruction is followed, without regard to genius, capacity, or probable situation in the commonwealth. [1]

Again, all the cults having to do with prediction and prescription — the astrologers, the palm and card readers, the phrenologists, physiognomists, mediums, and seers — recognized the importance of and were concerned with vocational adaptations. Was vocational guidance, like chemistry, astronomy, biology, and other sciences, born in pseudo-knowledge? If so, we must be alert in our study to search out the line of true progress.

In 1881 a little book was published which can perhaps claim to be the first book wholly devoted to the actual subject of choosing a vocation. It is a curious volume, but full of the need for vocational guidance and of the service to be rendered. The author, Lysander S. Richards, attempted to coin the word " Vocophy " for the title. The naïve point of view is shown in an extract from the preface:

[1] *Man of Feeling*, p. 48.

All we claim to perform is to bring order out of chance and chaos, and form or establish a system to enable a person to find the most fitting pursuit in which he can reap the greatest success that is possible for him individually to attain.

The book does nothing more than to point the need. Richards favors phrenology, though he points out its limitations. His aim was to have expert prescribers in each city. He made little provision for study of the occupations, and even in his study of the individual he tells chiefly what occupations to avoid rather than what to follow.

The Beginning of Genuine Vocational Guidance. — Frank Parsons is justly called the founder of the vocational-guidance movement, for it was he who began the work which has led to the present spread of interest. Parsons discarded the pseudo-sciences, used the systematic study of the occupations, and was sane and painstaking in the investigations of character and abilities which he made. Further, he wrote about his work, and thus gave to the followers in the movement an opportunity to build on his gains. His book, *Choosing a Vocation*, will perhaps have a permanent place in vocational-guidance bibliographies. Its critics recognize its value; at most only one objection to the method can be raised: Parsons was a bit too sure in his conclusions — too prescriptive in what he told the individuals who consulted him.[1] It should be noted that the scope of

[1] Bound up with this difficulty is the further fact that the "self-analysis" plan he used is over-elaborated and dependent upon a false psychology. His emphasis on choosing a vocation led many people to the belief that this is the sole function of vocational guidance.

the work and of the book is limited: guidance in the school, placement, and follow-up work, and guidance accompanying employment are not vital parts of the plan. The guidance Parsons offered was intensive, but it did not extend over a long period of the individual's life.

The Civic Service House, Boston, in which Professor Parsons began his counseling, was organized in 1901 by Meyer Bloomfield. In 1903 Philip Davis, the present director, came as assistant. They became interested in the writings, social outlook, and practical aims of Parsons, and under his direction the Breadwinners' Institute was organized. This work with immigrant young men and women brought to a focus all Parsons' latent interest in vocational guidance, and steps were at once taken to organize a vocation bureau. This was in the early weeks of 1908. On April 23, 1908, the organization of the Vocation Bureau was completed, with a substantial board of directors as sponsors for the movement. Mrs. Quincy A. Shaw (Pauline Agassiz Shaw), who aided many other progressive educational movements, financed the work. On May 1, Parsons made his initial report to the board. Just before the summer, students about to graduate from an evening high school were invited to confer with Parsons, and considerable counseling was carried on. In the fall he continued the work of the Bureau, at the Civic Service House, and also gave part of his time to similar work at other institutions. Late in the same year (1908) Parsons died.

During the early months of 1909 plans were perfected

for reorganizing and carrying on the bureau, and Bloomfield assumed charge of the work as director. At first several other civic organizations coöperated in the direction of the enterprise, but before many months the bureau attained to the dignity of an independent institution. It was very soon after this time that the bureau was asked to begin the organization of the work in the Boston city schools.

It was from these beginnings that the movement for vocational guidance has spread. The term " vocational guidance " is *new* — during the few years since 1908 it has assumed nation-wide significance. We shall now turn to an examination of the activities of the movement as expressed in various parts of the country, beginning with Boston, the birthplace.

The Vocation Bureau of Boston: Past Activities. — The Boston Vocation Bureau has done much important work. Among its activities may be mentioned the following:

1. Establishment of vocational guidance in the Boston schools, and of training courses for Boston teachers.

2. Summer-school courses in Harvard University, 1911, 1912, and 1913; and in the University of California, 1914 and 1915. Courses in Indiana University, the State Normal School at Greeley, Colorado; year courses at Boston University beginning 1913–14, and at Teachers College, Columbia University, beginning 1916–17.

3. Holding of First National Conference on Vocational Guidance, in coöperation with the Boston Chamber of Commerce, 1910.

4. Publication of *The Vocational Guidance of Youth*, 1911.

5. Publication of pamphlets and books on trades, businesses, and professions.

6. Investigation of vocational guidance in Europe and in Porto Rico, and publication of *The School and the Start in Life*, 1914.

7. Organizing of the Boston Employment Managers' Association, 1911.

8. Publication of *Youth, School, and Vocation;* and of *Readings in Vocational Guidance*, 1915.

9. Publication of *Business Employments*, and *The Shoe Industry*, 1916.

10. Correspondence, conferences, interviews, lectures, as noted in the list of present activities, below.

The Present Work of the Bureau. — At the present time the Boston bureau is not primarily engaged in giving vocational counsel to individuals, but is more especially concerned with carrying on investigations, publishing bulletins, drawing up plans for schools and school systems, and in others ways furthering the growth and development of the idea of guidance.

The duty of a bureau to aid teachers, employers, and school directors is thus stated :

It is the special business of a vocation bureau to organize that conscious and continuous service which takes hold of the child when the life-career motive has been awakened, and helps guide, strengthen, and protect it, particularly through the transition crisis between school and work.[1]

[1] Bloomfield, *Youth*, etc., p. 47. A systematic outline of the aims of the bureau is given on page 39.

Following is a partial list of the present attempts of the Boston Vocation Bureau to be of service in this field:

1. Correspondence about plans and policies.

2. Conference with persons wishing actual guidance.

3. Conferences with school people, employers, labor unions, social workers, legislators.

4. A course in Vocational Guidance at Boston University and at Teachers College, Columbia University.

5. Lectures by the director and assistant director for associations, schools, clubs, etc.

6. Investigations leading to publications on occupations.

7. Maintenance of a library of material on vocational guidance and vocational education, open to the public.

8. Conferences with and aid to students of colleges and universities who are investigating vocational-guidance.

9. Assistance in the organization and direction of employment managers' associations, in Boston, Philadelphia, San Francisco, and New York. (See p. 125.)

10. Assistance in planning vocational-guidance conferences and conventions.

11. Organization of a plan for vocational help to minors, for the New York public schools.

Counseling at the Boston Bureau. — The reason the bureau no longer aims to put the chief emphasis on extensive counseling of individuals is expressed as follows in the 1915 report:

The Vocation Bureau believes that the most effective vocational counseling comes through close association with individuals or groups. It does not believe that as a rule stranger can well counsel stranger. Therefore one main effort of the Bureau has been to secure the appointment and adequate training of those who are best situated for the right relationship with applicants for vocational help.

A counselor in a school system or in a business establishment is in a good position not only to observe the needs and growth of an individual but also to secure coöperation in judgment and personal service from those who are equally interested in a particular individual's welfare.

In spite of this policy there are calls at the bureau from persons wanting counsel, and these requests are not refused. Many come, however, for aid in finding work, and in such cases the Bureau can only refer them to other organizations. Applicants for advice are frequently counseled to seek the aid of responsible people of good judgment who have known them for a long period of time.

The following tabulation is based on a study of 133 case cards on file in the Vocation Bureau. They were chosen at random, and are only a portion of the many cases considered by the bureau.

INDIVIDUAL COUNSEL

133 SAMPLE CASES, VOCATION BUREAU OF BOSTON

Sex:		Ages:	
Male	93	12–16	20
Female	40	17–21	58
Place:		22–25	18
Boston	78	26–30	15
Others in Massachu-			
setts	50	31–40	2
Other states . . .	5	41–	2

Education:

Through elementary . 22

In high school . . . 10

Through high . . . 31

In college 7

Through college . . 5

Had plans for study . 44

Employment:

Misemployed . . . 25

Want advance . . . 5

Want work 8

Want advice about

getting work . . 49

Guidance on occupations sought:

Opportunities in specific lines 17

How to prepare for specific occupations 22

General advice about choice 11

Disposal of cases:

NOTE. — Only a portion of the 133 cases are here listed; many cards do not bear records when general information was given.

Referred to employment and placement agencies . . 34

Referred to people for advice on opportunity . . . 13

Referred to people for advice on preparation . . . 11

Referred to school and short courses 8

The foregoing tabulation shows that many persons have the impression that the bureau can help them find work. It shows, too, that there is a need for sources of advice and information for many persons far beyond the school age.

Requests for Counsel by Mail. — " It is absolutely impossible to give any vocational counsel by mail. Only harm can result from such an attempt." This is a sample answer of the bureau to one of the many letters requesting advice. Much of this correspondence came from those who had read Parsons' book, and some was the result of newspaper misdirection. For example, a

Sunday edition, in reporting the work of the bureau, made it appear that advice by mail was given. And an efficiency expert, writing in a well-known magazine, was guilty of this statement: " If you want to know what is your supreme talent, write to the Vocation Bureau of Boston." The resulting letters are pathetic in their appeal. One can imagine that great disappointment came to individuals who could receive no answer commensurate with their hopes.

Following is a tabulation of the characteristics of the letters, and of the replies to them:

Examination of the "Case-Letter File"

Vocation Bureau of Boston

1911–1915

Analysis of letters:

Number of letters examined	199
Ask information on finding their vocations	111
Ask how to study for specific lines	24
Ask about opportunity in specific lines	31
Ask other specific questions about vocations . . .	11
Request interviews	17
Request an examination to determine vocation . .	8
Offer to pay for information, examination, or advice	18
Relatives, teachers, or friends asking about others .	31
Teachers asking advice for school counseling . . .	3
Ask how to become a counselor	7
Ask names of employers for work	9
Ask names of counselors in their vicinity	8
Ask for literature	11
Ask general questions about help the bureau can give	12

Analysis of replies:

Told that advice cannot be given by mail 101
Advised to see Y. M. C. A. secretary, school people,
    settlement workers, etc. 106
Referred to schools and colleges for education . . . 15
Specific questions answered 33
Sent reports and other printed matter 17
Referred to literature 8
Referred to firms for placement 6
Told to come for an interview 14
Told that no interviews were immediately possible . 8
Advised to drop interest in phrenology 3

Only a few of the letters told about the education or employment of the writers: thirty-four said that they were at work but dissatisfied, eight that they were in school, eight in college, and sixteen out of employment.

The letters were from all parts of the United States, and seven were from foreign countries. Why should a boy about to graduate from a high school in Iowa write to Boston for information on finding his occupation? What are the resources for advice open to a man of 46 who has tried several occupations with indifferent success? These are serious questions with which the schools, the city, and the vocational-guidance people will have to concern themselves.

Occasional letters still come to the bureau in which the problems of a life are laid bare, and while schools are inadequate and economic conditions crassly competitive such letters are likely to be written to any vocation bureau. Since the reply is so eagerly expected and advice so sorely needed, and since a short letter may seem brusque and is always disappointing, it seems best to have a printed or stenciled form which can be sent in reply, in case it is not possible to send a personal note.

Future Plans of the Vocation Bureau of Boston. — The reputation of the Boston bureau has been carried far beyond the borders of this country, and the thought of vocational guidance has gone with the name. Recently there was received a book from Uruguay with translations from *The Vocational Guidance of Youth*, and Chinese pamphlets on vocational education have referred to the bureau and its work.

At the present time two important lines of work are being undertaken by the director of the bureau, Mr. Bloomfield : the perfecting of plans for an experiment in vocational help in three New York schools and a systematic study of the qualifications, duties and opportunities of the employment manager (Chap. IV). The director has recently given two courses in vocational guidance at Teachers College, Columbia University.

The assistant director, Mr. Frederick J. Allen, is devoting most of his time to the preparation of studies of the occupations. His book, *The Shoe Industry*, recently issued by the bureau, is of use not only as a guide to those who may wish to enter, and to intelligent workers in the industry, but to business men and manufacturers as well. His *Business Employments* aims to bring up to date, enlarge, and reprint the various studies made during the past six years. Allen divides the occupational field roughly into three sections: business, trades, and professions. *Business Employments* aims to survey the first field; *The Shoe Industry* is one study in the second; and *The Law as a Vocation* represents the third. It is hoped that the bureau may find opportunity to survey the last two fields — trades and professions — making three excellent texts for schools, vocational counselors, and other friends of youth.[1]

Vocational-Guidance Department, Boston Public Schools. — It was the establishment of the Boston Vocation Bureau which led to the work of vocational guidance in the Boston schools. The beginnings were explained by Superintendent Brooks at the first vocational guidance conference, held in Boston in 1910.[2] Brooks's report for 1911 advocated an investigation of the vocations of the community, an examination of the school system, work with parents and teachers, and follow-up. Committees coöperated, under the direction of the Vocation Bureau, many meetings were held, teachers giving time to the work, men drawn directly from occupations gave explanations of their field, high school principals told of the aims and methods of their schools, and later district conferences were held. The work has gone

---

[1] Through a plan recently consummated, Mr. Bloomfield now gives full time to industrial counseling, particularly in relation to the establishment of departments of employment management. The Vocation Bureau, now called The Bureau of Vocational Guidance, is under charge of the Division of Education and the Graduate School of Business Administration, Harvard University, and Mr. Roy W. Kelly, Instructor in Education, is the director.   [2] See *Readings*, pp. 83–91.

on continuously, in spite of the fact that counselors in the elementary schools have done their work without any allowance of time or money. The 1916 survey of the schools for the Finance Commission led to the following statement:

The work in vocational guidance is probably as well organized and administered in Boston as in any of our American cities. The work is undoubtedly of much value and deserves further study.

The committee believes that Boston will do well to expand its work in this field (Chap. VI).

The Central Office. — The vocational office, in charge of the director, Miss Susan Ginn, aims to be an aid to the appointed counselors in each school. These local counselors in most cases do the actual advising. Assistants in the central office are engaged in three kinds of work: investigating occupations, giving counsel to such students and working children as call at the office, and aiding in the placement of high school students and graduates.[1]

Much educational guidance is carried on by this department, the most striking evidence of which was the

[1] The central office is a coördinating force to draw together a body of information about practices and successes throughout the city. It is a clearing house for experimentation, methods, and ways and means. A few general conferences are held, and frequent district conferences, in which high and elementary school teachers exchange points of view, and needs of particular sections of the city are discussed and investigated, and typical cases needing direction are considered. At a recent meeting of the counselors, there were present about 300 teachers. Such a meeting argues well for the interest in vocational guidance in the Boston schools.

D

Annual Report of the School Committee for 1912. This report is addressed to the fathers and mothers of Boston, and is full of information about the schools: requirements, diagrams, pictures, vocational training, suggesting courses, special classes, etc. Miss Ginn maintains that with high school attendance assured, the problem of the vocational counselors in the elementary schools is concerned chiefly with aiding the child in the selection of a high school course.[1]

The counselors in the Boston schools have used the pamphlets of the Boston Vocation Bureau, and many of them have taken the training course conducted by Bloomfield, either in the classes under the auspices of the bureau and the school committee or in those maintained by Harvard University or Boston University. The work of the Vocation Department could probably be made more effective as a clearing house of information on guidance if there were a larger library at the central office. Each school has been furnished with a few books and pamphlets on occupations.

The Boston plan seems to lack effective centralization; the work is advisory and permissive. Were the director

[1] It is to be pointed out, however, that this selection cannot be made with intelligence and foresight unless the child has discovered his bent or probable occupation, and this for many is impossible at this age.

It is the plan in Boston, as soon as financial conditions can be met, to give time allowance to counselors in the grades, so that their work may be done more effectively. This was announced by Assistant Superintendent Thompson, in the meeting above referred to, as was also the fact that a booklet is being planned, so that some elementary statement of fact and policy may aid the counselor in the work.

able to require definite work in the elementary and high schools, especially in the giving of vocational information, better results might be expected. Voluntary work, nevertheless, shows interest, and a good foundation for comprehensive guidance undoubtedly exists.

Guidance in the Boston High Schools. — The Vocational-Guidance Department has little direct control over the guidance in the Boston high schools. During the closing weeks of the school year members of the staff personally interview each member of the graduating classes, and also make an effort to aid in placement. Aside from this help, however, there seems to be no direction given to high school work, each school working out its own plan. In most of the schools two or more teachers are allowed part-time for counseling individuals, but there seems to be no committee of coöperation between the several schools, and no attempt to supervise the work. It is well done or indifferently done, apparently, according to the interest and enthusiasm of the individual principal or counselor. Much profit would undoubtedly come from joint action in setting up a program of minimum requirement for vocational guidance.

In the schools which take greatest interest in guidance efficient work seems to be done. Superintendent Brooks describes the work as it stood in 1910.[1] Since that time there has been a growth of interest and effort, and the lectures, vocational talks, care in selecting high schools,

[1] See *Readings*, p. 83.

and summer and part-time work have been continued
and extended. A recent development is the Monday
and Saturday work in department stores by girls who
are in the last year of high school.

Many of the Boston schools make systematic efforts
to find places for their graduates.

Boston System Progressive. — The Boston work and
plans are commendable and promising. Effort is made
to differentiate the school program, vocational outlook
is widened early in the elementary school, advice comes
some time ahead of placement, efforts are made to keep
children in school, an attempt is made to safeguard
the critical time of school leaving, placement is carefully
done, and follow-up is provided for. Of late years a
corps of college students has given time to interviewing
employers for the department. The Boston School
Committee holds examinations for vocational assistants
— clearly a step in advance.

Before the Boston system can be said to have an adequate, city-wide plan for guidance, however, it would
seem necessary to work out a set of minimum essentials
such as we shall discuss at a later place, and then to
provide for authoritative supervision of the effort and
accomplishment.

Unguided Foreigners in Boston. — One of the guidance
problems yet to be solved in Boston, and in other American cities as well, is due to the presence of foreigners in
the schools, particularly in the night schools. It is
common knowledge among settlement workers that

adults come from Italy and other countries equipped with skilled trades, but must take to street work, peddling, or farming because they do not know the language or cannot get work. The drift of foreigners into certain unskilled trades is at present inevitable, regardless of their aims and abilities. It is reported that the girls who work in one of the Atlantic Avenue candy factories, looking out of the window at an incoming liner from Italy, remarked, " Here comes another load of chocolate dippers." These young persons must attend night school until they can speak English, and this would seem to be the opportunity for vocational guidance; but thus far little has been done. A sympathetic principal — one who believes in the races he is trying to help — should be given the resources to experiment with plans for meeting this need.

The guidance in the Boston continuation school and prevocational centers will be considered in Chapter III.

The Grand Rapids Plan. — The work in the Boston schools began with the Vocation Bureau, and thence was transplanted to the schools; that in Grand Rapids grew up in the schoolroom first and then was extended and organized in a central office.

The work in Grand Rapids is expounded in a recent publication.[1] This book is an invaluable aid to English teachers, for it shows in a practical way how written composition may be used to develop the interests of the child and to give him experience in and knowledge of the problems he will have to face. The plan is systemati-

[1] Davis, Jesse B., *Vocational and Moral Guidance.*

cally worked out, and proceeds step by step through the series of choices that the normal child has to make in the course of his education and economic progress. It is the result of conference and coöperation on the part of the teachers in both high and elementary schools.[1]

It is of interest to note that the work begins in a systematic way in the seventh grade. (We shall later show the reasons for an earlier start.) It seems particularly appropriate that the eighth grade child should study the value of further education, for this will encourage him to continue study even if he cannot attend the high school.

The Grand Rapids plan is very thorough in English, and since the publication of the book there has been some extensive development in the vocational use of the other studies.

The ideals back of the activities so far carried on seem sound, and the aims high. No narrow conformity

---

[1] The following statement of general aims or topics for each grade is of interest:

Seventh Grade: Vocational ambition.

Eighth Grade: The value of education.

Ninth Grade: The elements of character that make for success.

Tenth Grade: The world's work — a call to service.

Eleventh Grade: Choosing a vocation.

Twelfth Grade: Preparation for one's life work.

This list does not mean that the child is asked to make the decisions indicated at exactly the time each topic is being studied. It means simply that a concentrated attempt is made to set the child thinking about each of these problems. The choice of a vocation may not come in the eleventh grade; it may come in the eighth or the thirteenth. But during the eleventh grade the boy or girl has an opportunity to survey and check up the factors which should enter into that choice.

to present social and business conditions is involved. Witness Davis' statement on needed legislation on page 162. There has been organized in Grand Rapids, under the auspices of the Association of Commerce of that city, a Junior Association of Commerce which gives the boys of the high school an opportunity to come into contact with the commerce and industry of the city, and with the men engaged in these occupations.

The chief lessons of procedure from the Grand Rapids experiment are the following: use the studies of the school program to aid the child in understanding the vocational world and in making his choices and adjustments, lay broad foundations for the vocational bureau, and secure the coöperation of the moral and vocational interests of the community — library, school, occupation, and commercial associations.

The Grand Rapids plan, like that of Boston, seems still to be in process of growth. It becomes more and more apparent that vocational guidance can become a satisfactory system of procedure in a city only after it has been developed out of the knowledge, experiences, and interests of the individual teachers. Up to the present time no large city has succeeded in spreading the interest widely enough and in securing adequate funds to bring about what could be called a complete, city-wide plan of vocational guidance. For that, teachers must be instructed and encouraged, and they must be given time in the daily program for the work. Boston and Grand Rapids have gone farther than any other cities. Yet the latter, like the former, seems to be but little beyond the voluntary and permissive stage. Coöperative effort has led to good results so far; it would seem proper to take a new step in the near future, to work out a plan which will give every child adequate guidance, and to finance and closely supervise the operation of the scheme.

The Mishawaka Plan. One of the most interesting and well-rounded methods of guidance so far described in print is that used for three years at Mishawaka, Ind., and explained in the *School Review* of April, 1915.[1]

In working out the plan the teachers of the high school first made a survey in the light of which the high school courses were improved. Reading lists, assembly talks, conferences with seniors and eighth grade pupils, a course on vocations, and provision for placement, are used in the scheme. Entering students are well cared for, frequent enrollment blanks give vocational clews, and a system of follow-up work gives valuable information.

The chief virtue of this plan is that it shows how any school (or, in fact, any teacher) may make a safe and effective beginning in vocational guidance.

New York City. — The High School Teachers' Association of New York City has interested itself in vocational guidance since 1908. Investigations, conferences with graduating pupils, pamphlets, and provision for placement have been the chief kinds of work. So far, however, there has been no central bureau; most of the work has been carried forward by voluntary committees

[1] See Horton.

and at the individual schools. The Central Committee on Vocational Guidance published a booklet in 1912, and in the same year held, under its auspices, the Second National Conference on Vocational Guidance. Although a few individuals in New York City have devoted much time and energy to vocational guidance, it cannot be said that there is any plan for the city.

In the Sixteenth Annual Report of the Superintendent of Schools of New York City, 1915, five pages are devoted to this subject, and the superintendent recommends a plan for the city resembling that for Edinburgh described in Bloomfield's *The School and the Start in Life.*

During the winter of 1914–1915 Bloomfield was called to New York for part-time investigations, in connection with the Mayor's Committee on Vocational Help to Minors. This committee investigated the school history of boys and girls at work, the social environment of the children, the parent's estimate of the child's problems and progress, the employer's viewpoint about the children, and the opinions of the children themselves. The investigation was extensive, and at the same time was conducted with care, in order to keep close to actual individual cases. There were conferences in which boys and girls answered questions directly to the committee. The results of the investigation have not yet been published. On the basis of the investigations made, the committee has drawn up a comprehensive plan for vocational guidance in three schools in Manhattan, and the Board of Superintendents has approved the project.

Somerville. — Twenty teachers in Somerville, Mass., made preliminary investigations .for the establishment of a plan for vocational guidance. It has been found that even those students who are pursuing relatively narrow vocational courses in the high school, such as the commercial courses, are not at all sure of their choice of careers, and it is suspected that only a small number of graduates are following the work for which they were ostensibly prepared in school. The committee has investigated dropping out, has utilized the school's plan whereby each pupil in high school selects a teacher as an adviser, and has proposed a plan for systematic vocational guidance.[1]

Beginnings in Chicago. — In 1912 a committee on vocational training, of the Chicago City Club, reported the need of vocational guidance. As early as 1910 some work in guidance had been begun by the Chicago School of Civics and Philanthropy, and school people became interested. In 1913 the Board of Education gave office space to the work, and all children applying for employment certificates were directed to consult this bureau. Thus the effort has been from the first to aid those coming up for placement or for certificates to begin work. At the same time, however, a great deal of good has been done in returning children to school. Industries in Chicago are investigated, bulletins published, placement is put on a high plane, and children are followed in their occupations.

[1] See *Readings*, pp. 198–199.

In a recent survey of the Chicago schools made by the Chicago teachers, two committees took up the question of vocational guidance. Both recommended a central office, and one drew up a comprehensive plan for the work. Early in 1916 the Board of Education decided to take full responsibility for the central bureau, and progress may be expected.[1]

Work in Other Cities. — Buffalo and Los Angeles, through the school authorities or through committees of teachers, have issued lists of occupations open to young people. In one of the Los Angeles high schools vocational conferences were arranged by teachers in the English department, but no serious attempt was made to prepare these teachers for the work of counseling. Some investigation has been made in both cities, and in Los Angeles a useful bulletin was issued to post in the schools, showing what kinds of courses are given in each of the high schools, and to what occupations these courses lead.

Rochester has collected information about working girls, and used it to improve the school program of studies.[2] Bulletins on occupations have been issued. De Kalb, Ill., has instituted a very suggestive system of guidance.[3] Newton, Mass., has organized a plan connected with the work-certificate office.[4] Cincinnati,

---

[1] For Chicago references see: Proc. of Nat. Conference, 1912, pp. 14–18; Nat. V. G. Assn., 1913, pp. 59–64, 86–89; 1914, pp. 51–56; *Readings*, 542–556; 60th Report Chicago Schools, pp. 341–355.

[2] See Fletcher.   [3] See Giles.

[4] See Bloomfield's *Youth*, etc., p. 53.

Milwaukee, Philadelphia, and Boston are carrying on guidance in connection with continuation schools. The Los Angeles, Berkeley, and Rochester intermediate schools, and the Gary plan, at Gary, Troy, and New York City, provide differentiated courses in which children can discover their talents and aptitudes. Oakland, San José, and hundreds of other cities, are doing active guidance work in the high schools. Both the Oakland Technical High School and the San José High School have done pioneer work in organizing life-career classes, — school groups for the study of the occupations.[1] The life-career or occupations class seems to have been originated by Mr. Wheatley, almost as soon as Parsons began his work.[2]

Long Beach, Cal., High School offers credit for the continued study of one's vocational problems. A variety of exercises is included in the study.

The January, 1916, bulletin of the National Vocational Guidance Association prints a list of over 150 high schools which claim to have made beginnings.

Guidance in Colleges. — No systematic canvass of the guidance work of the colleges seems to have been published. The following notes will serve to indicate some of the work undertaken.

Wisconsin University holds annual conferences of women students, and the dean of women holds daily office hours for counsel. The character of the work is reported

[1] See Jacobs.
[2] See Wheatley, and Gowin and Wheatley, bibliography.

in the *Vocational-Guidance Bulletin*, of November, 1915. In the same bulletin is a short report of the guidance at Worcester Polytechnic Institute. There is provision in the institute for men to discover that they are not fitted to be engineers, without the traditional humiliation of failure in studies.

Vocational conferences for women students of the State College of Washington are discussed in the December, 1915, *Vocational-Guidance Bulletin*. Special stress is given to occupations other than teaching. The Women's Educational and Industrial Union of Boston, through its appointment bureau, has held conferences with women students of several colleges. The University of Minnesota has a faculty committee on vocational guidance for women, and for the year 1917–1918 a vocational adviser for women has been appointed.

One of the most systematic efforts to give educational guidance in a higher institution is that undertaken at Reed College in the freshman course called College Life. Among the topics included in this course are the following: the purpose of the college; selection of courses; principles and methods of study; the use of the library; student honesty; general reading and mental recreation; health; athletics; the relation of the college to the community; the choice of a vocation. Various members of the faculty contribute to the course.

College Courses in Vocational Guidance. — A recent article [1] on college departments of education names the

[1] See Bolton.

following colleges as conducting courses on vocational guidance: Chicago, Illinois, Iowa, Kansas, Washington, and Teachers College of Columbia University. To these must be added courses in Boston University, the University of California and Harvard University, besides summer-school courses in several other colleges. Los Angeles State Normal School is conducting a course for teachers in service. Without doubt many other colleges are giving full courses, and certainly all departments of education have courses in which the subject forms at least a part of the work.

Courses for Employment Managers. — During the past two years the Tuck School of Administration and Finance, the business division of Dartmouth College, has given a course to train men for the duties of the employment manager. The Wharton School of Finance of the University of Pennsylvania has organized similar work.

Guidance through Other Agencies. — What resources are there for vocational advice, for a person who is not a student at a school or college? The Vocation Bureau of Boston has had to face this question in answering letters from all parts of the country. In most cases there is no satisfactory solution; in few cities are there agencies whose business it is to give the misemployed worker the systematic counsel required to help him.

Guidance by Religious Organizations. — The Young Men's and Young Women's Christian Associations have general, educational, or employment secretaries who can

give counsel to their members, and these officers frequently accommodate nonmembers too.   But it is not
an easy thing for a person unfamiliar with the organization to bring himself to approach these busy officials.
Besides, it is doubtful if they can aid a stranger greatly
in one or two conferences.   For their own members,
however, these associations do good work in vocational
guidance, in spite of the occasional tendency to overemphasize character analysis.[1] The Boston, Buffalo,
and New York associations have given counsel to
thousands of young men.

Pastors of churches, writers, lecturers, teachers,
and superintendents of schools are often appealed to by
strangers needing vocational help.

Guidance through Governmental Projects. — A
searching investigation into the many activities of the
departments of the national government would disclose
a large amount of vocational guidance.   Much of it is
impersonal, in the way of bulletins, agricultural reports,
civil service manuals, and other documents: these are
studied by many persons needing vocational advice.

One of the most interesting experiments in guidance
was the summer camp organized in 1915 by the Recreation League of San Francisco, and conducted by
Forestry-Service officials of the national government.
Twenty boys were given three weeks of strenuous life
in the woods, and under the direction of experienced
rangers had actual practice in the duties of a forester,

---

[1] See Davis' *Vocational and Moral Guidance*, pp. 262–272.

from cooking and heliographing to putting out a fire a mile in length.

The work done by the Canadian and Australian governments, in financing men who wish to become farmers, is a practical kind of vocational guidance. The Homestead Commission of Massachusetts has repeatedly asked the legislature for funds to begin similar work, and a beginning is about to be made.

Work by Clubs, Settlements, and Libraries. — The need for vocational counsel is appreciated by every settlement worker, and guidance is a more or less important part of the program of every such institution. The Henry Street Settlement of New York City, through its Vocational Scholarship Committee, gives girls who would otherwise go into unskilled trades two extra years of schooling, and thus helps them to obtain skilled work.[1]

Public libraries were among the first institutions to understand the need for vocational guidance, and the lists of books, issued by the Brooklyn and Grand Rapids libraries, have been of great use to teachers and counselors. Miss Hall's paper, reproduced in Davis' *Vocational and Moral Guidance*, gives a general statement of what has been and may be done.[2]

Guidance through Placement. Placement in School Departments. — In a later chapter we shall discuss the advantages and disadvantages of guidance through

---

[1] See *Readings*, p. 322; also *Nat. Voc. Guidance Assn.*, 1914, pp. 59–61.
[2] See also Bloomfield, *Youth*, etc., p. 7.

placement (Chapter IV). We shall here note typical organizations for such work. We have already spoken of the Placement Bureau of Boston, which is now connected with the school system. Rochester, N.Y., and Lincoln, Neb.,[1] have placement bureaus which have induced certain employers to obtain all their help under eighteen years of age through the bureaus.

Portland, Ore., maintained a summer-employment office, under the supervision of the school board. High schools in many cities aid in placing their students.

Business Organizations. — Commercial associations have frequently used the term vocational guidance to apply to plans for placement organized under their auspices. Doubtless some guidance is given in connection with the placement. The subcommittee on industrial education and vocational guidance of the Chicago Association of Commerce has maintained a placement service since 1913. This subcommittee coöperates with the schools, aids in the effort to hold the child in school as long as possible, consults with parents, studies the aptitudes of the child, places him advantageously, and maintains a " follow-up " service.

Other Appointment Agencies. — Among other placement organizations which interest themselves in vocational guidance are the numerous associations for aiding college women to obtain employment. The Intercollegiate Bureau of Occupations, New York City, is the best known example. Other such agencies exist in

[1] See Leavitt, Dec., 1915.

E

Philadelphia, Pittsburgh, Chicago, and Los Angeles. Much helpful guidance is furnished by these bureaus. The Women's Educational and Industrial Union, of Boston, maintains an appointment bureau which gives vocational advice, and conducts short-term classes in certain occupations. A course in photography was recently given. A library on vocations for women is maintained. The Union has for the past two years conducted a class in vocational guidance.

Most colleges maintain appointment offices, and some of these have developed great efficiency. Their particular concern is to help graduates obtain teaching positions, but their work is by no means confined to this occupation.

Vocational Guidance in Foreign School Systems. — The European experiments in vocational guidance have been discussed at length by Bloomfield in *The School and the Start in Life*. Some of the salient characteristics from which American cities may learn, are these: the publication of brief, helpful books for youth and parents, giving vocational information about each of many occupations; progress in health guidance, particularly in preventing injurious labor on the part of young people; the organization of large voluntary committees for guidance of working children and youth. The needs growing out of the war have led to many new adaptations of the work of guidance in foreign countries.

Summary. — The plans discussed in this chapter will indicate the nature of the work so far attempted; they cannot indicate its geographical extent. Our survey

shows that there has been an effective start in many
schools in various parts of the country; that many of
these efforts have been preceded by a study of the occupational opportunities; that in each of a few cities there
is a central vocational bureau; that the colleges are
interesting themselves in the movement; that religious
associations, governmental offices, clubs, settlements,
and libraries have aided in the work of guidance; and
that there are many appointment agencies which make
an effort to give vocational guidance in connection with
placement. We know, too, that at the present moment
many American cities are laying plans for inaugurating
systematic vocational guidance.

The chief defects in the efforts for vocational guidance
so far made are of two classes, and grow out of two causes.
In the first group are those plans which are inadequate
mainly on account of the fact that they have not yet
reached maturity. In most of their characteristics these
are commendable so far as they go, and their present rate
of growth is healthy and hopeful. In the second group
are those plans which have set up the placement activity,
or have failed to put the guidance work where it obviously
belongs, — in the school department. In most cases,
apparently, satisfactory development can hardly be
expected without a reorganization of those plans.

It is characteristic of the men and women in charge
of the work in the first group, so far as we have been able
to observe, that they recognize the limitations of their
work, and are endeavoring to extend it as an educational

activity.   Those engaged in the work of the other plans, however, are more apt to look for immediate ends, and to fail to grasp the real need for offering vocational information and guidance long before the child is ready to leave school.

We shall now turn to the methods used in guidance. In the next chapter we shall consider the method of giving vocational guidance through educational guidance; in the fourth chapter we shall attempt to evaluate some other methods of counsel.

CHAPTER III

VOCATIONAL GUIDANCE THROUGH EDUCATIONAL GUIDANCE

THAT educational guidance is of prime importance is shown in the history of an actual case. The person concerned was the son of a mechanic with a large family, and early found it necessary to aid in increasing the family income. Two summers and one or two holiday seasons he served as cash boy in a department store. After school and Saturdays, during much of the time he was in elementary and high school, he worked as helper in his father's carpenter shop, and as helper and clerk in a paint store. A year out of his college course was spent in a grocery store. During all of this time he received absolutely no counsel of a definite or conscious kind about the work he was doing, save the instructions of the persons for whom he worked. Nor did he make any choice of vocation in this period. On the other hand, however, he did have *educational* guidance, from sister and teachers, as a result of which he was influenced to make the effort to begin and to complete his college education. In the course of time he became a teacher.

It is apparent that narrow vocational guidance without any educational viewpoint might have been a stum-

bling-block in this boy's way.   In Chapter V we shall
discuss the danger in the immediate kind of counsel
which attempts to sort out children twelve years old into
" thing-thinkers " and " idea-thinkers," and thereupon
to narrow their educational opportunity.   In the present
chapter we shall inquire how the school can widen the
vocational horizon of the pupil, aid him to make an intelligent choice, and advise him concerning his preparac
tion.   It will be evident, as we proceed, that a wide
outlook and a fixed desire for education will often rele-
gate present jobs to their proper place, as temporary
and never more than experimental.

We are to deal in this chapter with methods of vocational guidance as exemplified in educational guidance.
We shall be concerned with the following main topics:
(1) The child's place in the school; (2) School organization as related to guidance; (3) Possibilities for
guidance in the school program; (4) Possibilities for
guidance in the association of students with each other;
(5) The prevocational and continuation schools as instruments of self-discovery; (6) Definite preparation
for the occupation; (7) The development of good
traits of character.

The Child's Place in the School. — Why does the child
go to school?   Let us attempt to answer this question,
in the light of vocational guidance, first prefacing our
study with a reference to the early play of children.

Breadth of Experience through Earliest Play. — The
purpose of play in the child's life seems to be to enable

him to understand his world and to develop qualities that shall enable him to take his place in that world; it provides a tool through which he experiments and discovers the existence and methods of operation of materials, forces, and mental qualities. Apparently there can be no superstructure of educational guidance without the foundation laid by the child in his play.

Perhaps the chief way the young child begins to acquaint himself with the world is through dramatization. Joseph Lee has the dramatic age beginning at three, and among the first dramatizations of children are those which concern occupations. Let the postman or a plumber call, and the moment he goes the play begins. By entering into the fun — Mr. Lee shows that it is the child's most serious business — the parent can signally augment the educational effect. The tractable adult will find that the dramatization has elaborate and exact details, and will observe a growing sense of satisfaction and consciousness of success on the part of the child.[1]

[1] The vocational counselor must remember that this play is not for finding clews which point toward the occupation. Lee sets fourteen years as the earliest age at which vocational clews manifest themselves and states that in many cases none present themselves until much later. He says:

"And the first form of an instinct may be very different from that which it is destined finally to assume — a fact not yet recognized, even in this day of the apotheosis of evolution, by those educators, who, in their zeal for what they deem the practical, insist on pinning the fruit to the first sprout that appears above the ground. . . . Indeed there is almost a presumption that the spiritual force developing in any given play will not, in adult life, appear in anything resembling its present

The working out of these dramatic situations in his play at home and the assumption of various personalities, give the child an important preliminary experience, which becomes the mental equipment with which he later enters the school. Without doubt the complicated world of occupations discussed in his readers and his geographies will be better understood on account of the lessons learned in early play. Since an intelligent choice of vocation demands a broad vision of the field of occupations, the importance of this early dramatization is at once evident.

Aside from this form of growth through dramatization, the child's play before the school age should give him social contact and power of getting on with other children, and the habit of self-dependence and success in carrying out his legitimate purposes.

If play can be made to teach these lessons, the foundations for educational and vocational guidance will be well laid by the time the child reaches the school age.

How Schools Guide the Child. — Let us now turn to the school age, and consider first this question: How should the schools be organized and managed, for effective vocational guidance?

Educational institutions are organized to continue the lessons gained through systematic, serious play — to provide experiences useful to the individual and to

form. If it looks like a rose now it may develop into something very beautiful, but the chances are that it will not be a rose." (Lee, *Play in Education*, pp. 63–64.)

society. It is the business of the teacher to furnish an environment in which the pupils solve problems. The good school furnishes a sampling of life's worth-while experiences. This requires both manual and mental exercises — a combination of study and work — and the free play of the child's instincts. As Johnson pertinently says in reference to the serious purposes of the school, as related to the child's interest in play:

The efficient method is and must always be, in the nature of the case, from interests, activities, and achievements, to subject matter and not the reverse. The problem of elementary education is not to put play into the curriculum, but rather to put the curriculum into play.[1]

Let us see how the methods of teaching, the plans of organization, and school studies can be made to serve these principles, and how the vocational interests of the child may be given appropriate consideration and development.

Methods of Teaching should early be related to Vocations.— The principle of beginning with the child is making headway in the organization of many schools. The designation of certain types of schools as "lifesaving stations" and of others as "self-discovery schools" shows the attention being paid to the child by the modern teacher. Dewey's *Schools of To-morrow*, and Burk's *In Re Everychild vs. Lockstep Schooling* show the progressive teacher how the work of moving the focus of attention may be carried on. True educa-

[1] Johnson, *The Place of Play*, etc., p. 5.

tional guidance is impossible to the teacher who sees the subject before he sees the child.

The child and his needs must be the teacher's point of view, and vocational needs are not to be lost sight of. Beginning with the fifth grade, at the very least, the child should occasionally be regarded as one who will ultimately have an occupation in life, and as one who will sooner or later have to make his choice. We may well be generous in the breadth of experience in play and work in the kindergarten and the early grades in consonance with the thought that vocational outlook (as well as many other good things) comes from such experience. Nor need we narrow the scope of experience in holding that definite preparation for choice of occupation should find a place in the school plan from the fifth year on. Indeed as Eliot maintains,[1] habits of listlessness toward studies, and laziness, too, may arise from failure to appeal to the " life-career motive."

School Organization as Related to Guidance. — The development of men and women is the purpose of the school, and the selection of and preparation for the occupation is one of the important features in this development. The schools must therefore be organized with the vocational guidance of the child as one of the aims in mind.

Elementary-School Organization for Educational Guidance. — What organization shall school board, superintendent, and principal give to the first six grades of

[1] *Readings*, p. 1.

the elementary school, if that school is to carry out its vocational-guidance purpose? In Chapter II, Standards in Education, of Hanus's *School Efficiency*, the whole question of aims and elements of organization is tersely discussed. Unity of aim has more place in these lower grades, though there must be provision for flexibility in the rate of promotions, and for special classes and special schools whenever needed.

The work of the first six grades may comprise reading, writing, effective speaking, simple computation, construction of simple articles out of paper, wood, and clay, the domestic arts, singing, drawing, games, dramatics, and stories of history.[1] Geography, chiefly concerned with occupational opportunities, may begin with the fourth grade. All of the work of the first six grades may be called vocational in that both the so-called tools of knowledge, and the breadth of experience derived from the other studies are essential to success in the occupation.

Differentiation in the Intermediate Age. — Beginning with the sixth or seventh grade there must be provision for differentiation. Many American cities have made significant strides in the improvement of the upper elementary grades. Los Angeles has eleven intermediate or junior high schools which take children upon the completion of the sixth grade, offer them the choice of

[1] For excellent suggestions to show how play and manual work can widen the knowledge of occupations in the early grades, see Parsons, *Plays and Games*, and Dopp, *The Place of Industries in Elementary Education*.

many studies and provide secondary school methods, special teachers, and several studies formerly taught only in the high school. Boston has provided "prevocational centers," to which are admitted those boys and girls who might drop out if forced through the regulation routine. Many cities have experimented with the "transfer class," an attempt to help pupils who have reached the high school age but have failed to complete the elementary school. And many cities have seized the opportunity for schooling adapted to the blind, the dumb, the backward. Several progressive school systems in the country have been influenced by these recent changes.[1]

Besides the improvement of the upper grades, the organization of continuation schools gives promise of our realizing the ideal that before long our young people will never entirely "quit school." The prevocational centers and the continuation schools are of such direct importance for vocational guidance that we shall refer to them later in the chapter, after we have discussed the subjects of the school program.

High School Organization for Educational Guidance. — As in the case of the elementary school, a recognition of the problems of individual differences is prerequisite to that organization of the high school most favorable to vocational guidance. The aims and methods of the high school need not differ from those of the elementary

[1] See Briggs, Wright, and Com. of Educ., 1914, pp. 11–12, 21, 25, 93–96, 258.

school, except in so far as to provide for the fact that individual pupils differ more widely in their interests as we go upward in the school — the effect of learning (or increased practice) on the "curve of learning" is to widen the curve. Hence we need opportunity for greater differentiation.

For the purposes of vocational guidance the character of the differentiation should depend on the aims, interests, and future opportunities of the students. It is important to know both the pupils and their environment before organizing the school or drawing up the program of studies. It is idle to say, as some superintendents may, that each high school principal should personally do this work — should study individuals and environment for the purpose of giving the pupils educational and vocational guidance. The principal is ordinarily too much occupied with teaching or with the routine duties of his office either to get intimately acquainted with the pupils or to spend time enough in field observations and investigations to give him the needed outlook toward the occupational opportunities of those who are to leave the school.

What then can the organization provide? It should provide what the Boston, Grand Rapids, San José, Mishawaka, and many other high schools provide: one or more teachers whose chief business in the school is to make himself of special use in investigations of this sort. Such a person should be one who can leave the school for an hour's visit to a factory, store, or office when necessary, study the points of view of persons of various occupations and various life philosophies, summarize significant vocational information in such a way as to make it available for busy teachers, be at the call of any teacher to help solve a difficult vocational problem, give time to consultations with parents, give helpful talks about typical occupations, and conduct classes in the study of opportunities. Ordinarily, there will be at least a man and a woman teacher in each high school for such work. While such a division of labor is undoubtedly advisable, yet if the whole school program is to be related to the vocations, and if we are still to adhere to the policy of coeducation, every teacher must be prepared to do his or her best in capitalizing, for the benefit of the students of both sexes, the vocational values in every study.

Flexibility in Organization Necessary for Guidance. — Perhaps no element of successful organization is of such importance as that of flexibility. If failure begets failure, and if the habit of success is of vital importance for the pupil, then it is the business of the school to see that circumstances make possible the hourly, daily, and ultimate success of every pupil. The task should always be within the grasp of the boy or girl. Principals and teachers must be willing to modify the course of study rather than spoil the boy.[1]

' [1] In a Los Angeles intermediate school, a boy gave difficulty to the teacher and to the class in a recitation which began shortly after 11 o'clock each day. It was found that this was his fourth academic recitation each morning, that he gave no trouble in earlier classes, that he was

Boys are sometimes advised to interrupt their schooling for a year's working experience. This advice is mentioned by Davis, on page 87 of *Vocational and Moral Guidance*. Would it not be better, however, to increase the choice of subjects and the kind of activities so that the boy will not be exposed to the temptation which comes with earning money — wanting to keep on working? It is the experience of boys'-club workers, and of observant teachers, that many boys "learn the value of money" (a little money) too early in their careers — so early that it cuts short their schooling.

We shall find in a later chapter that the rigid school program drives boys and girls from school and into the great army of unskilled workers. A program adapted to their needs might save them for more education and more intelligent choice of vocation.

School Organization should not Relieve the Child of Responsibility. — The danger latent in the whole tendency to adapt the school organization and program to the child is that we may make conditions so easy for him that he will become a creature of whims, drifting, and dependence. Prudence and good judgment, therefore, are necessary in the administration of the elective system and the provisions for flexibility. These devices should never be used by a boy or girl to evade

fond of athletics but was assigned to the gymnasium class only twice a week. Here was obviously an opportunity to change custom. In spite of administrative difficulties the boy's program should have been altered, and daily physical training given him.

an obvious duty, to avoid the necessary consequences of a careless choice, or to withdraw from a half-completed undertaking.

On the positive side, what can the organization do to foster character development? It can provide for breadth of experience through many different kinds of tasks, and it can require success in these tasks as a condition to participation in the more advanced and attractive activities of the school. Further, it can seek out the aims and ambitions of the boy or girl in his own field of interest and show him what an amount of effort and persistence is necessary to success. Thus, the boy who wishes to learn to play the bass drum may be given lessons and allowed to try with the school orchestra, where he will readily see the need for application, attention, and study. Teaching him to do the broad jump correctly, using the proper marks to get his step, will mean months of study and practice for him. The girl who wishes to " go on the stage " may be assigned a part in a school play where she may be shown the necessity for a long course of training as a prerequisite to success.

The habit of hard, willing work in "play" can certainly teach good lessons needed in the occupation, and these lessons can be transferred to the schoolroom and to after life, if the teachers will make a serious attempt to see that the transfer is made possible. Later we shall show how some organizations have used student or club activities for this purpose.

How Certain New Plans of Organization Stimulate and Aid Vocational Guidance. — New plans of organization inevitably stimulate guidance, for they involve a reëxamination of the aims and methods of the school. The Gary plan widens the experience and opportunity of the child, and so aids in the discovery of his interests and talents.[1] Further, the practical nature of the shop work gives excellent preliminary knowledge in several trades.[2] The flexible daily program gives opportunity for outside experiences which widen the vocational horizon.

The longer school day is another plan which is favorable to better guidance, for it involves more play and more manual work.

The supervision of the child's experiences in the winter and summer vacations is a fruitful method of guiding him. This plan is used in many school departments, among them Portland, Oregon, and the High School of Commerce, Boston. Dartmouth College has recently inaugurated such a scheme.

Summary. — Our survey of school organization leads us to conclude that much of the recent progress has been directly in line with educational and vocational guidance, in that teachers are led to turn their attention to the welfare of the individual, provision for differentiation is made, and certain newer plans are opening the

[1] It has been suggested by Dewey that the enriched opportunity in the Gary plan will make actual guidance unnecessary. This question we shall discuss in the next chapter.

[2] See Com. of Educ. 1915 report, pp. 27–30; also Burris.

F

way to more efficient guidance. We shall now turn to the consideration of the studies of the school program, as instruments for educational and vocational guidance.

Possibilities for Guidance in the School Program.[1] — One of the writers on vocational guidance maintains that the subjects of the school program which have no occupational value are of little use. We need not agree with him, but we must hold, if the child is to be regarded by the teacher as a prospective worker, that each lesson having something to contribute to the vocational efficiency of the child should be taught with that fact in mind. The vocational uses will appear in almost all of the studies and will predominate in many of them.

English used for Guidance. — No doubt many teachers would object to displacing the present list of literary masterpieces which form the basis of the course in English. But these books themselves have vocational implications. Witness the lessons in qualities necessary to success in such works[2] as *Captains Courageous, Paul Revere's Ride, Treasure Island, Horatius, The Last of the Mohicans, Tom Brown's School Days, Old Testament Stories*, Bacon's *Essays*, Emerson's *Essays*, and *A Tale of Two Cities*. Witness, too, the actual vocational information and lessons in vocational guidance in *Silas Marner, David Copperfield, Oliver Twist, Snow-*

[1] For references on the vocational aspects of the school program, see the following: Bonser, Fletcher, Giles, Richards, Leavitt, Wheatley, Wile.

[2] These names are selected from the course of study of a city which is doing almost nothing in the way of conscious vocational guidance.

bound, Franklin's *Autobiography*, and Parton's *Captains of Industry*. The vocational questions arising in such books would serve as bases for interesting discussions which would put more life into a study which now often contributes notably to the process of eliminating children from school.

Some schools require book reviews of pupils in connection with the English work, and the available list is composed almost exclusively of fiction. It would at once add to the interest and breadth of the English work if books on vocational subjects were added to this list.[1]

The elimination of such material as useless formal grammar and long spelling lists would give room for more practical work in the language and literature classes.

Written Composition. — The work at Grand Rapids has been noted; it stands as an example of effective use of composition. Contribution No. I in Davis' book, which concerns work in the seventh and eighth grades, offers several interesting samples of pupils' work.

Undeveloped Possibilities in Oral English. — One of the Grand Rapids teachers[2] raises objections to the use of long biographical books, and gives her experiences in classes formed into clubs and arranging their own programs. The classes have made a specialty of " local

[1] See Davis's *Vocational and Moral Guidance* for lists of such books.
[2] Eaton, V. G. Bulletin, Jan. 1916.

heroes," interviewing persons in their own city, and reporting the results orally to the class.

Moreover, there may be a danger involved in attaching vocational guidance unthinkingly to the written composition lesson. Some teachers of composition concern themselves chiefly with the mechanics of writing, with the twofold result that subject matter is subordinated, and students dislike the work. It would be a pity for such a teacher to add vocational themes to the slaughter. Red ink, liberally applied, will kill even a subject as interesting as the choice of a vocation.

Why should we not approach vocational interests through Oral English, and wait until the students themselves express the desire to put ideas into written form? All the topics listed in the Grand Rapids suggestions are appropriate for oral work. Spoken English offers rich opportunity for experimentation and self-discovery. If the pupil is allowed to select his own subjects, he will be found explaining scientific and mechanical processes, telling about inventions, discussing current events, and arguing about vocations. He can be induced to learn to draw as he speaks, to give simple business talks with demonstrations, to take part in debates, and to organize impromptu conversations, interviews, and plays, in which problems like those in real life are presented and solved. In all this work he will make two gains: he will grow in confidence and speaking ability; and he will discover his interests. If something closer still to the vocation is desired, interviews may be arranged in which one pupil applies for work or promotion,[1] and afterward the class may discuss and criticize. Nomination speeches, announcements, the oral advertisement, technical descriptions, the introduction of a speaker, and mock trials offer valuable educational guidance.

Parliamentary law is of special importance. It trains the same person to lead and to follow. It is used in all organizations, whether business or social, into which the children will enter.

Oral English is used in connection with every vocation; hence its importance.

Arithmetic. — Such subjects as partial payments and cube root are going out of the arithmetics because they have little vocational use.[2] It is being recognized that spelling, writing, and arithmetic are for practical everyday needs, and that time spent in trying to find unrelated " culture " in them is waste time. It is the business of the teacher to relate the arithmetic as closely as possible to the obvious vocational needs of the boy and girl. The schoolroom, yard, store, and home offer wide opportunity for problems in arithmetic. In the upper grades it may be wise to offer sample problems from each of several common occupations. It may also be advisable to give the boys some arithmetic which will

[1] Artificiality and tiresome realism may be avoided by dramatizing a plot in connection with the application, thus making the interview into an extempore play.

[2] See the fourteenth Yearbook of the National Society for the Study of Education, Part I, pp. 61–130. University of Chicago.

not interest the girls, and the girls some problems connected with homemaking.[1]

Geography. — Geography has manifold possibilities. Related to human life, it can serve to introduce discussions on such topics as the following: Why do people live here? What do they do for a living? What has the topography to do with the habits and occupations of the people?[2] What are the resources of this place or that? How can we account for commercial and industrial differences between two places? Geography may be related to arithmetic by the use of time tables and graphs. Stereoscopic pictures, moving pictures, visits to museums, travel, and reference books all may be used in connection with the geography lesson.

Commercial geography is a profitable high school subject of great vocational value. Another name sometimes used is Industrial Geography, and the phrase Occupational Geography is coming into use, though textbooks have not thus far covered that field.

Social Studies: History, Economics, Civics, Sociology. — Fortunately, history is becoming less a fixed body of knowledge, and more a thing to be studied in the light of present events. Textbooks are emphasizing the beginnings of industries, changes caused by inventions,[3] the facilities for transportation, the educational re-

---

[1] See Leavitt and Brown, pp. 73, 176, 185–191, 220.

[2] See Chamberlain, Jas. F., for a plan.

[3] Prof. Bonser points out that industrial heroes are as worthy of consideration as military heroes.

sources of the people, the manners, customs, and occupations. This gives the teacher the opportunity to show the causes which were at work and to show that these causes in many cases are operating to-day. Thus we lead to the student's attempts to estimate the effects of these forces, both in the present and in the future, which is perhaps the chief use of history.

No better exercise can be given a pupil in the history class than the task of finding out all he can about the history of a chosen occupation. Throughout the course he can collect and record information whenever it can be found, and may make interesting reports to the class.

Community civics is rapidly replacing the civics which concerned itself largely with constitutions, terms of offices, and salaries of officers, and now children may study the complex, practical relationships of their own environment.

Boys and girls must be taught the elementary notions of political economy, for the reason expressed by Jevons:

If people do not understand a true political economy, they will make a false one of their own. [P. 11.]

Occupational life should not be entered by the child until he has been given some idea of its problems. He should have an elementary knowledge of how he as a worker helps to pay taxes, how the tax money is spent, what rent includes, what profit is for, what are the problems of the employer-employee relation, the elements of production, examples of coöperation, the advantages and disadvantages of competition, causes of unemployment, thrift, and conservation. The work may be a combination of sociology, civics, and economics. Segregations in and definitions of the three fields are unnecessary; the consideration of practical problems is more important.

Such studies cannot be postponed till the high school, because all our citizens need them.[1]

How Science is Related to Vocations. — The last ten or fifteen years has seen a marvelous change in the teaching of elementary science, as a comparison of text-books will show. Formerly, curiosity was the chief interest appealed to; now use is becoming the test. Courses in nature study which classified insects and named curious botanical specimens have their place for children who find satisfaction in this kind of work. At the same time, however, the science which ties natural causes to their effects in street, stream, mine, factory, and farm also should have its place in the school.

Drawing and Design. — The head of a high school art department is fond of saying that we neglect an important fact about the Greeks: though it is true that they adorned their homes and temples with beautiful statues, they also put artistic expression into the pots and pans of the kitchen. The courses in applied art and applied design reflect the modern desire to couple

---

[1] Some suggestive references, either for the pupils or teachers: Davis (*Field of*, etc.), Dunn, Gillette, Barnard, Pritchard, Haynes, Bate.

theory and practice, ornament and use, appreciation and execution, " culture " and vocation. Drawing should be intimately related to manual training, and it should be freely used in studies like oral and written composition, science, geography, and arithmetic. The ability to make a rough sketch is useful in many occupations. Many schools do efficient work in drawing, both in the elementary and in the high schools.[1]

Higher Mathematics. — Much algebra and geometry as now taught is purely theoretical and might be supplanted by problems related to needs. It is now recognized that a student may be taught to use the law of signs with perfect accuracy, even if he cannot explain its principle. The formula for the ratio of the circumference of a circle to the diameter may be grasped by analogy, without all the tedious drill on the logic, and time for practical applications may be gained.

Other Studies may Become Vocational. — Any study, whether Greek or geology, is a vocational study for the few or many in the class who may find their interest to lie in that work and decide upon an occupation for which this study is a requirement. This is an argument, obviously, for a wide range of opportunity in school and school system. Further, higher vocational courses often require certain high school subjects, such as Latin and mathematics.

The Manual Arts. — We shall speak in a later section about the high school subjects which are intentionally

[1] See bibliography, Haney.

vocational; here we shall consider the manual training of the elementary grades.

In the city of Los Angeles [1] there is an enrollment of about 5**,000 in the first eight grades, not counting those in the intermediate schools. For these children ninety minutes weekly is devoted to manual training. About one hundred and six teachers are engaged full time in the work, besides nearly a thousand grade teachers who assist. In the first and second grades the following are the activities: sand-table work, clay work, bead-stringing, seed-stringing, paper-tearing, cutting and folding, ruler work, paper construction, spool knitting, hand crochet, slat-weaving, paper-weaving, jute and raffia weaving, and knotting. The handwork is closely related to the drawing, music, nature study, gardening, and arithmetic. Woodwork extends from the fourth through the eighth grade. From the sixth grade on cement is used, and reed and textile work. Supervision and assistance is given to the work which boys and girls do on their own account at home. Shoe repairing is taught at two schools. At another school all the work of the school restaurant — cooking, sewing, laundering, and cleaning — is done by the students. Sewing is carried on in all the grades, and cooking in the last three.

In addition to the above described manual training, one hundred and one schools are doing work in gardening and elementary agriculture, with twenty-two special full-

[1] See School Report for year ending June, 1914.

time teachers. Each of nearly 12,000 pupils has a garden, with a total of eighteen acres under active cultivation.[1]

These activities show what can be done in the regular school, and the vocational values are evident. No better educational guidance can be given than the combination furnished by the manual arts, with the studies of the ordinary school program related to the vocations. As Eliot says, in discussing what studies the school should offer:

The elements of the arts applicable in ordinary households and in various trades and callings ought to be carefully taught in all schools, public, endowed, or private, such as drawing and designing, domestic science and art and home economics, carpentry and joinery, and, in rural communities, agriculture.[2]

It is important that manual work be made practical if it is to have any great effect in discovering aptitudes. Not " manual dexterity," but rather the ability to grasp and solve problems is the aim — to repair a leaky faucet or a broken rake. The stage should be set for the occurrence of such problems. Occasionally the pupils should be brought face to face with a complex situation such as is presented in the farm or factory. The dramatization of actual trade conditions offers opportunity for relating the manual arts to the other

[1] Note that these figures relate to conditions before the world war began. The 1917 figure was 1800 acres.

[2] *Readings*, p. 7. See also Cole.

work of the school. The importance of such manual training to vocational guidance is so great that it may almost be said that broad and practical manual training in the elementary school is indispensable for adequate guidance. Vocational counseling cannot be founded on a narrow school program.

The Use of Museums in Connection with School Studies. — An undeveloped field in most cities is the use of museums. The 1915 report of the Commissioner of Education, Chapter XXII, surveys the work of museums, and a 1914 Bulletin [1] explains the work of the St. Louis museum. Such organizations as the Boston Children's Museum minister to the interest which children have in the entertaining and curious, but they have little vocational significance. The Philadelphia Commercial Museum supplements the work of the schools in geography, commerce, and industry, and is of much greater use for vocational purposes than are collections of shells, stuffed animals, botanical specimens, insects, and the like, good as these may be. American curators still have much to learn from European institutions, where attention is paid to both kinds of exhibits. In the scientific museum in Munich one can see the X-ray, diagrams of the chemical composition of common substances, the full-sized model of the shaft of a mine, models of canal-locks, pulley systems, ships, agricultural machines, bridges, etc., besides machines to illustrate the principles of many sciences. In the

[1] No. 48, Rathman.

Museum of Arts and Crafts in Paris are shown industrial processes, safety devices, and models of factories and mines. In the South Kensington Museum of London, besides the extensive collection of scientific and industrial subjects, there are scores of models of machinery which may be set in motion by the pressing of a button. Here boys may study the steam locomotive from one model upside down, another cut into a vertical section in the middle and set up against a glass, and another with a section cut through one of the cylinders.

So far as is known to the writer, no American museum, unless possibly that at Philadelphia and certain exhibits in the new National Museum at Washington, can compare in vocational helpfulness with any of these three European examples. Here is a big field for progress in our methods of teaching. Will not the museum and the moving picture teach much about geography and manual arts in the future school and thus play a large part in vocational guidance?

New Subjects for the School Program. — The most important new study needed in the school program is a course on vocations. This course is needed in the elementary school, and it should be continued in the high school. As stated by Woods:

We teach our youth about the characteristics of geographical regions, the properties of numbers, and the peculiarities of language. As they go on with their studies we teach them the characteristics of chemical elements and compounds, the physical properties of bodies, the texture and mechanism of organic structures, both vegetable and animal, and their young minds unfold in the presence of a world richer and more complicated than they had ever dreamed. But about the qualities of men demanded by the world's work, about the rôle played by tact, by ability to meet men, by differing traits and tendencies of mind, as related to individual success in specific present-day tasks, we teach little. That the demands of one profession or craft are radically different from those of another, that the application of individual endowment to its appropriate task is a tremendously difficult thing, they learn only in the wasteful school of experience. . . .

Every boy before leaving the elementary school should be given an accurate idea of the nature of the principal kinds of human work, the qualities demanded by them, the preparation required, the rewards offered, the advantages and the opportunities for usefulness which they afford. He should, moreover, be taught the rudiments of self-appraisal from the vocational point of view and should have the benefit of counsel with a professional vocational counselor who is thoroughly informed with regard to the industrial opportunities of the community and the means of entrance thereupon.[1]

Bloomfield states the need thus:

Now real selection is impossible where the world of occupation is a dark continent . . .

It is in our centers of population, in the apartment and tenement-house districts, that the masses of children are to be found. Here is much need for unfolding the panorama of occupations to the quick intelligences of the young people.[2]

[1] *Youth*, etc., pp. 4–6.   [2] *Readings*, pp. 27–28, 30.

A school course in vocational information should aim to give needed direction for advanced education as well as for vocation. The course in the elementary school should aim to afford opportunity for an intelligent choice of a high school, and for the choice of the particular course. References such as the Boston School Committee Report of 1912, the Los Angeles Vocational Bulletin No. 1, the charts of educational opportunity in the Richmond and Minneapolis Surveys for Vocational Education, the Boston charts of the Women's Municipal League, and the recent Philadelphia publication should be studied as texts for the course, and visits to the schools be a part of the work. In a similar way, the high school course in vocations should use the catalogues of colleges and technical schools. The high school should make the necessary connections with the elementary school, so that the advice given may be followed in the high school. Freshmen students in the high school need careful educational guidance.

Turning to the high school course in vocational information, the Grand Rapids plan, with the modifications we have noted, may be followed. Another suggestive plan is that described by Superintendent Wheatley of Middletown, Conn., in the March, 1915, number of *School Review*.

In a later place we shall outline a proposed plan for a life-career class.

Possibilities for Guidance in the Association of Students with Each Other.—It seems likely that students obtain more usable experience and information from contact with each other than they do from adults. The "student activities," which are frowned upon by many teachers as "interfering with school work," have great vocational significance.

We have already noted the serious and valuable lessons from early play, in imparting experience and interpreting to the child both himself and the world. Later play continues these processes, and brings out vocational tendencies. Philip Davis speaks of the need for the vocational counselor to take account of traits developed on the playground.[1] Not only do athletics, if rightly conducted, furnish necessary and proper excitement, but they test, select, and train, and this without the failures and disappointments often attending failures to pass in school work. The activities carried on by the Boy Scouts and the Campfire Girls have the same good effects as athletics — everybody gains by trying the games and tasks proposed in their handbooks, even if he does not excel.

The summer camp is a microcosm of the industries of a community, and may be made to offer unsurpassed opportunity for guidance.

Competitions, such as those in growing corn and pigs, held by the state and federal departments of agriculture and by the General Education Board;[2] organizations such as the Junior Association of Commerce of Grand

[1] *Streetland*, p. 249.
[2] See Secy. of Interior, Report, June, 1915, p. 141.

Rapids,[1] dramatics, and boys' and girls' clubs, all furnish preliminary and tentative specialization of an advantageous kind, and disclose vocational clews.

Opportunity for participation in student government not only helps to teach civic rights and responsibilities, but it also gives play for tact and human intercourse which is important in the vocation.

When shall we have, as a student activity or as a regular part of the school program, an organization and assignment of the janitor and gardening work about the school? Professor James's celebrated pamphlet *The Moral Equivalent of War*, suggests the question, and if a beginning is to be made the schools must make it. Miss Lathrop[2] maintains that the janitor should be a teacher, and that the work of caring for the school should be done by the pupils as a regular part of their work. Claxton believes that the school should organize the labor of the pupils in such a way as to make it contribute toward their support.[3] Many schools have made a beginning: furniture for the school department is made in the shops of the school, books are bound, printing done, automobiles kept in repair, lawns cared for, and heating plants managed, each as a part of the manual training of the school.

How Club and Student Activities Enable the Child to Discover his Powers. — We shall now present some specific instances to show how the boy discloses his aims

---

[1] See Davis, p. 286.   [2] 1914 Proceedings, pp. 49–50.
[3] *Ibid.*, p. 46.

G

and abilities, to himself and to others, by means of these activities which are not a part of the regular school program. The boys from whose experiences we have drawn are or were members of the Columbia Park Boys' Club [1] of San Francisco.

GUIDANCE THROUGH CLUB AND STUDENT ACTIVITIES

SUMMARIES OF ACTUAL CASES, TAKEN FROM CORRESPONDENCE

1. F. C. Studied electricity at a trade school, and became interested in the school paper. Went on Australian trip, and wrote constantly about the trip. Wrote a $75 story about Hawaiian Islands. Took up work with Boy Scouts and wrote scout news for papers. Often went out on news details to accommodate one of the editors; finally went into the newspaper office as reporter for the waterfront

---

[1] Speaking of the work of the club, as it relates to vocational guidance, Major Sidney S. Peixotto, the founder and president, says: " I consider that the school studies have absolutely nothing to do with the vocational end of a boy's life; I mean by this, no matter how good a boy is in study periods, it is really no positive indication of his . . . vocation. The true vocational guidance comes from the educational play given a boy. I include in this list of educational play: Dramatics, Dancing, First Aid, Gymnastics, Handicraft Work, Military Training, and Outdoor Athletics. Until the school includes most of these subjects, the difficulty of advising boys by teachers will be great. By studying a boy in his play activities, and by giving him serious tasks to perform in achievement work, I am able to decide upon a boy's natural bent and to act as his guide in shaping his thoughts for life work. . . . It will be necessary for the schools eventually to go into the achievement idea, because it is only by example or illustration of actual conditions that children learn anything, especially those traits which are necessary to success in any vocation, — energy, work, and the need of long and careful preparation."

district. Sees literary possibilities and intends to devote his life to writing. States that very few of the boys who studied in the trade school have followed the lines they studied. "The architects seem to be the most consistent."

2. J. C. Joined club when very young. "I owe the shaping of my early life and the commencement of my progress . . . to the environment and activity of the club." Graduated from grammar grades and took a job driving a butcher wagon, with hours so long that night school was impossible. Was placed in another position by the club, and went to night school. "It was through the spirit of the club that I took full advantage of this, and I do not believe the education I received would have been obtained had it not been through this influence." Has "been with several importing and exporting firms, but never deviated from this line of business." Now managing one of the offices of a trading company. "It is needless to say that I cannot speak too highly of the club's work. It puts the right kind of optimism and enthusiasm into a fellow that works wonders in after life."

3. M. S. Decision to study medicine was primarily due to home influences, "greatly augmented through my club experiences." Was called "Doc" in club, on account of facility in bandaging blisters on walking trips. Club workers encouraged the ambition. Now taking a medical course, and earning $70 per month as a signal towerman at night, a position which gives opportunity for study. "I believe that the club has been the most important influence in that with such a wide range of opportunities it gives one a chance to choose a line to which he feels best adapted."

4. H. R. "I acquired more confidence in myself, gained broader views and ideas through association with people of

higher intellectual standards than my own. The influence of the club was on the moral and social side (social in its broader sense)." Now a civil engineer, and teacher in a technical evening school.

5. A. J. T. States that the club offers opportunity for its members to become broader in ways often neglected by the other methods of schooling. "All the teaching takes place through actual practical experience. It does not instruct its members what to do when they go out of the club, but actually goes through all this work with them. . . . The club has been the means of putting all my other education into good and practical experience." Professional cornetist. Got his start in the club band.

Some Implications for School Authorities, from Club and Student Activities. — The obvious lesson from the guidance furnished by the activities of boys and girls outside the classroom, is that school authorities should systematize, organize, and encourage them so that they may have their full effect. Every schoolman or woman should read on scouting and play, school credit for home work[1] and such works as Denison's *Helping School Children*. Too often the interests of children are exploited by persons with goods to advertise, or directed by other persons who lack the educational aim. The only preventive is to substitute school control. Many principals have long used these interests as leaven in the school. In Chapter XII of *Vocational and Moral Guidance*, Jesse Davis outlines a plan.

Student and club activities have too often been called

[1] Alderman.

the " side shows " of the school. Pending the awakening of the teachers to the real opportunity these activities offer, students who have seen both the side shows and the " main show " will need to be convinced that the latter is the more valuable.

The Prevocational and Continuation Schools as Instruments of Self-discovery. The Prevocational School. — The theory back of the prevocational idea has already been made clear. Parsons says that " a knowledge of each of the great classes of industry by practical contact is the right of every boy." [1] Goodwin says that there is a general agreement among those who have investigated the subject that but little can be done for the pupils who do not go on to high school, except as prevocational training, manual in character, is introduced into the elementary school.[2] The prevocational school is the so-called " self-discovery school." It aims to widen experiences, to present problems, to set the attention on projects, to teach the academic studies and the manual subjects in intimate correlation, to give children a well-planned " jack-of-all-trades " opportunity.

Prevocational Education in the Public Schools, by Leavitt and Brown, goes into the subject so clearly and succinctly that we shall here call attention merely to two or three salient features, and answer some possible objections to the work, and some questions which arise.

The extent of the school program, in a typical plan, is shown by the Boston list:

---

[1] *Choosing a Vocation*, p. 61.   [2] P. 130.

Academic studies: English (including penmanship, composition, spelling), arithmetic, history, geography, hygiene, science, drawing.

Manual studies for boys: Printing and bookbinding, metal work, electricity and power, shoe and leather work, clay and cement, woodwork, textiles, paper work, agriculture.[1]

Manual studies for girls: Cooking, dressmaking and millinery, household management, textiles, sewing.

Some distinctive features of the prevocational work in American cities are the following: the employment of teachers who have had actual shop experience; visits to factories, shops, and stores; assignment of projects away from the school premises, with boys in charge as foremen; competitions in workmanship; the use of commercial magazines and catalogues for study. The Boston prevocational centers have a Foreman's Club, and publish a magazine called *The Workmaster*.[2]

Another feature must already have become obvious — that here is an ideal setting for effective vocational guidance. The teachers have shop connections, have few pupils and can become well acquainted with them, know the requirements of the occupations, and have abundant opportunity for observing the abilities of the boys. Naturally enough therefore, vocational guidance is a vital part of the work.

[1] It must not be thought that more than two or three of these subjects are offered in any one school, or that any great proportion of pupils are enrolled. The work is still in its beginning.

[2] Leavitt and Brown, p. 235. See also App. E of the Minneapolis Report.

One or two possible misconceptions concern our study of vocational guidance. First, is the prevocational work for the relatively dull boy? Practically, the work is expensive and cannot at once be thrown open to all; hence those who do not do well in the ordinary classes are often selected for the prevocational classes. Here many show at once that it was the work of the regular classes which was the misfit, rather than the boys. As a matter of future policy, no doubt all whose parents desire it should be allowed the broader program of the prevocational school. Second, are there boys with the " motor type " of mind who should be discovered and assigned to this work? In answer to this question we must say no; our reasons we defer to a later chapter. Third, is the name " prevocational " well used, to describe this work? Bawden in the 1915 report of the Commissioner of Education raises this question.[1] The criticism of the term is just : these schools are for self-discovery, and in any given case a boy may discover here that he should be a teacher, lawyer, salesman, or merchant rather than a plumber or a printer. In this connection it is interesting that in one of the Boston classes in June, 1915, all of the fifteen graduates went on to high school.[2] Fourth, is this the same as or different from " manual training " ? The discussion as to the aim of manual training is too large in its implica-

[1] P. 223.

[2] See Bonser, "Is 'Prevocational' a Needed or Desirable Term?" His point is well taken: the intermediate or junior high school should do prevocational work.

tions for adequate consideration here. We may infer, if past development is to be continued, that manual training will cease to be justified by its supposed friends on the basis of its so-called " training " or disciplinary value, that it will become more and more practical, and that it will finally be indistinguishable from what we now call prevocational work. Fifth, and last, is this kind of education for the boys alone, or for both boys and girls? Our answer is similar to that given to the first question. The work is new and more expensive than that of the ordinary classes; the girls have protested less against the all-academic program, therefore they must endure it longer. Their turn for a broader program will come — indeed it has come in some schools.

Continuation Schools, in their General Effect on the Vocation, are Similar to the Prevocational Schools. — Wisconsin, Ohio, and Massachusetts are the three states which have done most with continuation schools. So much experience has been gained that we are now referring less and less to European example.[1] This experience is convincing us that the continuation school, though completely different in organization from the prevocational school, must do the same work — must help the child to find himself. The data for this conviction are so clear that it has been said that the continuation school should not even be called a finding but rather a reclaiming school (see statistics, Chapter

[1] Some of the limitations in the German continuation schools have recently been pointed out; see Myers, Geo. E., pp. 9–11, 14, 16.

VI). Assistant Superintendent Thompson of Boston says that four fifths of the working boys under sixteen are merely messengers. President Miles of the Wisconsin State Board of Industrial Education states that " from fourteen to sixteen, eighty-seven per cent of working children are in dead-end, blind-alley jobs." [1] Thompson says that about one half the girls in the continuation school are actually engaged in industrial pursuits, and that some real continuation work can be done for them, as well as for the few boys who are in machine or printing shops.[2] It is evident from these studies that the children of the continuation school have not found themselves, and that the manifest duty of the school is to assist them in just such a way as does the prevocational school or the " regular " school with the enriched and varied program. " General improvement " classes are organized in Wisconsin and in Massachusetts (Boston) continuation schools, and vocational guidance naturally forms a large part of the work.

It is not necessary to ignore the present employment of the continuation-school pupil; it should be used as a probationary experience. Children should be trained to be efficient in to-day's work, to broaden their vision and their business experience in their work as errand runners, to select their real vocations wisely, to prepare

[1] Nat. Assn. Manufacturers, p. 30. See other data in Chapter VI.

[2] Wisconsin experience in regard to girls has led to a different conclusion; see Wisconsin State Board of Industrial Education, 1914, pp. 476–483, especially p. 479. Wisconsin has recently extended the continuation school age to 17.

themselves definitely, and to recognize and seize opportunities which present themselves. These things the continuation schools are trying to do, with what success may be judged by an examination of the growing literature on these important experiments.[1]

Definite Preparation for the Occupation. — We have so far considered the child's place in the school, the school organization as related to vocational guidance, the possibilities for guidance in the curriculum and in student and club activities, and the prevocational and continuation schools as instruments of self-discovery. We now come to the consideration of the actual vocational training given by the school — the preparation for the occupation.

Our study of the continuation school shows us that as a matter of general policy it is impossible to give real vocational training before the sixteenth year. And even if we begin our definite preparation at that age, experience shows us that we must still be ready for changes of mind and must provide also for the large number who may not yet have reached any decision. Thus we must constantly be ready to apply vocational guidance. With these provisos, what shall be the nature of the education which our secondary schools shall offer? Obviously, the high schools must offer continued experimentation or broad curricula for those who do not yet wish vocational training, and diversified voca-

---

[1] For an account of the Boston work, see Circular of Information relating to Continuation Schools, Boston Public Schools, No. 26, 1915.

tional preparation for others. Hence the need for educational and vocational guidance throughout the high school is evident.

What should be the nature of the vocational training? Fortunately there is a body of experience from which to draw. Schneider, Hanus, Gillette, Snedden, Leavitt, Thompson, Lapp and Mote, Eaton and Stevens, and the Richmond, Minneapolis, and Cleveland Surveys have put into available form what has been learned.

It is needless in this book to treat of the many kinds of vocational education which are actually in operation, and of the problems yet to be solved. On these problems are working both the layman and the educator, and in the newer plans, employer and teacher are joining in the guidance of the high-school student. We refer, of course, to the coöperative or part-time plan explained in Schneider's book, and now in operation in many parts of the country.[1]

No one can say what will be the terms upon which this coöperative labor and education will be carried on, when experience has taught us. Devine said at the Second Vocational Guidance Conference:[2] "Education and industry should get together, but it should be on education's terms, not on industry's terms." It is the paramount duty of the school and the employer to agree on such terms as will be beneficial for both the future worker and society. In this coöperation

[1] See also McCann and Stimpson.
[2] Page 1, quoting Henderson in *Pay Day*.

it is certain that both industry and education have much to learn, and that both will profit from the association.[1]

With all the efficiency developed in vocational training, the surprising fact must not be forgotten that many boys and girls decide on a vocation, learn the elements of that vocation in a high school, and succeed in their school work, but in the process of the learning broaden their horizon and choose another occupation. It would seem that even specialization must not be too narrow — vocational training must not close the door of opportunity — it must open several avenues at once. The boy or girl is likely to experience a progressive rising and clarifying of the vocational aim.

The Development of Good Traits of Character. — We have already discussed the questions of responsibility and persistence, and we have shown how play and student activities aid in the development of persistence, habits of success, initiative, responsibility, and power to coöperate. All these, however, good as they are, relate in the main to personal efficiency : their bearing on the habit of kindness and unselfish living is not so direct. We shall see in a later place that mere personal efficiency will not of itself solve the perplexing problems of our social life. The teacher and the counselor, therefore, must strive for a social efficiency which relates itself to the commandment to love one's neighbor as oneself. No student of vocational guidance can tolerate the unsocial scramble for money or power.

[1] See Schneider, *Education for*, etc., pp. 75-76.

It is the business of the school to make character count; without it all guidance is vain.

Some educators are fond of saying that this ideal is a matter of religion as distinct from morals. Be this as it may, the school cannot escape responsibility for the habits developed by the children in the school. In the first place, the school can help to prevent the many breaches of good taste and kindness due to thoughtlessness. By example, discussion, systems of self-government, and punishments the school can put before the pupil the duty of consideration for the welfare of others. In a well-ordered school atmosphere it should be made hard for the selfish person, and unselfishness should have the reward of approval, respect, and satisfaction.

In the second place, the school should plan coöperative tasks, both in academic and in manual work, so that the pupils will have training in joint action. This coöperative action should be so ordered as to show the pupils their own interdependence; for example, an investigation in community civics or the construction of a dozen desks may be planned in such a way that the advantages of coöperation become apparent. Team work, obedience to rules and principles of conduct, and loyalty to aims, motives, and ideals may be taught in these ways, as well as in the play and athletic efforts of the pupils. "School spirit," with its loyalty to the worthy purposes and activities of the institution, furnishes a large opportunity for the wise teacher, principal,

and vocational counselor. No doubt these loyalties
are far more efficient and lasting than any based on mere
personality.

Third, the attitude and habit of service may be cultivated. In the manual training work articles may be
made by the younger children for the use of the older,
and *vice versa*. Useful tasks for parents, city, school,
and companions may be planned and encouraged in
many of the classes; and the civics and history recita-
ations may bring out the thought of service among
adults. There should be no cant in the teaching; the
teacher may deal with conditions in the business and
industrial world candidly, but may point out the better
way and the many indications that progress is being
made.

In dealing with questions of personal morality and
self-control the task is more difficult. Negative advice
— abstinence — has been to a large extent the traditional method. Such a method has little effect unless
it can be grounded on concrete facts. Thus, there may
be cited the large and growing number of firms which
object to the use of liquors on the part of their employees.[1]
On the other hand, negative advice based on physiological considerations is notoriously dangerous. There is
almost always an inevitable exaggeration of physical
effects, which for many boys vitiates such advice. Again,

[1] Some of them reject all users of liquors, but use a decoy question in
their application blanks: "Are you a heavy or a moderate drinker?"
or "Do you drink liquors? To what extent?"

fear does not deter, nor does mere knowledge; it is known that some men who know in detail the harmful effects of dangerous drugs fall victims to their use.

Substitution is no doubt the safer and more effective way. If self-respect, honesty, and temperance can be learned through actions in which they play an important and necessary part, the opposite qualities would be avoided, in part if not altogether.

The development of good traits of character should be the ubiquitous concern of the vocational guide. Though our discussion here is brief and inadequate, the character motive should be read into our treatment of all the other topics of the book.

Summary. — The aims of education, and of educational guidance, from the viewpoint of vocational guidance, are as follows: to study each child as a separate problem; to make the school organization flexible and to provide for the teacher's playing the part of counselor; to turn to account the vocational possibilities of the school program and to add to the program an effective course on occupations; to encourage and direct such student and club activities as will contribute to the finding of vocational clews; to use the prevocational and continuation school for self-discovery, conservation, and reclamation; to provide in schools of secondary and college grade definite preparation for the occupation; and to develop, with all, good traits of character. We have seen that much progress toward the realization of these aims has already been registered.

Our next task is to study the methods of guidance which are directly concerned with individual counsel. It will become apparent, as the study proceeds, that the task of counseling is much more difficult than the task of guidance through educational experiences. This fact will present two implications: there is need for keeping boys and girls under the school influence as long as possible; and there is need for making that school opportunity count for educational and vocational guidance. When hundreds of boys say that they left grammar school before completing the eighth grade because they did not think it worth while to graduate, as they actually said in a recent New York investigation, it discloses the character of the problems ahead of us.

These problems are being attacked, with more and more approach to a systematic method. In the approach, we find the study of conditions in the occupations helpful. To a review of these conditions we shall come, first examining the plans for counseling individuals which are in common use.

CHAPTER IV

VOCATIONAL COUNSELING AND THE WORK OF THE COUNSELOR

The Need for Counseling Individuals. — " If I had had vocational advice when I was a boy," recently remarked a college professor of sociology, " I should probably have been guided into being a gardener." The purpose of the statement was to show the danger in vocational direction. Admitting that an error would have been made in the case of the professor, is that a reason for no guidance? If the speaker had examined his own past experiences, he would without doubt find that he did have vocational counsel — that he had advice, encouragement, and direction while taking all the important steps in his career. Then how about the millions who drift blindly into and out of jobs? Shall we fear the error of making one less teacher, and thereby create scores to join the army of the misemployed?

It may be replied that with the plans outlined under our study of educational guidance the individual will be enabled to find himself, and no actual counsel in the shape of personal conferences will be needed. There are several negations of this position. First, the enriched

program often means increased bewilderment to individual pupils unless they have sympathetic aid in
making the decisions which the large range of choice
entails. The course on vocations must necessarily be
general in its scope; applications must be made concrete
and individual, and this involves personal conferences.
Vocational guidance cannot stop with furnishing a wealth
of knowledge of opportunities and occupational information; valuable as these are, they may still leave
the boy or girl far from the desirable goal. The teacher
who sets out to conduct a course in occupational information will soon find individuals coming to him for
personal advice; thus counseling becomes unavoidable.
Educational guidance will probably mean not less but
more counseling.

A second reason why counseling will be needed is that
with the best the school can do the child cannot be made
fully to understand the importance of his decisions, and
cannot be induced to make the most of his opportunities.
There will be boys and girls who will derive little benefit
from our elaborate plans while in school, but will be ripe
for counsel after they have tried three or four jobs. Then
the counselor must be at hand.

Third, until we perfect our educational guidance there
will be work enough with those who are employed but
in great need of advice. As one of the letters to The
Vocation Bureau states it: " I notice that your book,
Choosing a Vocation, is widely circulated, but cannot
think that it is of much advantage to the individual

unless he has direct connection with some vocation bureau." [1]

The Questions with which Counseling Deals. — We shall confine our study in this chapter to the legitimate and valuable factors of the process of counseling individuals, leaving to the next chapter the criticism of some questionable practices which often pass for vocational guidance. We shall here consider the following topics: (1) The use of tests; (2) Analyses of personal qualities; (3) Record cards; (4) Guidance through placement; (5) Employment supervision; (6) The work of the employment manager; (7) Some special plans; (8) The collection, classification, and use of occupational information; (9) The equipment of the counselor.

The Use of Tests. — Almost any kind of a test is called a " psychological test " nowadays, and the usual effect of the term is to give such tests a vogue without proper inquiry as to their utility. This overestimation of the potential and actual value of laboratory tests has done much harm to the cause of vocational guidance, and will be discussed in the next chapter. We are concerned here with what *can* be done.

Dr. Ayres, writing in October, 1913, says:

Even after all allowances are made, the inevitable conclusion remains that in vocational guidance the greatest field

[1] For further discussion of the need of counseling, and the coöperation required, see Maclaurin, *Readings*, pp. 16–17; and Hanus, *Readings*, p. 92.

of immediate development for psychological tests is in choosing persons for positions rather than in selecting positions for persons.[1]

Now since the teacher, the counselor, and the young person himself are concerned with the second of these two operations, that of finding a vocation or position for a boy or girl, psychological tests do not appear to offer help to them. Rather the tests seem to aid only the employer, who of course has the position and wishes to select the person to fill it.

On the same topic, Bloomfield, in *Youth, School, and Vocation*, says:

It appears that if facilities for competent research are provided, the general decision concerning relative fitness for (1) advanced education for expert scientific, technical, or professional service; (2) clerical or office work; and (3) mechanical or trade and factory work can be based in part upon a psychological inventory taken as early as the age of fifteen (pp. 60–62).

These two statements seem to be the most hopeful views of the situation with regard to the present contribution of psychology to vocational guidance. (Some others seem to be too sanguine and are treated in the next chapter.) Let the counselor get what comfort he may from these hypothetical advantages; the fact remains that much is yet to be done before practical use can be made of psychological tests.

[1] Proc. of Nat. V.-G. Assn., 1913, p. 37.

What then can tests do? In the first place, investigations such as those being carried on in Cincinnati may finally give helpful results to guide us. Mrs. Woolley's plan is to make frequent tests of groups of children in school and at work — tests which are of great variety and several times repeated — and to keep a record of the successes of these children in the occupations. She then hopes to be able to find a basis of correlation between the records in the tests and in the occupations.[1] This experiment suggests a point so far almost completely neglected by the psychologists — the testing of a person's capacity for improving. Perhaps general " improvability " cannot be tested; clearly, however, it is more important in a beginner than present knowledge or skill, and frequently bears little relation to initial performance.

In the second place, laboratory tests may for the present be abandoned, so far as vocational guidance is concerned, and actual standardized work tasks substituted. The records of the child in such tasks, and his capacity for improvement, if a series of tests can measure it, may be taken as a basis for forecasting

[1] See her plans and preliminary report in the references in the bibliography. (Her conclusions that there are types of mind will be discussed in the next chapter.) It is only fair to note that the tests Mrs. Woolley has used are those for psychological ages, and not at all for vocational aptitudes. Further, even psychological ages tests have not been standardized or agreed upon for a period of years. Again, even if positive correlations between tests and occupational success are found, we can never be sure that other occupations might not have proved more successful.

probable success.[1]   The achievement tasks and prevocational work, of which we spoke in the last chapter,
would go far toward becoming adequate tests of ability.
The part-time or coöperative plan will serve as an actual
trial of the worker's ability, if the entrance into the work
is carefully supervised.

School examinations may be much improved, and may
in time become the best of all " psychological tests."   If
the psychological investigations were made in the actual
schoolroom in coöperation with the teachers, it seems
likely that much more progress would be made than we
can hope to make with researches apart from the school.
Thus the psychologist may study the interests of pupils
as expressed in their choices of studies, games, and subjects for oral and written composition; aid the teacher
in grading for difficulty a series of lessons in arithmetic;
study the correlation between school marks in English
and in science; help the teacher in planning better
examinations in geography; plot individual learning
curves for records in a series of examinations in stenography.   The coöperation of the trained psychologist,
the vocational counselor, the teacher, the employment
supervisor, and the employment manager, may in time
yield some examinations which will aid in the work of
selecting a vocation.

Analyses of Personal Qualities. — The attempt to
name and classify the human virtues is as old as the time
of Homer; we shall not try to add another schedule.

[1] See Thompson, 1915 Report of Comm. of Educ., p. 291.

The review of long lists of desirable qualities is a favorite exercise of the business man who is asked to address a body of high school students. But what the students need is the experience of actual situations in which these virtues play a part. Thus, a better lesson can be drawn from a class discussion on the question, " What would you do if you found a counterfeit half-dollar in your pocket? " than on the question, " Why is honesty necessary in business? "

In the Grand Rapids plan " the elements of character that make for success in life," are taught through biography, discussion, compositions, and self-analysis. (Davis states that the last must be used with discretion.) The book, *Vocational and Moral Guidance*, contains directions, sample compositions, and bibliographies.

Several high schools (*e.g.* in Los Angeles and Boston) attempt to obtain a composite judgment on each pupil, as a basis for office information in regard to him, and for possible recommendation to an employer. A list of pupils is presented to each teacher, the names being followed by columns labeled at the top: Reliability; Scholarship; Initiative; Appearance; General Character, etc. The marks used designate Excellent, Good, Fair, and Poor, and the teacher fills the columns for whatever students he knows well enough. The results are tabulated in the principal's office. They show, for example, that three teachers have marked Harry White excellent in initiative; ten have marked him good; and two, fair. Such judgments should be of value, though too often the teachers have a very limited experience with the children.[1]

It must be noted that virtues are specific things and not general; they are carried over from one situation to another only as the two situations have similar characteristics, or as special effort is made to secure the transfer. Thus, a boy who is industrious in his school work will be industrious in his home duties only as the two situations are similar, both possessing such elements or ideals perhaps as emulation, graduated progress, intelligent supervision, and satisfactory results. Much of the "moral suasion" used on children is based on the theory of general discipline, as we shall see in the next chapter. Children are told that they must learn persistence, as if this quality could be absorbed from following the plow and then automatically transferred to the task of studying Latin. It is now seen that good habits must be consciously and persistently related to the second field of action before there can be any great likelihood that they will be transferred.

Self-analysis, too, should be based on one's measuring himself by concrete tasks rather than by qualities abstracted from their environment. An illustration from the experience of Miss Ginn, Director of the Vocational Guidance Department of the Boston schools, will indicate a legitimate and helpful method of self-

[1] Teachers who have had to fill out a statement upon a boy who has applied for a bond will realize how little the classroom work tells about him.

analysis. When she was in charge of an eighth grade class of girls she asked them to state what they intended to be, and eighty-five per cent gave stenography as their choice. After a few days had passed the girls were asked in a class exercise to make a list of the qualifications of a good stenographer. They responded with many items, all of which were placed on the board and allowed to remain some days. Then the girls who had chosen stenography were asked to measure their own personal qualities by the requirements there stated. The same exercise was carried out with other occupations. A few weeks later, when another poll was taken, the per cent of stenographers had dwindled to eleven, showing that the exercise had made the girls more critical in their thinking.

Character analysis, then, like psychological testing, must be based on the actual tasks which children will be called on to do.

There are two characteristics, or habits of conduct, or states of mind — whatever they be called — which seem to be present as common elements in most of the situations of life. Therefore they may be spoken of in general terms, and they possess a large degree of transferability. We refer to the habit of coöperative service and the habit of succeeding. Manifestly it is the school's duty to see that these powers have play in all legitimate ways.

Record Cards. — The best practice seems to indicate that the counselor rather than the child should fill in most of the answers on the record blank. If the child does the work unaided, either the question may be misunderstood, or the answer made to fit what the child thinks is wanted, or the temptation to vary from the exact truth may be presented. Frequently the counselor will find it necessary to ask three or four questions, in order to obtain a satisfactory statement to fill one space.

What questions shall be asked? The literature of vocational guidance is full of sample record cards,[1] and the total list of questions asked would range from the now notorious, " Does your mind concentrate or skip around? " to the query, " What service to the community are you planning to render through your vocation? "

Of all these blanks the simplest are the most workable. For the average child two thirds of the questions on a card with many spaces to fill have no significance whatever. It seems best, therefore, to ask a minimum number of questions and to allow space for comments on other significant facts discovered in the conferences. Thus the teacher or counselor and the child are enabled to save time and to concentrate on vital matters. The blank with forty or fifty questions is usually never all filled in, and is unwieldy for actual use.

The Boston cards on pages 192–193 of *Youth, School, and Vocation* are concise and workable. This question might be added, perhaps; Use of time outside of school

[1] Parsons, pp. 17–46; Bloomfield, *Youth*, etc., pp. 179–206; *The School and the Start in Life*, pp. 39–69; *Readings*, p. 131; Report of U. S. Com. of Labor, 1910, Chap. XV, p. 441; Davis, *Vocational and Moral Guidance*, pp. 78–80, 143–144, 253–272.

hours, in work, recreation, and clubs. The question on future vocation may be broadened to include the three to five occupations which are under consideration, arranged in the order of present preference. At the bottom of the card could be filled in the composite record of teachers' opinions suggested above.

It is a serious question whether or not unfavorable data should be put on cards. There are some strong reasons against the practice. First, the cards should be transmitted through the grades, and it is unfair to the child to prejudice him in the eyes of a new teacher. Second, the importance of unfavorable comments, if placed on record, is likely to be exaggerated — they strike the attention of the reader and suggest more than they should. Third, we guide the child by means of his successes and not through his errors; his mistakes may often best be forgotten. Keeping them on record after they are corrected is a poor policy.

Even such questions as those relating to physical disabilities, past sicknesses, and " hereditary " weaknesses are open to objection, on similar grounds. Hurried judgments on these objectional questions are useless if not injurious. Some cards examined recently bore such statements as: hereditary tendencies — rheumatism, scar over eye; past illnesses — measles, appendicitis, scarlet fever (no other statement). Such statements tell nothing about the vocation. There is no general agreement on the complex questions of heredity, and it seems useless to parade before the child the possibility of duplicating in his life the diseases of his parents. Teachers are ordinarily not well enough informed to be discriminating, and frequently attach more importance to the influence of heredity than do those who have studied the subject more deeply. An examination upon entering every job, as is enforced in Boston, and a general question on the child's blank, such as, " Are there any common occupations or kinds of work he should avoid? " would seem to be sufficient.

Religion should not be entered on a card. If placement is the issue, a general question about regular work and holidays will serve the purpose.

We have said above that the record cards should be passed on with the pupil. This does not mean that they should remain unchanged. Horton[1] tells of the advantages of a new card each semester, and Mrs. Woolley speaks of the child's being followed through the school by a kind of cumulative judgment of his various teachers.[2] The Boston card provides for changes of plans. The card should bear spaces for additional information at any time, and for the date and significant facts of each conference between the child and his counselor.[3]

Guidance through Placement. Its Advantages. — The placement office has undeniable advantages for

---

[1] P. 40.   [2] Proc. of Sec. Nat. Conference, p. 85.

[3] This counselor may be the child's teacher, though there should be provision for distinguishing in the record the occasions when the pupil is counseled by the specialist in vocational guidance in the school or vocation bureau.

exercising guidance: the applicant is receptive to advice; the officers are in close touch with the needs of occupations; placement saves the young people from the dangers involved in wandering about in the streets and offices looking for work; the placement officers are in a position to do good "follow-up" work; the reaction on the school can be made effective for better school work.

The Disadvantages of Guidance through Placement. — On the other hand, there are certain dangers involved in guidance through placement. In the first place, the name placement itself suggests inactivity on the part of the applicant, — that he is a pawn to be moved into his space. "Pegs" are to be fitted into "holes." If we could see certain economic and social conditions improved, it might be far better for young people to find their own places. This proposition we shall discuss in Chapter VIII.

Second, placement is never finished; it is a process which must be so often repeated that the machinery for adequate placement in a city would be so unwieldy as to be very likely to fall by its own weight. The Boston Placement Bureau manages, apparently, to keep sight of the individual, but the report of the continuation school shows that the bureau secured places for only one and eight tenths per cent of the children enrolled in the school. In order to place and to follow up even this number an elaborate card system must be prepared and kept as nearly up to date as the facilities of the bureau will allow. No one can prophesy what kind of records would be needed for placing all the working children of Boston, or whether it would be possible to organize the work in one office. It seems certain that a system so extensive would lose sight of individual problems.

Third, placement does not begin the guidance soon enough. The placement bureau cannot be said to give effective guidance if it has no conferences with the boy or girl before he or she comes to find work. It should become an axiom of vocational guidance, that effective direction demands long-continued personal acquaintance, advice, and occupational preparation before the time for work arrives, and supervision and counsel during at least the start in the occupation. Mere placement of the child, even when well done, deals with a very limited part of the problem.[1]

Fourth, placement officers are tempted to take the viewpoint of the employers and this tends to have an unfavorable reaction on the school. The good-will and coöperation of the employer is desirable and important. But his needs should not be set up as a sole measure of school efficiency.[2] An employment agency of any kind,

[1] Jesse Davis has well stated the complexity of the problem of placement, showing how it fails if it does not come as a step in the larger welfare of the child (p. 156). Davis maintains that there is no "best" job for a fourteen-year-old child.

[2] In a recent continuation school lesson much was said about obeying orders, being respectful to superiors, being worth what you are paid, and the like. Loyalty and obedience were enjoined, and the lesson plan proceeded from parents to employer to God. One might have imagined himself in a Munich school.

even if it be a public institution, is likely to harbor the idea that the school is or ought to be training children exclusively for efficient employment. True, this is a desirable by-product, but even if all children were destined for permanent positions in subordinate employment, it does not follow that they should be trained with this in mind as the goal.

Fifth, placement under present circumstances, competing as it must with private employment agencies, does much for the employer without being able to demand much in return. A placement officer recently spent a day's time in filling four places. The work was well done, and a considerable amount of money was saved to the employers. If anything is given by these employers in return it is at best intangible, voluntary, and subject to reversal at their pleasure. Under a system of genuine employment supervision, the employer might be required to chart the jobs, to maintain healthful conditions of employment, to pay adequate wages, and to call in the counselor for a hearing before discharging the boy.

Sixth, a final objection to a placement bureau in connection with guidance is that it behaves as did the Arab's camel. Vocational guidance should be the master; placement should serve the vocation. But the act of getting the boy a job seems such an important achievement (justly so, in many cases) that the deeper problems are relegated to a subordinate place. The results of placement are easily appraised: " This office last year placed 145 persons in positions with aggregate earnings of nearly $15,000." Such a report seems to be a tangible one when read by the practical man. The work of the vocational counselor cannot be put on paper in any such shape. Well may he say, to school committee or tax-payer,

> After such argument what can I plead?
> Or what pale promise make?

Yet we know that the need for adequate vocational guidance is a pressing one and that it can be defended successfully to any school committeeman who will consider the whole problem broadly.

Are the Placement Bureaus Efficient in Guidance? — We come now to the practical question: Do the placement agencies use even those facilities for guidance which they have? Miss Odencrantz, to whose article we have already referred, states that her investigations in New York City give her evidence which " may be taken as an indication of the lack of realization on the part of these workers that they are actually undertaking any sort of vocational guidance. It likewise indicates limited efforts in relating the child to the proper kind of work. It is nearly always a case of any job that may happen to come up for any girl who happens to be at hand." She states further that even the organizations which are carrying on the work of placement more or less definitely do not perform one of the fundamental duties and

[1] P. 176.

responsibilities of the noncommercial placement agency, — the duty of making preliminary investigation of the industry or establishment, before sending girls into it.

Obviously, then, if the placement bureau is to hold any advantage over the commercial employment agency, its organization, equipment, and ideals must be improved. Perhaps the greatest advantage possible to the publicly managed bureau is its power in many cases to put children back into school. Dr. Edward T. Devine puts this point as follows:

There is a great deal of sound doctrine in the idea that the only place to put people under eighteen years of age is in school, and we assume a serious responsibility if we in any way seem to give prominence to the idea that the chief task is to put people into positions rather than to keep them out of positions.[1]

The experience of placement bureaus suggests the need for scholarship funds, and for an investigation to determine whether or not the bureaus actually find for the average boys and girls better jobs than they could find for themselves. There are degrees of placement activity: some systems allow for independent action on the part of the applicant, while others exercise unwarranted paternalism.

The Cleveland office has a staff of fifteen persons, and aims to return children to school whenever possible. No boy or girl is placed without a study of his school record, and the attempt is made to give all attention

[1] Nat. Conference on V. G., 1912, p. 1.

possible to the vocational aims and abilities of the applicant, and to follow his progress in the occupation. The office is under state and city control.

The Cincinnati Department of Child Labor is under the supervision of the school board. It is intimately related to the schools and to industry, and aims to provide vocational guidance beginning with the application of the child for a work certificate.

The Boston Placement Bureau [1] is intimately related to the work of the Vocational-Guidance Department, and the placement feature seems here to have something like its proper subordination. The director was formerly in charge of the placement bureau, and states that of the three functions of the vocational-guidance department — guidance, placement, and follow-up — placement is the least important. Assistant Superintendent Thompson, who is in general charge of the work, says that just now follow-up is the most important, for through this the school gets guidance — it sees the causes of its own failures and successes, and learns how to improve its own work.

Employment Supervision. — It seems fair to state to employers of labor that theoretically all children should be in school, and that if they are allowed to work, on account of economic needs, their labor should be supervised by school authorities. The age for compulsory attendance has been progressively raised, and there

[1] This organization has now been taken over by the school committee and incorporated into the Vocational-Guidance Department.

seems to be no reason for believing that the limit has been reached. Minnesota has now set the age at sixteen, and Wisconsin requires continuation schooling for workers up to the age of seventeen.

The Need for Employment Supervision. — From the economic and social standpoint, the worker needs the protection which a supervisor can give. The factory or mercantile system does not automatically protect its workers — the interest of the managers is directed into other lines. Hence the demand that somebody actually representing the public be appointed to follow the child's career in the occupation. It is true that the more progressive firms are organizing employment managers' departments. But these represent the firm and not the children; when adjustments seem difficult to make, the settlement finally agreed upon in every case should be for the public good.

Most of all, the employment supervisor is needed as vocational counselor for the young person who is in an occupation for which he is not adapted — who feels that he is a misfit. Again, the supervisor can counsel when advice is wanted on any of the problems which arise: when to ask for a promotion, which of two opportunities to choose, what processes in a given industry to learn, what advanced study to undertake, what openings there are ahead and how to prepare for them, when to seek a new place.[1]

---

[1] To take a concrete instance from the files of the Boston Placement Bureau, — a boy quit work because he decided that it offered no future

The Advantage to the Employer. — The enlightened employer welcomes such supervision, for it enables him to call in the aid of an understanding friend whenever advice is necessary. It has been the experience of men and women engaged in such supervision that employers desire to be fair to the boy or girl, and are willing even to see him leave for a better place.[1] No doubt the system of competition in which employers find themselves offers temptation to unfairness. But the evils of this system itself would be greatly ameliorated if adequate supervision for young people in employment were widely enough extended.

Follow-up Work. — The first step toward employment supervision is taken when school people investigate the experiences of those who have left school, as did the teachers of the Mishawaka high school when they looked up the graduates for ten years back to find out about their work and wages. Strictly speaking, this form of follow-up does not involve actual supervision. But the expression " follow-up " is often used to mean over-

opportunity; the firm, however, stated that the boy had a good opportunity for promotion. Here is the place for a conference to see what definite proposition can be made to the boy. Another employer asked the bureau for a messenger boy. The placement officer got him to admit that there was no opportunity for promotion, and then had him agree to the plan to take a boy with the understanding that in a year's time he was to leave for a better position, and a new boy be supplied. (See Breckenridge, for further data.)

[1] Experience has so far been limited; it is not possible to infer that this kindly attitude would be universal. If supervision is needed for educational and sociological reasons, it must come regardless of the attitude of those who represent narrower interests.

sight as well as investigation. Investigation should precede and lead to supervision.

Examples of Employment Supervision. — Though the simpler forms of follow-up are now very common,[1] it is difficult to find examples of employment supervision with authority and equipment for adequate work.

The most elaborate employment supervision yet worked out is that which is a part of the coöperative or part-time plan. The system is explained by its originator, Dean Schneider of the College of Engineering, University of Cincinnati, in Chapters IX and X of his book *Education for Industrial Workers*.[2] The work of the "coördinators" is treated on pages 56 and 57. These officers are employment supervisors; their duty is to see that the shop work is educative and the school work practical. They have authority to protect the worker: "No girl or boy may be exploited by over-zealous foremen, as the visits of coördinators prevent this."

Other cities which have coöperative or alternate-week plans which involve the supervision of the start in industry are Dayton, Rochester, Buffalo, Boston, Fitchburg, Chicago, and Solvay, N. Y.; and many other cities have made beginnings.

There is, of course, extensive inspection and supervision of industry in connection with the enforcement of the

[1] See Boston Circular; Nat. Conference, 1912, pp. 24–31; Nat. Voc.-Guidance Assn., 1913, pp. 59–66; 1914, pp. 52–55; Bloomfield, *Readings*, pp. 220–233; pp. 485–503; *The School and the Start in Life*, p. 54.
[2] See also Com. of Educ., 1914, p. 259.

labor and health laws of city, state, and nation. Though this inspection is not concerned with the educational welfare of the workers, much can be learned from its organization and method. In Chapter VIII we shall outline a possible plan for employment supervision.

Vocational Guidance through the Employment Manager. — Perhaps the most hopeful improvement within industry itself is the recent organization of employment departments in many establishments. These departments are directed by employment managers, who attend to hiring and discharging workers, training the new employees, supervising the conditions of labor, adjusting work to workers, carrying on social work among the employees, and otherwise aiding in making the workers efficient and satisfied.[1]

The Kind of Work Accomplished by the Employment Manager. — In the factory of the Dennison Manufacturing Company at Framingham, Mass., progress has been made in charting or " blue-printing " particular jobs. The employment manager, Mr. Philip J. Reilly, can tell in advance just what each of the one hundred and fifty jobs requires and offers. For example, it can be specified that the girl who is to work at covering jewelry boxes must have small, fine, but strong hands, not too ill-used by housework, be right-handed, have had a better education than the average, and have a good sense of color and design. Other jobs present significant

---

[1] We do not here refer to Scientific Management. See Chapter VII for a treatment of that subject.

specifications: one requires standing; another hammering; a third the use of glue, with its disagreeable odor; another knowledge of the use of fractions; another the use of inks and dyes. A special effort has been made to transfer persons from one department to another, to avoid dissatisfaction, discharge, or leaving. During the year 1915 ninety-two per cent of the transfers were successful, and there were only 13 cases of voluntary leaving, out of a force of 2300. In the same year forty per cent of the transfers were to better positions. This company has taken stock of the educational opportunities of the community open to workers, for the purpose of advising its employees.

H. P. Hood and Sons of Boston have an elaborate system for teaching the duties of milk-delivering to new employees. The plan is a model of definiteness and good pedagogy — an improvement over the old method of "trial and error." The operation of the plan is supervised by the employment manager. A council of employees hears appeals and complaints.

William Filene's Sons Company of Boston have developed many democratic features. Teaching new employees, hiring, transfer, cases of discipline, and discharge are under the supervision of the management, but an appeal may be taken to a council elected by such workers of the store. Further details in regard to the plans will be reserved for our study of conditions of employment in Chapter VII.

The reaction on the men acting as employment managers is one of the most significant features of the work. The humanizing influence in securing satisfied employees is in evidence. One of these employment managers recently spoke of the responsibility in connection with discharging a man who earned no more in a week than he, the manager, earned in one day. Another manager stated that a worker earning only nine dollars a week should not be subject to discharge by the whim of any one person. A third remarked: "Most of us are everlastingly good bosses but very poor teachers." It is not claimed by these men that they are doing their work for humanitarian reasons. Mr. E. A. Filene recently remarked that there is no occasion for any gratitude on the part of employees; they are not getting any more than they are giving.

Employment Managers' Associations. The Boston Association. — Boston, New York, Detroit, Chicago, Philadelphia, and San Francisco now have organizations of employment managers, meeting regularly for conferences on current problems. The Boston Employment Managers' Association was the first organization in the field; it was formed in December 1911 by the Vocation Bureau. The membership is about 125. It holds monthly meetings with programs of talks and discussions arranged in advance by a program committee. Occasional meetings are held at the places of business of the members, for the purpose of observing the methods of handling the employment problems in the various stores and factories. A paid secretary has recently been employed, and a systematic program of work has been planned. A recent circular letter to the members outlined the scope and character of the problems, and work of the association.[1]

Other Employment Managers' Organizations. — In New York, the Society for the Study of Employment Problems plans to study the following topics: sources of labor supply; selection of employees; analyses of jobs; conservation of employees, including methods of training, ways and means of promotion, physical conditions, records of employees, and means of remuneration; reasons of and methods for discharge.

In Boston the women interested in these subjects have organized the Employment Problem Association, and are making similar investigations. Some of their meetings will take the form of joint meetings with the Boston Employment Managers' Association.

The associations in the other cities are working along similar lines.

Coöperation of the Associations with Education. — All of these associations admit educational people to their membership, and there is much promise of genuine coöperative effort toward a solution of the perplexing questions of employment. It was the work of the Boston association which led to the college course in Dartmouth, which we have noted in Chapter II. Recently the

[1] See Annals, *Personnel Problems*, pp. 78–81, 114.

Massachusetts Institute of Technology has organized courses to train men for the business management of engineering establishments.

The first national conference of employment managers was held on January 19 and 20, 1916, at Minneapolis, in connection with the ninth convention of the National Society for the Promotion of Industrial Education. This meeting was addressed by persons representing colleges, factories, commercial organizations, and the United States Department of Labor, besides the associations of employment managers.[1]

Some Special Problems and Methods of the Counselor. The English Plan. — The English plans for counseling proceed on the assumption that no central office in a large city can keep in personal touch with the individual child. Hence their provision for large volunteer committees. Each child is put in touch with an adult who will take a personal interest in his school, home, and working affairs, and who will do everything possible to foster his development and progress. The children are assigned to these " helpers " about three months before the school-leaving time, and the helper undertakes to keep in touch with the child for about three years. Only a few children are under the direction of each helper. Conferences with parents, teachers, and employers are frequent. Helpers keep records of their

---

[1] The proceedings of this meeting and of later conferences at Boston and Philadelphia were published by the United States Bureau of Labor Statistics.

work, and a central office holds conferences and correlates the work.[1]

Superintendent Spaulding advocates the adoption of this use of volunteer help in America. After speaking of the part to be played in guidance by pupils, parents, and teachers he says:

> In my judgment they must all take a part, but their work to be successful must enlist the coöperation of high-minded and public-spirited men in the busy world who are ready to give society the benefit of their experience and aid the rising generation by their suggestions and advice. Such men can help enormously in this great task.[2]

Methods of Inducing a Young Person to Change his Aim. — How shall a boy or girl be induced to reconsider a determination to be lawyer or doctor or engineer, when it appears that he has no conception of the battle ahead of him? The obvious thing to do is bluntly to say to him: " You have no chance to be a lawyer." But that such a statement is the wrong one to make has been abundantly proved, for the strangest things have happened to make success possible.[3] Direct counsel of a negative sort is inappropriate; a different method must be used. That employed in the case of the girls who chose stenography is suggestive (p. 104). Another

[1] Explanations here apply particularly to Birmingham, whose plan is typical of the best. See Bloomfield, *The School and the Start in Life,* pp. 47, 65–75, 81–83; *Youth, School, and Vocation,* pp. 127–136; or *Readings,* pp. 679–703.

[2] *Readings,* p. 17. See also Martin.

[3] See Breese.

good method is used by F. M. Giles [1] — the method of giving information which will show the difficulties as well as the advantages of the occupation. Many decisions of children have been made on insufficient data, and therefore more data are required, especially about other desirable occupations. When the teacher as counselor has done these things he had better let the pupil do the rest. Either he will have experiences that will teach him or lead him to change his mind, or he will succeed at the occupation he has chosen, regardless of apparent handicaps.

Counseling in Grand Rapids High School. — Six teachers of the Grand Rapids High School have three recitations each, daily, and give the remainder of their time to the work of counseling. Each is responsible for the educational, moral, and vocational guidance of about 250 pupils. They keep record cards for these pupils, and act as a cabinet of vice principals for the advice and assistance of the principal.[2]

Policies of Counseling in Boston. — The Vocational-Guidance Department of the Boston schools holds that no vocational counselor should take the responsibility for telling a boy or girl what he can or cannot do. The director believes that just as a guidepost tells which turns must be made to get to certain places, but leaves the decision to be made by the traveler, so the vocational guide should tell what must be done to reach any

---

[1] See Bibliography.
[2] Leavitt, *Examples*, etc., p. 252.

occupation (and what the occupation offers), and must leave the final choice to the boy or girl.

The Civic Service House, in which the modern vocational-guidance movement originated, has recently outlined a plan to be used in the conferences held with its members:

EDUCATIONAL AND VOCATIONAL GUIDANCE

CIVIC SERVICE HOUSE

1. Preliminary interviews are held, to discover experiences, successes, abilities, and aims. Parents and house workers are sometimes present. General advice is given, perhaps in regard to reading on occupations, advanced study, or visits to schools or other places.

2. Investigations are made by the house workers, to determine the desires and resources of the parents.

3. A conference committee, made up of the house workers and the officers of the Vocational Bureau, holds monthly meetings at the Vocation Bureau for the consideration of cases.

4. The recommendations of the committee are carried out, so far as possible. The resources of the house and of other organizations are used in whatever way seems necessary to extend the education and the opportunity of the persons who are counseled.

At What Age should the Vocation be Chosen? — Counselors are sometimes asked this question by anxious parents or " practical " friends of the child. It is impossible to answer; generalization here is quite gratuitous. Yet the dangers connected with too early or too late choices are serious.

The enrichment of the school program will undoubtedly furnish an educational guidance which will disclose aims and abilities much sooner than would the narrow program. Yet the child has only a child's experiences, and there are certain occupations whose requirements and opportunities can hardly be appreciated by a person under twenty-one; for example, those of the lawyer, the statesman, the social worker, the college teacher.

The problem can be solved only by opening wide the opportunity for education and range of choice: by increasing the vocational infancy of all those young persons who are likely to profit by the delay of choice. The test to be applied should be progress in profitable lines of applied study. The prevocational age for certain occupations may be extended into the twenties. Note that the prevocational idea involves *work*. There is only gain to the individual and to society from profitable, supervised work, if such work is educational in its functioning and effect. Thus, the future statesman may run errands, the lawyer wire a house, the preacher lay a cement sidewalk, and the college president work as clerk in a store, all with educational profit to the individual and to society.

Do early choices persist? Peixotto (p. 82) thinks that vocational clues of a reliable sort begin to manifest themselves between the ages of eleven and fourteen years. Thorndike has computed for 100 individuals the resemblance between relative interests and relative capacities as 0.9, and between interest in the last three years of the elementary school and capacity in the college period as 0.6. He concludes, " These facts unanimously witness to the importance of early interests." [1]

It is always unsafe to apply conclusions based on averages — or on 60 or 90 per cent — to the individual case. We can never know which is the exception. Too many " average " boys and girls have broken the rules of averages. A case from a current magazine illustrates the way late choices are made. The Polish novelist Stanislaw Przybyszewski went to Berlin in 1889 at the age of twenty-one to study architecture. He soon changed to the study of physiological psychology, but in 1891 became editor of the *Berlin Arbeiter-Zeitung* and leader of strikes in Silesia. In Berlin he began to write on philosophical subjects, at the age of thirty became editor of a literary magazine in Cracow, and thence went to Warsaw and devoted himself to drama. He is now engaged in writing novels and in lecturing.[2]

As we remarked in another place, a person's aim is likely to change as he proceeds in study and work, and his period of vocational exploration may be extended so long as he is occupying the time in ways profitable to himself and society. A forced choice might lead to unhappiness and disaster.

Making Alternative Choices of Careers. — Apparently one precaution worth taking, in order to prevent early mis-choices, is to suggest to the youth that he select

---

[1] *Readings*, pp. 386–395; Kitson, *Interest*, etc.
[2] See *Current Opinion*, Dec. 1915, p. 424.

from three to five occupations for consideration and study. He may then keep in mind throughout his life one or two occupations other than the one he decides upon, so that if a change ever seems desirable, it may be made without too much diffculty.

The Collection, Classification, and Use of Occupational Information. — In order to do effective work, the teacher and the counselor must know about the world of occupations into which the children are to enter. He must collect, classify, and use significant vocational facts.

Collecting Information. — In the collection of occupational information much may be learned from the methods employed in recent surveys of school systems, and of surveys for vocational education. The Portland, Oregon, Survey devotes two chapters (VI and VII) to the vocational needs of the city, and the Cleveland survey devotes nine of the twenty-five booklets to the occupations of that city in relation to schooling. The Richmond, Minneapolis, and Indiana Vocational-Education Surveys come nearer still to our purpose: all are full of information very much needed by the counselor in his work.

Much as these surveys are to be commended, they have a slightly different aim from that necessarily taken by the counselor. The survey for vocational education aims to find out (1) what are the occupations of the community, with the requirements of each; (2) what the vocational-education opportunities are; and (3) what educational advantages should be provided to meet the requirements. The survey is not necessarily concerned with asking whether or not the occupations should be improved, whether or not there should be supervision of employment, what provision for placement there should be, or what system for guidance should be inaugurated.[1] The vocational-guidance survey wishes to know all that a vocational-education survey can tell, and is interested besides in such problems as those noted above.

Comprehensive surveys for the express purposes of vocational guidance are rare, though the surveys made by the Vocation Bureau while training the Boston school counselors were for explicit use in vocational guidance. We have spoken of a follow-up investigation in which a high school finds out what its graduates are doing. Such a study involves visiting stores, factories, offices, shops, and other establishments, asking questions about the occupations, and then using the information so obtained in improving the school and guiding pupils. Such an investigation is a rudimentary vocational-guidance survey, and has no doubt been attempted by many schools. A city or school system survey for the purpose of vocational guidance would be of national help and importance.

[1] On page 8 of the Minneapolis Survey is given a statement of the aims of the survey. It should be noted that this particular study (as well as the Richmond Survey in some particulars) goes further than its aims require: it is critical in its examination of the occupations, and makes frequent recommendations of great significance to vocational guidance. Chapter XXIV makes some suggestions for a program of vocational guidance.

K

What Information shall be Collected? — The first requisite is to know what to ask. Dr. Richards, Director of Cooper Union, gave an adequate answer to this problem at the Second National Conference on Vocational Guidance.[1] He classifies the necessary questions under the following heads : the economic data, the effect of the occupation on body and character, the data on opportunity for beginners, and the relation of the occupation to school training. Following is a brief summary of the questions he proposes :

WHAT WE NEED TO KNOW ABOUT OCCUPATIONS

I. Economic data :

1. What is the size and importance of the industry, nationally and locally?

2. Is it a growing or a diminishing field?

3. Is the occupation overcrowded?

4. Is it stable, or likely to change on account of invention or the whim of the public?

5. What are the hours of labor, and the rules about overtime ?

6. Is the pay by time-work or piece-work ?

7. How is the work in the occupation subdivided? What proportion of the work is desirable?

8. What physical and mental qualities are necessary for success and efficiency?

II. Physical and hygienic conditions :

1. Is the work carried on indoors or outdoors?

2. Does the worker sit or stand for long periods, or move about ?

3. Is there ample room and good ventilation ?

[1] *Report of Sec. Nat. Conf. on Voc. Guidance*, pp. 35–44; also *Readings*, pp. 504–514.

4. Is the worker exposed to heat or cold or sudden changes of temperature?

5. Is time allowed for dinner, and is there opportunity for warm meals?

6. Does the work involve strain to eyes or nerves?

7. Are there dangers from machinery?

8. Are there dangers from dust?

9. Are there any special unhealthy conditions which might lead to occupational diseases?

III. Influence of the occupation on the character and growth of the workers:

1. Is the occupation stimulating, or deadening?

2. Are the influences surrounding the work morally deteriorating?

IV. Opportunities for beginners:

1. What are the ways by which the occupation is entered?

2. Do employers want trained workers? Are they willing to take untrained workers?

3. What is the age for entering the occupation?

4. What are the beginning wages, and the normal rate of gain?

5. What per cent of the workers leave in the first year?

6. What per cent remain in low-paid work at the end of six years?

7. What per cent are advanced to more skilled and responsible work at higher wages?

8. Has a beginner opportunity to learn more than one process?

9. Are there opportunities for transfer from one department to another, and for showing ability to transfer to better work?

10. How are skilled or high-grade workers recruited?

11. Does the worker receive any instruction from the employer?

12. Is there an apprentice system? What percentage of young workers are apprenticed?

13. What are the trade-union restrictions as to apprenticeship or helpers?

V. The relation of the occupation to school training:

1. Is school training beyond the legal requirement an advantage in the occupation? Beyond the grammar school?

2. Is high school training an advantage? Vocational school training?

3. Which are of greatest help: General knowledge? Industrial and economic intelligence? Specialized technical knowledge? Manipulative skill?

4. How should the instruction be obtained: Before entrance to occupation, or after? In evening schools? Part-time school? Are there facilities for such schooling? Are employers willing to allow part-time schooling, without reduction in wages?

Dr. Richards' paper is well supplied with examples to illustrate the points covered in this outline. He remarks that these data are not needed alone for vocational guidance, but also for the general improvement of social and economic conditions. A significant statement is his observation that the work of vocational guidance need not wait until these facts are fully collected.

The questions in the above outline cover the ground in comprehensive fashion. The variations in the requirements, as given by various writers, and as applied in actual surveys, may be noted by referring to the literature of the subject.[1]

[1] Literature on surveys or investigations for vocational guidance (see Bibliog.): Nat. Conference, 1912, Stevens, Richards, Fitch, Woolman, Perkins. Nat. V. G. Assn., 1913, Ayres, Giles, Richards, Leavitt; 1914, Wheatley. In Bloomfield's *Readings*, Ayres, Lewis, Dearle, New York, Schneider, Talbert, Montgomery, Breckenridge and Abbott, Richards, Parts III and IV. Bureau of Labor Statistics (Richmond). Nat. Soc., for Prom. of Ind. Educ. (Minneapolis). Cleveland Survey, Bryner, Fleming, Lutz, O'Leary, Stevens, Shaw. Bloomfield, *Youth*, etc., Chap. VIII, pp. 65–86; *School and Start*, pp. 70–72. Davis, *Voca-*

Selecting Significant Facts. — The complexity of the occupational world makes it absolutely necessary to select from the mass of facts those which have special bearing on the work of the school and especially on vocational guidance. The field schedules for the vocational-education surveys are very complex; a glance at the large tables in the Richmond Survey will show how necessary is the selection and emphasis of significant facts, if the counselor is not to be lost in a maze of irrelevant details. The field investigator himself may aid the selection by underlining or checking items of special significance as he gathers data, and by making some general comments about the occupation or establishment. Field books should provide space for these comments.

After the facts and comments are gathered, they should be studied and put in shape for use. Vocational specialists may want to have access to all the facts, while teachers, parents, and children want brief statements and significant conclusions. The returns from the surveys must therefore be reduced to a form appropriate for general use. This seems to have been the aim in the reports of the Cleveland Survey; not only are there eight booklets each devoted to one group of occupations, but there is also one book devoted to the findings for all. The Rochester school department has utilized the

tional, etc., Chap. VII, p. 139. Parsons, Part II. Eaton and Stevens, Gowin and Wheatley. Hill. Myers's Bibliography. Pamphlets of Chicago, Boston, Portland, Ore., New York, Rochester, London, Munich, and other cities.

Chamber of Commerce survey from which to summarize for vocational guidance the main facts about several occupations, in very brief form. Bulletin No. 3, *Clothing Industry for Girls*, has five pages of text, and treats of the following subjects: size of the industry, divisions of the trade, the season, the kind of girl desired, the pay, hours, labor laws, location of shops, and where to learn operating and buttonhole making.[1]

Frequently the Chamber of Commerce of a city may be induced to assist in the publication of the booklets, if not in the expense of collecting the information. Thus the Gesellschaft zur Beförderung der Künste und nützlichen Gewerbe of Hamburg stands sponsor for booklets so economically gotten up, in the printing and binding, that they can be revised and kept up to date with a minimum of expense.

Too often in the past the sole printed matter in connection with painstaking surveys has been the large volume called the report — a forbidding document except to a few experts. It is now recognized, apparently, that new methods of disseminating the findings are needed, and brief, popular summaries should do much toward making vocational guidance practicable and systematic.

Who should Make the Surveys? — We have indicated already that the vocational-guidance department of the school board or committee should follow the children

[1] See also the Chicago bulletins reprinted in Bloomfield's *Readings*, pp. 542–556.

into the occupations, and should supervise their employ-ment. In connection with these processes they should make investigations which can furnish information for counseling children still in school. This information should be systematically gathered, tabulated, verified, and kept up to date, and should serve the purposes of a vocational-guidance survey.[1]

The occupational information should be kept ready for reference in a central office, and may there be accessible to state and federal officers. The State Bureau of Labor Statistics should sift and tabulate the information collected by local authorities, publish exhaustive reports, and issue brief bulletins of a popular nature useful to parents, teachers, employers, workers, and school classes. The Federal Bureau of Labor Statistics, in turn, should collect, compare, correlate, tabulate, and disseminate the material from all the states, and should issue popular bulletins for the use of all classes of people.

These reports, of course, should by no means be limited to mere facts or statistics; in spite of the name Bureau of Labor Statistics, used in the case of state and federal boards, a glance at their reports will show a very wide range of powers. These bureaus are well equipped to aid the movement for vocational guidance.

[1] As a matter of fact it should be better than a formal survey, for the latter is apt to be thought of as completed, while the information should be always growing and being revised. The formal, occasional survey is useful when information is lacking on account of past neglect, but it is not an ideal plan for keeping information about occupations up to date.

Coöperation of the most far-reaching nature should be practiced in collecting the occupational information. The following organizations, among others, should contribute: employers' associations, labor unions, chambers of commerce, manufacturers' associations, employment managers' associations, teachers' organizations, state commissioners and superintendents of education, health boards, employment bureaus, professional and civic clubs, settlements, private schools, newspapers, civil service commissions. Of special aid will be the Bureau of the Census, the Bureau of Education, and the Departments of Commerce, Agriculture, and Labor.

Until such time as facilities for collecting the appropriate information are adequately provided, the teacher, principal, or superintendent can do what the Boston Vocation Bureau has done: investigate typical, important occupations, write concise explanations of them, submit the copy to employers, workers, and economists for correction and suggestion, and publish the resulting material in the form of pamphlets or booklets.[1]

A glance at the current Manual of Examinations of the United States Civil Service Commission [2] shows what might be accomplished by a more extensive use of agencies already in operation. For example, the following is an extract from the stated requirement for Press Feeder in the Government Printing Service: [3]

---

[1] See the interesting plan by which high school boys gather information for themselves: Westgate.

[2] Spring, 1916, pp. 108 and 121 ff.   [3] Sec. 227.

No application is accepted which does not show that the applicant has had either (1) at least three months' experience and has fed, at the rate of 1200 sheets per hour, sheets not less than 24 by 38 inches in size on a cylinder press or sheets not less than 14 by 17 inches in size on a platen press, or (2) at least three months' experience in packing and banding cards of approximately 3½ by 5¼ inches, at the rate of at least 300 packets per hour.

Any boy studying the work of the press feeder may measure his potential abilities by these standards. In Section 249 of the same bulletin the specifications for stenographer and typewriter are outlined, sample tests are published, and definite standards set. No source of information gives more promise than that represented by federal and state departments of government.

Classification of the Material for Use in Counseling. — The classification of occupations must be simple and brief, if it is to be used with young children to aid them in getting acquainted with the world's work. Two such classifications, one for boys and one for girls, are given by Davis on pages 67 and 69 of *Vocational and Moral Guidance*. The divisions for boys are: agriculture; business; professions; industry; unclassified. For girls: household arts; agriculture; business; industrial arts; professions; special occupations for women. Bonser accepts the fivefold division: professional, commercial, agricultural, industrial, and household.[1] Woods has eight classes for boys: professional, mer-

[1] *Readings,* p. 110.

cantile, petty mercantile, clerical, artisan, laboring, agriculture, miscellaneous.[1] The census classification has nine divisions, and if home making be added, ten: agriculture, forestry, and animal husbandry; extraction of minerals; manufacturing and mechanical industries; transportation; trade; public service; professional service; domestic and personal service; clerical occupations.

All of these classifications are open to the objection that they are logical rather than pragmatic; they do not aid the child by relating the occupations to his own life, abilities, and ideals. The counselor may therefore enlist the aid of the young people, and they may build up classifications of their own, based on special points under consideration. For example, the members of an oral English class debated in an informal way about the usefulness to society of certain special occupations, after which they took a vote of first, second, and third choices. Another classification interesting to young people is based on these questions: What occupations are so important that organized society manages them? Which ones are so important that voluntary organizations manage them without making any profit? Which are so necessary that society officially recognizes and regulates them? Which are privately managed, but held as necessary? Which have to do with mere luxuries? Which are prohibited?

Other bases of profitable classification are suggested

[1] *Readings*, p. 26.

by these questions about a given occupation which a boy or girl might be studying: Is it a purely automatic process? Does it take semi-attention? Does it take occasional thinking? Does it require continued think-ing? Does it take strength, size, use of eyes or ears? Still another basis for study is indicated by such questions as: What occupations are open to a boy equipped with a good knowledge of chemistry? Mechanical drawing? [1]

The work in agriculture fostered by the Massachusetts State Board of Education is planned so that the exercises are graded with the easiest first and the most difficult last. Thus the pupils have a useful classification within the field of agriculture.[2]

Certain classifications once useful but now of no practical value should be avoided, for example that based on the materials used in the occupations: the woodworking trades, the iron trades, etc. Materials are no longer of sufficient significance: certain processes in wood, metal, and leather may all involve the manipulation of machines requiring almost identical dexterity.

No doubt the life-career class may consider the common classifications of occupations. The pupils should be shown, however, that there are many practical problems not at all settled by such classifications, and that they can hardly choose a vocation without a much more

[1] Another suggestive classification of the grades of workers in an industry was published recently in *School and Society* (Garnett). See also Richards' questions, above.

[2] Stimson.

significant analysis of its characteristics than any these classifications furnish.

The Use of Vocational Material in Counseling. — Bloomfield, in speaking of the work of the counselor, says:

> Prolonged, earnest effort on the part of the counselor is imperative, and a corresponding effort on the part of the applicant, or the service fails of results.[1]

One of the chief duties of the counselor is to assist the pupil in a systematic study of the occupations which he is considering. Attractive reading matter must be assigned, both general and particular in scope and nature. The use of this material must not be limited to local opportunities, for Ayres' study of thirteen-year-old boys in seventy-eight cities shows that only one half of them were living in the city of their birth, and of the fathers but one in six.[2] As the pupil proceeds in the study of his occupation, he must have the benefit of frequent conferences with the counselor. He should be encouraged to discuss his problems with parents and friends, to talk over with other pupils the reading he does, and to make it the basis for some of the work in the composition and oral English classes. Literature sent to the parents, with an invitation to a conference, will aid in the work materially.

The use of vocational material in life-career classes has been discussed in the chapter on educational guidance.

---

[1] *Youth*, etc., p. 57.   [2] *Readings*, p. 154.

The Equipment of the Counselor. — The " blue-printing " of the task of the vocational counselor has been adequately and acceptably done by Professor Bonser in the article to which we have already referred.[1] Four specifications are named : information, experience, appropriate personality, and capacity for constructive research. Of special significance for our purpose here is a study of the equipment of the counselor as expressed in the judgment of men who have had years of experience in the work — such men as Parsons, Bloomfield, and Davis ; to the writings of these men the reader is referred.[2]

An attempt to add to these statements about the equipment of the counselor, or to formulate a new set of specifications based on the present study, would involve a summary of the topics of our entire book. We shall therefore defer further consideration of the subject until we have completed our study of the conditions in the occupations and have come to the discussion of normal school and college courses to prepare for counseling.

The Teacher as Counselor. — It is hoped that Chapter III has made it clear that every teacher of the school has opportunities to give vocational guidance. The present chapter aims to show that individual conferences are needed by the children — conferences with persons specially equipped to give more nearly adequate guidance.

---

[1] *Readings*, pp. 109–116.

[2] *Choosing a Vocation*, pp. 94–95; *Youth, School, and Vocation*, pp. 55–57, 60–65, 87–94; *Vocational and Moral Guidance*, pp. 137–152.

What should be the relation between the teacher and the trained counselor? Obviously the supervision of the work should be under the direction of a man or woman trained for that work; obviously, also, the classroom teacher should do all he can in guiding the pupils, because he is nearest to them. It seems safe to say, then, that the trained counselor's function is to direct the work, to furnish teachers with whatever helps he can, to meet with and advise pupils whose problems need more attention than their teachers can give, to conduct life-career classes, and to attend to the activities which have to do with employment supervision.

No matter how efficient and enthusiastic the trained counselor may be, however, the success of his work will very largely depend on the attitude of the teachers of the school system toward the work. It is to be hoped, therefore, that the increased professional training of teachers will help to equip them for an interest in guidance and an ability in counseling. In the last analysis, perhaps most of the actual counseling should be given by the child's teacher, and the director should devote the greater part of his time to the effort to train special teachers in each school for the work, and to aid all the teachers in developing the viewpoint of vocational guidance in the studies of the school program.

CHAPTER V

Pseudo-Guidance

In our study of pseudo-guidance we may concede that most intentions are good, and we shall not go so far as to label all the methods discussed as entirely false and pernicious. But we shall maintain that experimentation should not be considered as vocational guidance, and that no method should be adopted into a plan for guidance until it has adequate foundation in logic and in good educational practice. Vocational guidance is still in the experimental stage, — that is very true; but enough experiments have been carried on, in certain lines, at least, to show better ways than these we shall consider in this chapter.

The many questionable practices in attempted vocational guidance may be classified for our purpose by the theories or points of view on which they rest. We shall distinguish the following: (1) Belief in the unproved theory that there are fixed and well-marked types of mind; (2) Overestimation of what psychological tests can at present do; (3) Belief that qualities of mind are general and transferable, rather than specific; (4) Overestimation of the importance of physical characteristics; (5) The encouragement of morbid self-examination; (6) Overguidance; (7) Commercial agencies; (8) Lack of social perspective; (9) Control of vocational guidance by other departments or by non-educational organizations.

Belief in the Unproved Theory that there are Well-marked Types of Mind. — Are there distinct types of mind? It must be admitted that the evidence, from authority, at least, is imposing. Let us see if it is confirmed by experiment, note how the theory works in practice, and judge it by its fruits.

In our treatment of this subject we shall consider first, the common classification into object-minded and symbol-minded, second, other classifications by types, and third, the educational implications of the theory of types.

Are there " Thing-thinkers " and " Idea-thinkers "? — A New England superintendent of schools said recently that at the age of thirteen two types of children are discoverable — the bookish and the manual. In another city the school psychologist has organized a " practical-arts " class for the " object-minded," leaving the " symbol-minded " in the regular classes. Another classification has it " motor-minded " and " mind-minded;" another " concrete-minded " and " abstract-minded; " another " dynamic " and " sedentary." Sincerely interested in the vocational guidance of the students, an enthusiastic vice principal wrote an article for the school paper, in which occurred this statement:

Are you mechanically dexterous? Are you a handy boy? Then surely the industrial world with its crafts and its trades, its manufacturing, and its mechanic arts, should be your choice.

Mrs. Woolley, in her recent preliminary report of the Cincinnati investigations,[1] distinguishes four types:

1. Low in mental and physical tests of ability.
2. Low in mental but good in manual ability.
3. High in mental but low in manual ability.
4. High in mental and manual ability.

It is to be noted that the second and third of these "types" are respectively the "finger-minded" and "idea-minded" of the other classifications, and that the first and fourth classes violate the theory of *distinct* types. Mrs. Woolley does not tell us the proportion of children in each of the four classes. An attempt to do this would probably break up the classification. She does tell us, in another article,[2] that 149 children were tested with regard to their simple motor and mental abilities, and it was found that those who were best in the mental tests were also, on the whole, best in the physical tests and in physical development.

Types of Thinking vs. Types of Mind. — That there are types of thinking no one doubts, nor that there are boys and girls who like to use their minds through the use of their hands, nor that some boys and girls are more practiced in one kind of thinking than in another. But so far in the study of "types," there seems to have been

[1] New Scale, etc., p. 533. [2] *The Present Trend*, etc., p. 46.

L

no investigation made regarding the causes of these variations. As a substitute for such investigations, it has invariably been assumed that because John likes to think by means of driving nails we know that he is manual-minded, or, put the other way about, John belongs to the manual-minded type, therefore he likes handwork rather than bookwork.

We still have no proof that these explanations do any more than travel in a circle. It may be that bookwork has been made unattractive, that the wrong kind of reading matter has been set before the boy. We know how assiduously many a boy has read about electricity, because he was constantly using his hands in making and installing electrical apparatus. May it not be that it is the business of the school to balance the kinds of activity for the child, rather than to unbalance them? At least this proposal has as much evidence in its favor as the other, and that it leads to a sound organization of the school program is shown by the fact that nowhere has prevocational work led to the exclusion of the " symbol-thinking," but always to a strengthening and vitalizing of it by relating it to the manual work. The implication seems to be that the symbols in the old school were symbols of vague things, while those in the prevocational academic work are to be symbols to represent pragmatic things — chairs, processes, acts of helpfulness, success in planning and in working, concrete and satisfactory accomplishments.

If our school work can offer to all pupils a varied

program of really *useful* studies, shall we not have less need to ferret out types of minds to put into different kinds of schools?

What Experiments have Shown. — Thorndike has summarized the arguments against the theory of distinct types, and has given the experimental data on both sides of the argument.[1]

In the first place, it is significant that almost every experimental study of types has led to two findings: first, there are many more individuals between or combining the types than there are in the types themselves; and second, various intermediary types are discovered. In the studies of imagery the division into auditory, visual, and motor types, on which methods of teaching spelling have been based, has given way to intermediate classifications which include most of the children. Thorndike quotes Meumann as stating that no child of pure type has been discovered, and Segal as introducing a type called " visual-auditory-motor-intellectual!"[2] Between two so-called types there are so many other cases that the total representation approximates the curve of normal distribution. So far as can be found out, no distribution by groups has been found true for any mental quality, unless special training or accident be the obvious cause.[3] Thorndike concludes his examination of certain experiments:

---

[1] See his *Educational Psychology*, Vol. III, pp. 360–363, 367–371, and Chap. XVI.

[2] Thorndike, p. 374. [3] Thorndike's *Briefer Course*, pp. 404–410.

Intermediate conditions are in some of these cases demonstrably, and in all cases probably, more typical than the supposed type. [Vol. III, p. 381.]

Again:

It is highly probable that, when actual measurements are made, mediocrity — . . . moderately *everything* will be found to be the one real type. [P. 375.]

Mrs. Woolley's conclusion that ability in manual and mental activities are in positive correlation is borne out by Thorndike's review of the experiments. He finds that desirable qualities stand in positive correlation to each other, — that it is not proved that there are "mental antagonisms," a person being good in manual skill but poor at abstract thinking. "The good external observer may be excellent at introspection, and the man with a strong interest in his inner life of thought is much more likely than the average man to have a strong interest in external affairs." [P. 382.] "It is very, very hard to find any case of a negative correlation between desirable mental functions." [P. 362.]

What shall be done with the "Manual Type"? — Without doubt the student of vocational guidance wishes to foster the introduction of more handwork into the schools; without doubt also, however, he must protest at assigning a thirteen-year-old boy to a class which will become for him an educational blind alley. There are teachers, college presidents, dentists, lawyers, and preachers who would have been called " object-minded " had they in their school days fallen into the hands of an enthusiastic " psychologist." How can we know that the boy who is just now disinclined toward Scott's *Lady of the Lake*, and toward a classification of sentences into simple, complex, and compound (symbols which probably no one can show him have any value), — how can we know that he should therefore be guided into a mechanical career? Perhaps he should cultivate his manual powers, but at the same time have an education so broad that the way may be kept open for him to become a teacher of manual work, an industrial manager or foreman, a manufacturer, a salesman, a chemist, a surgeon, a patent lawyer, an employment manager in an industrial plant, a scientific farmer, or, indeed, a professor of philosophy.

Not only, as suggested above, is there a likelihood that we should find upon investigation that the habit of thinking most practiced by a given boy is due to influences in his past and present environment, but there is also a possibility that an individual changes his habit of thinking as he grows older. Thus Winch [1] found evidence that children change their imagery from auditory predominance to visual. As there are times and circumstances in every day when one favors either abstract or concrete thought, so there are likely to be periods in his life given over to one kind of thinking

[1] P. 460, see bibliography.

more than to the other. If such an hypothesis be even a remote possibility, it is unwise for us to limit the opportunity of any individual.

The way should be kept open for any development which may arise in the child's manner of thinking; he should be trained to both kinds of thinking by both mental and manual work, and should be taught the value of abstract thinking about the hand work he is doing. Correlation of the kinds of activity is the task of the teacher.

Finally, too much stress should not be put on the boy's present stock of aptitudes, in his choice of vocation. As Thompson [1] says from his experience with Boston boys:

> Grit and courage, I believe, have more to do with success-ful adjustment to the job than special aptitude . . . Moral attitude has scored to count more than fortunate mental and physical gifts. What vocational counselor would have advised the youthful Demosthenes to study oratory?

Other Classifications by " Types." — Classification is such an alluring temptation that it is not surprising there should be a liberal assortment of categories into which to pigeonhole any particular individual. Thus we find Schneider, from his experience in Cincinnati,[2] proposing sixteen ways of dividing twenty-year-old boys into two classes:

[1] *Vocational Guidance in Boston*, p. 18.
[2] *Selecting*, etc.

(a) Physical strength
Physical weakness

(b) Mental
Manual

(c) Settled
Roving

(d) Indoor
Outdoor

(e) Directive
Dependent

(f) Original (creative)
Imitative

(g) Small scope
Large scope

(h) Adaptable
Self-centered

(i) Deliberate
Impulsive

(j) Music sense

(k) Color sense

(l) Manual accuracy
Manual inaccuracy

(m) Mental accuracy (logic)
Mental inaccuracy

(n) Concentration (mental focus)
Diffusion

(o) Rapid mental coördination
Slow mental coördination

(p) Dynamic
Static

Schneider hastens to warn us of the danger of hasty judgment, and to state that one may belong to both types, — may be "both mental and manual, or both an indoor and an outdoor man"; and that "further, one may not possess either characteristic to any marked degree." Like Mrs. Woolley, however, he does not estimate the relative number belonging to well-marked types and not belonging to such types.

We are given in this article no concrete data; only the opinion that such types exist, based on the author's experience in the coöperative schools in the University of Cincinnati. We can hardly adopt it without more evidence. It is a characteristic of the writings of Dickens that he puts the people of his stories into sharp lights and deep shadows, so that we find in his books well-marked types which we do not find in real life. Dickens saw and magnified the peculiarities of men. Such a habit of mind may prove delightful in a novelist, but it can hardly be of use to a vocational counselor. Perhaps Dean Schneider realizes this, for he says just before his conclusion:

I am of the opinion that for the present, vocational guidance can only point out in which types of occupations an individual will in all probability *not* be successful.

It is to be regretted that the authors of a new high-school textbook for life-career classes (Gowin and Wheatley) should have used and elaborated Schneider's classifications.

Another classification has been proposed by Professor Giddings, in a recent address at Teachers College, Columbia University:

Does the child that you are watching begin to lead, to dictate, to suggest, to set examples, or does he show, from earliest years, that he is a born imitator, a copyist, a follower? . . . If you are a teacher, if you are a parent, if you are interested in the child, the sooner you discover to which of the classes your child belongs, the sooner you will be on the right track in guiding the further development of his character and his mind.[1]

"Born imitator," we are told, and, "the sooner you can discover." Thus we are not dealing with types of twenty-year-old minds, but with types determined before birth! The address contains little attempt at

[1] Giddings, p. 24.

evidence, the rhetoric being of the hortatory " type " rather than the scientific. Moreover, nothing is said about accidental circumstances which determine, influence, or alter a child's behavior : what kind of parents has he to live with ? has he older or younger brothers or sisters ? is he equipped with educative toys ? has he had early playmates, and were they older or younger ? Neither is anything said about those children who may reside comfortably between these two " types " and show no marked tendencies to either extreme.

No doubt we may find, if we divest ourselves of the mania to classify and find types, that a given child is " directive " at one moment of the day, and meek at another ; aggressive about his own toys, but submissive in strange surroundings ; willing to lead in games he knows, and to follow in others. We can agree with Professor Giddings in his conclusions about the need of socializing the individual, but we can maintain that neither for that nor for the purposes of vocational guidance is it necessary to read into him a classification unfounded on facts.

Another classification (Blumenthal) [1] is stated as follows :

There are three types of school children :

I. The coarse type.
II. The fine type.
III. The medium type.

[1] Central Committee, pp. 14-18. Puffer's book is founded on the type idea, as also on an exaggeration of heredity; see pp. 59, 62, 83.

The context suggests that the classification is to be undertaken when the child is four years of age. For every type there is a positive and a negative. No estimate of relative numbers belonging to the different types is given. After describing each type the author proceeds:

Now after the teacher has classified the types, and any teacher of average intelligence can do this easily, he will be anxious to group the types according to their quality — their mental and physical standards. Grouping the types is very interesting work [*sic*]. For this some practical psychological knowledge is required. The easiest way for a beginner is to group his types in the following classes:
1. Mentally strong and physically weak.
2. Physically strong and mentally weak.
3. Physically and mentally weak.
4. Harmonious — mentally and physically well-balanced.
5. Advanced or degenerate.

Such a classification, presented without evidence, should, after what we have said above, furnish its own refutation.

The notorious classification of persons into round pegs and square pegs has fortunately almost disappeared from the modern literature of vocational guidance. It is significant that the references to types of mind are diminishing in the literature of vocational guidance. Is it not now the time to abandon them altogether, as having no evidence in their support, as tending to crystallize the procedure of vocational guidance into a machine-like operation, and as helping to obscure the fact that every child is entitled to be treated so far as possible without reference to the characteristics of other children?

Classifications should be known by the company they keep: it was the business of astrology, palmistry, and phrenology to pigeonhole into fixed classifications the individuals who applied to them. For the typical kinds of brains, as described in Fowler's *Phrenology*, we are now asked to substitute typical kinds of minds — kinds that correspond more or less closely with the phrenologist's categories.

Educational Implications of the Classifications. — The reason for attempting a classification is that we may subject the children in the two classes to different kinds of educational treatment. That this aim is a desirable one is shown by all the progressive efforts to differentiate courses for children — to take account of individual differences, in the administration of the school and its program. For this work the child's requirements must be studied. But there is neither need nor justification for using fixed or questionable classifications in making this study. Individual differences in mental traits are rapidly being measured, and they approximate the normal distribution. The teacher needs neither to try to diminish nor to accentuate the deviation of any individual from the mean. He need only provide for the child's development, adjusting the curriculum to his present requirements, and keeping the way open for a change of treatment at any time.

Overestimation of what Psychological Tests can at present Do. — Our second class of false guidance has to do with tests. We have already quoted Bloomfield and Ayres [1] regarding what these tests can do. Their statements, conservative as they are, seem to be too sanguine. Ayres [2] states as the substance of achievement up to October, 1913:

At the present time we possess a rudimentary knowledge of the qualifications demanded in four occupations — those of inspector of bicycle balls, motorman, telephone operator, and typewriter.

The evidence, even for this modest claim, is not very satisfactory. There is nothing to prove, for example, that testing the reaction time of the girls who sorted the bicycle balls was as good a test as would have been an actual trial at the exercise which that occupation demands.[3] The second and third sets of tests are drawn from Münsterberg's experiments.[4] Yet his experiments were designed to show a method rather than a result, and have never been adopted in commercial life.

[1] Chapter IV.   [2] Nat. V. G. Assn., p. 36.

[3] This bicycle-ball test is now abandoned, but the report of it promises to go on for an indefinite time echoing through the writings of those searching for help from psychology. So little does the science teach us yet, and so much are short cuts sought after!

[4] Professor Münsterberg's tests are criticized in the article in *The Unpopular Review* (Breese), especially that for sea-captains. The test is not explicitly designed as an adequate method of selecting captains, yet each page of the chapter is headed "Ship Service." This test has been won on speed alone. It is based on the naïve assumption that accurate, quick judgment in sorting cards can measure good judgment in managing a ship!

The " typewriting test " is based on an experiment by Professor Lough.[1] His theory is that typewriting involves habit-formation; therefore as a test in habit formation sheets of paper are given out, each sheet containing rows of letters and bearing at the top a key in which each letter of the alphabet is represented by another letter as a symbol. This exercise is given as a test of speed in transcribing and learning the key, twenty tests in as many days, and it is assumed that the results will show who is fitted for the typewriting occupation and who is not. But this conclusion rests solely on this one experiment, whose results when correlated with school marks in each of four studies, German, mathematics, typewriting, and business forms and stenography, show a high degree of positive relation with typewriting. He concludes that from such tests in habit-formation " it would be possible to select those who are likely to succeed in typewriting, and to give a vocation to those who would not succeed." Here is a curious compound *petitio principii*. In the first place the tests are not measured against real success in the occupation of typewriting, but only against school courses in the subject. In the second place, the school marks in the classes in typewriting are used as the standard to validate the test, after which the test is to be used to supplant the school marks and provide a short-cut method of determining capability for the course and the occupation. If our previous conclusions are correct,

[1] See Nat. Conference, pp. 89-96.

we must raise three serious objections to the method. First, habit-formation is but one of the mental elements in learning to typewrite, and perhaps not the most important. There are spelling, neatness, common sense, and general education to be reckoned with. Second, certain moral qualities may enter in such a way as to upset completely conclusions based on such a test, — persistence, for example, may finally win out against great odds.[1] Third, as we shall see in the next section, habit-formation cannot be regarded as a general quality, to be transferred at will from a substitution test to typewriting.

The statement by Bloomfield may prove true — it may be that tests will aid a fifteen-year-old boy in choosing between professional, business, or mechanical study. So far, no tests have been adequate to prove or disprove the hypothesis. As Bloomfield says, tests can hardly show ability to influence men [2] and, as we have noted in another connection, they have not yet shown general improvability.

The whole question of the danger in overestimation of what psychological tests can do, as well as the theory

[1] Professor Lough suggests the desirability of testing emotional control, but outlines no method. Added to the above strictures, this observation seems to have escaped the experimenter, — that some who study typewriting have no intention of making it their calling. It seems desirable that everybody should learn to typewrite at least as fast as he can write. Finally, one wonders whether twenty trials at typewriting itself might not prove a better index of ability than those here used, if an index must be sought.

[2] *Youth*, etc., p. 62.

of types, is discussed by Dr. H. D. Kitson, University of Chicago. His two articles form an excellent antidote for the conception we are combating. (See Bibliography.) He quotes approvingly Professor James's observation that, " However closely psychical changes may conform to law, it is safe to say that individual histories and biographies will never be written in advance no matter how ' evolved ' psychology may become." [1]

Other recently written papers indicate that a saner view is being taken. In *School and Society* for June 26, 1915,[2] Hollingworth discusses the various kinds of tests and concludes that Mrs. Woolley's records may prove of value, but that others are open to question. He concludes:

It is essential that interest in this eminently practical use of the psychological laboratory be sustained among those who are responsible for the further promotion of its methods and problems. It is equally undesirable that public expectation should be strenuously directed toward the laboratory before it has done more than outline a series of problems and attempt a few trivial and preliminary efforts toward their solution.

In the issue of June 19, 1915,[3] Hancock of the University of Cincinnati says that Dean Schneider and Professor Breese, after three years of experimental work, have

[1] *Principles of Psychology*, Vol. II, p. 576.
[2] Pp. 920, 922. Hollingworth's book, *Vocational Psychology*, is helpful and conservative. However, one wonders whether there is yet any real body of vocational psychology.
[3] P. 899.

so far been able to find no correlation between the results of the psychological tests and known abilities.

Employers have been particularly credulous regarding psychological tests and gullible about actual chicanery, but we find Richard A. Feiss, general manager, The Clothcraft Shops of the Joseph and Feiss Company, Cleveland, Ohio, saying that outside of such practical examinations as the color tests for railway engineers psychological tests will not aid materially in the problem of employing.[1]

There seems to be no reason for amending in any way Mrs. Woolley's statement at the second conference that " an intelligent interest, extending over the early years of school life, ought to furnish a more adequate basis for judgment about the child's future, than any set of laboratory tests could supply. Experimental psychology is, as yet, a coarse and clumsy tool, attacking a very difficult, delicate, complex problem." [2]

Superintendent Thompson, speaking at the Richmond Convention, said : [3]

The few scientific tests for vocational aptitudes that we now possess give us more of concern than of promise. . . . For the present, at least, the vocational counselor will obtain greatest advantage from the study of the general employment situation of his community. . . . Common sense, broad sympathies, and knowledge of adolescent tendencies will prove of more worth to him than acquaintance with intricate psychological procedure. The practical methods

---

[1] *Scientific Management*, etc., p. 3.

[2] Nat. Conference, p. 85.   [3] Nat. V. G. Assn., 1914, p. 19.

to be at once adopted by vocational counselors are those which are obvious rather than obscure.

The next thought in Superintendent Thompson's paper, as quoted above, is one with which we may conclude this section: that " the school records of pupils if properly kept and reasonably comprehensive furnish enough presumptive evidence upon which effective guidance can be tentatively based." The psychologist may help vocational counsel best by aiding in the improvement of the school examinations in the various subjects: the laboratory should be the schoolroom and the exercise the regular work of the class. And he may help civil service commissions and business establishments in devising standardized tests based on the actual work the employees will be called upon to do.[1]

The Belief that Qualities of Mind are General and Transferable, rather than Specific. — Vocational guidance has still another score to settle with a pseudo-psychology, and this is the belief in the " spread " or transfer of mental qualities. Can *the attention* of a boy be tested, so that the conclusion can be drawn that he is attentive or inattentive? Can a simple examination be devised to test the powers of observation? Can honesty in examinations qualify a girl for the label, " honest girl " ? In short, are such activities as attending, observing, con-

---

[1] Scott's " Salesmanship Test " tests general cleverness, but has little relation to salesmanship. Seashore's tests for musical ability are profitable as showing what may be done in fields requiring a high order of specialized ability. The testing carried on in the army proved its value as an emergency measure.

M

centrating, persisting, using energy, being fair, being honest, remembering, analyzing, etc., if applied to one situation, likely to be applicable to all? We are, of course, touching on the whole question of general training or formal discipline. It is the belief in the general nature and transferability of mental and moral qualities that is at the bottom of the beliefs that we have just been examining: the beliefs in types and in the efficacy of laboratory tests.

A glance at a few of the blanks used in vocational guidance will show how common is the assumption.[1]

The doctrine of general training has recently been subjected to experimental tests, and while many psychologists hold that the data are not yet conclusive, few persons who have examined the modern literature of the subject can maintain seriously that mental qualities are general enough in their nature to justify the educational practice of developing a quality in one department of life in order that it may spread to another one more desirable.[2]   Rather, the valid practice is to train specifically for the particular quality desired.   Thus, as has been pointed out, the manual dexterity required to guide a bicycle is quite different from that needed by an engraver.   Courage in facing a baseball pitcher is likely

---

[1] See Parsons, pp. 37–43, 104; *Readings*, p. 131; also references in Chapter IV.

[2] Following are some important references on the subject of general training: Moore, Chap. III (gives a historical sketch and a résumé of the argument against the theory); Pillsbury and others; Thorndike, *Educational Psychology*, Vol. II; Heck; Bagley, Chap. XIII; Judd.

to be entirely unrelated to that required in facing an audience. Even memory is now held to be specific: a good memory for athletic records does not of itself mean a good memory for poetry. Observant school people have always known that any pupil's standards of truthfulness, honesty, courtesy, kindness, good use of English, attention, and all the other virtues, vary with time and circumstance. Personal qualities are specific rather than general. The writer knows of a person who is deliberate in deciding to go to the theatre, but hasty in choosing what to eat; fond of both indoor and outdoor work, with no preference for either; abstract in his religious thinking, and skillful with carpentry tools; inaccurate in arguments, but accurate at figures; careless in handwriting, but careful in typewriting; dependent in buying clothes, but " directive " in buying books; observant of names, but very unobservant of faces; attentive to political arguments, but excessively inattentive to narrative and to music.

Is it not true that emotional elements, such as the desire for success, self-confidence, excitement, competition, accidental associations which are stirred up, strangeness of the laboratory, — and so many others that nobody can estimate their number or influence, — are at all times hidden denials of our records in such tests as those for " verbal memory," " auditory retentiveness," " left-hand steadiness," " cancellation accuracy," and " index of fatigue "?

Until we measure the index of fatigue in an actual

football game, the hand steadiness in making something the child very much wants to make, the accuracy in throwing a ball, the verbal memory for sentences vital to the child, and the retentiveness for something the child wishes to retain, our laboratory measures cannot have very much psychological accuracy or general utility in school and shop.

What substitute procedure can we follow? In the first place, we can select situations which illustrate human virtues, and we can then make a conscious effort to point out the ways in which these principles can be applied to other situations. Thus neatness in arithmetic papers gives certain benefits; such and such of these benefits hold true of papers in composition. In the second place, we may seek concrete situations, and, instead of asking a boy if he is honest, ask him what he would do under certain hypothetical circumstances, and why. In the third place, we ought to define " efficiency " and " success " with our pupils, and should strive to give them the habit of succeeding in repeated instances of socially useful tasks. Then, if we wish measured results, they should be computed on the basis of the success of the boy or girl in these tasks.

What we need to do, in other words, is to cultivate desirable habits in every activity and relation of life, without depending on the transfer of qualities from one department of life to another.[1]

[1] Artificial tests may yet discover short-cut methods of judging character; the point here made is that they must, for the present, be disre-

Overestimation of the Importance of Physical Characteristics. — The fourth kind of questionable guidance is based on an exaggeration of the importance of physical qualities. Not only have we forgotten Plato's true doctrine that a good body will not by its own excellence make the soul good,[1] but we have also grown into a materialistic centering of the thought on bodily characteristics. There are courses for business men in which blonds and brunettes, brown eyes and blue, aquiline faces, small lips, and tapering hands, are discussed in their vocational significance. It is supposed that employment managers can by this means find short cuts to " size up " applicants and tell which to hire and which to reject. Current magazines are supplied with the advertisements of the people who furnish such information. A new book has recently appeared, in which is told how to analyze character and ability at first sight. The effect of these experiments goes deeper than mere loss of money and disappointment; it involves the injustice of misjudging men. This teaching goes on in spite of the fact that not even criminals can be discovered by their faces; if they were, the work of detectives would be easier. Some men say they can tell whether or not a man is a good workman by the way he picks

garded for vocational guidance, and they must free themselves of their dependence on the transfer theory. It is to be noted here that we are not discussing the subject of psychological tests for determining mental backwardness; the best of such tests are founded on specific items of knowledge.

[1] *Republic*, III, 403.

up a hammer, and Fullerton tells about an employment manager who judges boys by whether or not they respond to certain arbitrary orders and mental suggestions he throws out.[1]

The schools cannot coöperate with employment managers who taint themselves with such doctrines. Yet who does not know a teacher or two who occasionally makes snap judgments, or " sizes up " her pupils the first day? Even the counselor may sometimes be tempted to say: " This girl is too short to be a good teacher," or, " That boy is not strong, so he ought not to do indoor work." No such statements have a place in vocational guidance. The physical requirements have not yet been standardized even for athletic events and professional baseball. Further, the physical examination, as such, can tell nothing about the person's courage, perseverance, kindness, ability to coöperate, nor even much about his ability to gain in physique.

The best way would be for the counselor to tell the requirements for the occupation, and to raise the question of physique, general health, or apparent defect as a problem likely to be met and therefore necessary to consider. Advice is appropriate; prophecy must be avoided. The person himself must decide.

It is reported that some of the members of an occupational bureau in New York City are taking one of

[1] See Bibliography. He offers no evidence that the psychological or other tests are valid.

the courses given by a leading exponent of character analysis and vocation-determination-at-the-first-interview, their excuse being that while the theories and practices expounded in the course are very largely "rubbish," nevertheless the teacher herself is a woman of great common sense and gives them some valuable information which they can use in their placement activities. This shows the dangers to which the vocational-guidance movement is exposed by those supposed to be its friends. Here are educated persons, who, instead of making painstaking study of the educational, sociological, and economic aspects of their problems, resort to admitted charlatanism for the purpose of finding a short cut. Just at the time when more and more employers are making a scientific study of their problems and are abandoning rule of thumb on the one hand and mystic methods and guesswork on the other, these people are going back to methods no better than astrology and phrenology. What an assumption of superiority, besides, that they can separate the good from the evil! The movement for vocational guidance has had quite enough, already, of the method of mixing good and evil. It is time now for a separation between those who wish to study and learn and those who wish to juggle and dream.

Regarding the sanguine beliefs in mystic short-cuts, — beliefs which die hard, — David Spence Hill, who expresses a particularly sane viewpoint on the difficulties and dangers besetting the vocational counselor, says that we must " know the individual by a method more sure than casual observation, phrenological chicanery, or physiognomic delusion." [1]

Morbid Self-Examination. — The fifth error in some plans of vocational guidance, overemphasis of self-analysis, seems to be based on the theory that somewhere in the world there is a niche for every person to fit into, and that misfits are those who fail to find their destined places. It is known now, however, that there are no such fixed niches, and that jobs need more analyzing and adjusting than do people. Boys and girls need a record of successful accomplishments in a variety of useful fields ; this the schools of the near future will give them. A list of useful acts is as much better than a list of qualities as works are better than mere faith.

That vocational guidance must free itself from those questions which overemphasize self-analysis must be evident through an examination of the blanks used in present practice (see references, pp. 106, 162). Questions on manners [2] are not so objectionable, though they may foster the attitude of the Pharisee. But such questions [3] as the following serve no good purpose in a

---

[1] Nat. V. G. Assn., 1914, p. 37. We have spoken of the misuse of hereditary influences, in Chapter IV. Puffer's book furnishes extreme examples, pp. 59–62, 83–86. The counselor can find no practical use for investigating family trees.

[2] Parsons, p. 32.

[3] Note that most of the objectionable questions are based on the general discipline theory.

printed blank: " Do you consider yourself absolutely honest? " " What vices do you have to fight down in yourself? " " Are you stubborn? " " What are your limitations and defects? " Questions of this nature lead to statements like these two taken from the case-letter file of the Boston Vocation Bureau: " I always like to joke and to improve things." " I feel unrest, due to the conviction that I am cut out for something big and fine."

Self-analysis has the hypnotic effect of fastening on us the qualities we set down; to a great degree we have the qualities we think we have. This is illustrated in the paper on Self-Analysis by High School Girls [1] in which the girls chose their vocations partly on the basis of classifying themselves as " thing-thinkers " or " idea-thinkers."

So far as may be discovered, no concrete evidence has been presented to prove that the young person's analysis of himself is valid. We know that we adults encounter frequent surprises, both in ourselves and in others whom we know best, and that we can never be even approximately sure of success in a new venture until we have made an actual trial. Yet we ask the fourteen-year-old boy to tell us his talents and characteristics and then to choose his vocation. Even adults cannot be trusted in self-analysis. In the words of Burns:

> "O wad some Pow'r the giftie gie us
> To see oursels as ithers see us!"

[1] Nat. Conference, p. 101.

Three substitutes for detailed self-analysis may be tried. We may first obtain the question and rating sheets from business houses in the community, using these as a basis for showing the qualities demanded, and for suggesting that each person must prepare himself to meet the scrutiny of these questions. Second, we may arrange our school program, and the occupational experiences of persons entering upon work, so that each bad trait or defect, so far as is humanly possible, will be crowded out by the development of an appropriate good habit. Finally, we may adopt the plan of obtaining composite opinions of teachers and others interested in the child, as suggested in Chapter IV. These opinions are built up out of the special qualities the child has shown in the varied work and play of the efficient school, and they will no doubt prove a far better index of the character of the child than will his own self-analysis.

Overguidance. — Two high school teachers, both college graduates, went out of their way to " take an interest in " and advise a certain pupil, and both of them told him that on account of various limitations it was useless for him to think of going to college. He had already made himself an expert salesman, working afternoons and Saturdays in a large clothing store, was an excellent student, and was a leader in the affairs of the high school. Here was an obvious case of gratuitous and erroneous advice. The boy did well in college studies, serving as assistant in economics, and is now studying in a graduate school and trying to decide between law, teaching, and business. Naturally he does not remember kindly the attempted guidance these teachers gave him.

Overguidance may be either positive or negative. Though perhaps the attempt deliberately to discourage a student's choice is the more common kind, yet frequently cases occur in which the counselor is tempted to be sanguine, or too sure in the advice which he has given. Thus, Parsons' cases[1] sometimes show more confidence than seems warranted.

Overguidance is frequently implicitly advocated by writers who apparently have not weighed the consequences of what they are saying. The following quotation, for example, makes it appear that the children are permanently stamped with distinct qualities, and that they should, like so many pawns, be put once and for all into their places:

A guidance bureau should be like a type-distributing machine, which will take a hopperful of type, of all the letters of the alphabet, and place each in its particular niche, in the one place of all places where it fits.[2]

The way to avoid overdirective influence is indicated in much that has been said in preceding pages. Kitson speaks for the "monitory type" of vocational guidance which states facts and frees itself both from intuition without knowledge, and zeal beyond the evidence.

---

[1] *Choosing a Vocation*, Chap. XV.   [2] Kelley, T. L., p. 85.

Commercial Agencies. — Probably no person other than one receiving pay from the applicant would ever say, " This is your vocation." Such an agent is bound to produce something tangible at the first interview, in order that he may send the applicant away feeling that the visit has been worth money. The honest counselor cannot at the first interview produce final results for a stranger. Hence arises the need for protecting the public by having all the guidance done under public auspices, or by agents responsible to boards of well-known and trusted directors.

As has been noted in an earlier chapter, children often get their ideas of guidance from newspaper advertisements, and are often induced to read and use material which is worse than trash.

If vocational guidance will free itself from all extravagant claims, and from the use of methods not yet valid — for on these claims and methods the commercial agent thrives — there will be little chance for the counselor who charges a fee to deceive the public. The school courses in vocations should touch on this kind of " guidance," so that young people may be forewarned.

Lack of Social Perspective. — " The Efficient Optimist," is the title of a recent magazine article [1] which commences as follows:

The first idea to be drilled into the mind, heart, soul, and body of every human being is the firm assurance:

" You can ! "

[1] Purington, *The Independent*, Nov. 22, 1915, p. 309.

This advice is of the sort so often given to young people, couched in such expressions as, "develop personal efficiency," "be a leader," "strengthen your will-power," "never admit failure," "get the success-habit," "be a director, not a follower," "manage men," "you may be the kind of steel that is made into rails for people to run over, or you may make yourself into a watch-spring and run the whole works!"

Many of these ideals [1] appear to put success before righteousness; they base success on power to do things, without first determining whether or not the things are worth doing at all. What is there in human will power, that we should so urge our young people to cultivate it? Is a strong will, *per se*, a desirable quality? These questions cannot be answered here, but they are worth better consideration than the efficiency experts have given them. Will power is necessary, no doubt, in all worthy undertakings; but it has also been at the bottom of nearly every act of murder, lust, and unrighteous war. Will power needs the check of education, conscience, and social aim. [2]

[1] It is true that the author of our first quotation includes in his test sheet the question, Is your final ambition unselfish? But this is not enough. The writer knows of a gentleman whose final ambition is to help the cause of prohibition. While waiting for a "more convenient season" he is engaged in some questionable real-estate speculation, and occasionally patronizes the liquor business.

[2] An interesting study in this connection is based on the question, Is the use of the will more necessary in selfish or in unselfish undertakings? Compare, for example, the works of Jesus or Socrates with those of Alexander or Napoleon. The answer is not far to seek, — "Not my will, but thine, be done."

Mere material success cannot be the goal of vocational guidance: moral guidance must accompany vocational.

Another kind of guidance which shows a lack of social perspective is that in which the boy or girl is repressed and his individuality subordinated to the will of another. It is to be noted that the motto " I can " means for multitudes " I cannot." Mere personal efficiency, as we shall see in a later place (Chap. VII), is likely to benefit the few at the expense of the many. The acceleration of the competitive struggle means many tragic failures but only a few spectacular " successes." Both kinds of error, unless checked by our educational programs, will only aggravate the hatred between the classes, and add to a problem already very acute in America.

The unsocial doctrines to which young men are exposed is well shown by the questionable methods being taught in salesmanship. For example, a widely circulated book, *Influencing Men in Business, The Psychology of Argument and Suggestion* (Scott), is dedicated " to the young business man . . . who is studying to make his arguments more convincing and his suggestions more coercive." The book teaches that suggestion has greater influence than argument, and that suggestion excludes comparison and criticism (p. 147). The author shows how suggestive questions may be used to force a customer to decide to buy, and states that such methods " when properly used . . . are most effective " (p. 168). The book concludes:

If in persuading men we wish to depend upon the working of suggestion we must relieve them, so far as possible, of the distressing necessity of deciding, and we must also relieve them of all difficulty in the steps necessary to carry out that which we have been trying to suggest they should do. The man who is able to relieve his prospects in these two particulars is the man skilled in carrying his suggestions to a happy conclusion. [P. 168.]

It would seem that if such doctrines are to be taught under the name of salesmanship, courses in " buymanship " should be taught as an antidote and protection. At any rate, the vocational counselor can do nothing but condemn such a dangerous attempt at vocational " efficiency."

Control of Vocational Guidance by Other Agencies. — What is of greater importance than the " vocational guidance of youth? " Is it the granting of work certificates; the enforcement on truants of the compulsory education law; the placement of children who are unfortunate enough to have to leave school; the securing by business men of adequate help; the promotion of vocational education; psychological research in the schools?

That vocational guidance, like many another movement, needs to be protected from its supposed friends, is shown by a statement by Healy in his book *The Individual Delinquent.*[1] He is discussing the difficulty involved in inducing the children to come to his labora-

[1] Pp. 47–48.

tory to be examined for possible deficiencies, and states that a good plan is to tell them that they are to be examined for their vocational abilities, " which indeed they are." He continues that the examination may begin with vocational questions, and may then gradually lead into the mental and medical fields. If this sort of thing goes on, vocational guidance will not only lose its identity; it will take on all the associations of pathological psychology, and will be thought fitting for only those who " have something the matter with them." Cannot those genuinely interested in vocational guidance issue an injunction against such practices?

Probably it will be admitted that nothing less than the problem of education considered as a whole is of greater importance than vocational guidance. If this be true, then its work should not be directed by any other subordinate department. Vocational guidance must be controlled by the main organization for education, the school committee or board, through the superintendent and his assistants, but it should not be controlled by any lesser power. For the same reason that associations of business men should not control the vocation bureau, neither the work-certificate office nor the placement bureau should control it.

Vocational guidance must develop its own point of view. Its problem is at best a very complex and difficult one. It must not be hampered by having to see its problems through the eyes of an office with a different purpose.

Conclusion. — No errors are eradicated by merely fixing the attention on them without turning the effort into the right channels. The errors must, however, be recognized, and then denied opportunity for operation. Genuine and systematic study of the complex problems of vocational guidance, no matter on how small a scale, is more to be desired than attempts to find by-paths and short-cuts. Mystical and futile activities should be abandoned and energy directed into improving the school environment of the child, studying the occupations, or other legitimate efforts, if real and permanent progress is to be made.

One of the most necessary activities for the teacher-guide is the study of occupations, for of them he will ordinarily have had least experience. Our inquiry will therefore proceed into that field. The next two chapters will deal with the conditions under which young people enter work and the problems of employment, together with some economic and social aspects of vocational guidance.

N

CHAPTER VI

The Young Worker

" At least two million boys and girls in this country between the ages of fourteen and sixteen are working for wages. They are unskilled at that age and unable to take responsibility. Few occupations open to them offer any training that enables them to develop.

" This does not include the additional army of children in some of the Southern States leaving school at the tender age of twelve. During the present year at least a million more childish wage-earners upon reaching the age of fourteen will enter the ranks of industry. More than six out of ten of this multitude did not finish the work of the elementary school. More than three out of four of them did not reach the seventh year of the schools and more than one out of two, the sixth. Almost half of them had not completed the fifth grade work. Great numbers of them were barely able to meet the test for illiteracy necessary in order to secure working certificates, which in most of the States is a test on the work of the fourth grade.[1]

This quotation, based as it is on census reports and on trustworthy studies of elimination from the public schools, suggests the subject matter of the present chapter. We are concerned with five questions: (1) Why

[1] Bulletin of Nat. Soc. for Prom. of Ind. Educ.

do children leave school? (2) How do they obtain work? (3) What kind of work do they do? (4) What are the opportunities offered by their work? (5) What proposals have been made to remedy existing evils? That these problems are important is attested by the fact that scarcely a legislative session in any state fails to grapple with one or more of them. They are the burden of two important bills recently passed by the national Congress, the bill for federal aid to industrial education, and that to prohibit interstate commerce in child-made goods.

Why do Children leave School? — Two industrial surveys[1] of recent date present tables showing the reasons given for leaving school:

CAUSES OF WITHDRAWAL MINNEAPOLIS ELEMENTARY SCHOOLS	%	REASONS GIVEN FOR LEAVING RICHMOND SCHOOLS	%
Left the city	23	To go to work	42
To attend private school .	11	Wanted to	10
Death	1	Poor health	9
Economic pressure . . .	3	To support family . . .	8
Illness of pupil	5½	Had to go to work . . .	5
Illness in family	2	Graduated	4
Physical defects	1	To learn a trade	4
Incapacity (mental) . . .	2	Failure in studies . . .	3
Indifference	2½	Moved	1
Failing promotion . . .	1	Disagreed with teacher .	1
Went to work	44	To accept position . . .	1
Unexplained	4	Miscellaneous	2
		Not stated	10

[1] Minneapolis Survey, p. 25; Richmond, p. 19.

Figures are changed to per cents. All such tables are open to question, as Van Denberg has shown (see Bibliography) and the classifications contain overlapping items. Nevertheless they suggest opinions and tendencies. For additional data see Bloomfield, *Readings*, pp. 119, 123, 238–239, 404, 449; Davis, Jesse B., p. 153; Bloomfield, *Youth*, etc., 16, 19; Ayres, *Laggards*, etc., p. 101; Reed, *V. G. Report*, pp. 95–97.

The Boston Continuation School publishes the following table:[1]

REASONS FOR LEAVING THE REGULAR SCHOOLS. BOSTON.

In per cents.

	Boys	Girls	Both
Related to economic conditions in the home	35.0	46.4	40.2
Related to conditions in the school . . .	56.8	42.7	50.4
Related to personal feelings of child or attitude of parent	6.2	8.3	7.1
Related only to vocational opportunity offered	.2	—	.1
No reason given	1.8	1.2	1.6
Will probably work only during vacation .	—	1.4	.6

At the second national conference on vocational guidance Miss Colleton of Boston stated (p. 156) that about one third of those leaving school needed to for financial reasons, but that another third left because they or their parents were dissatisfied with the work of the school. Mrs. Woolley at the same meeting declared (p. 30) that every investigation of economic need among families of working children, except one in the stockyard district of Chicago, has shown that three fourths or more of the families do not absolutely need the earnings of the children under sixteen years of age. She states that the chief factor in sending children to work is their own desire to go, and that the chief reason for this desire is retardation in the school.

[1] Circular, p. 23.

Children leave school, it appears from these studies, largely because the school fails to attract them. They leave " to go to work," sometimes pressed by economic need, it is true, but more often because to quit school for going to work seems to be the ordinary, expected thing to do. Three remedies suggest themselves: better school program and methods, scholarships to help needy children, and part-time work. These plans we shall discuss later.

To the question, Does industry need the labor of children? a rapidly increasing multitude of testimonies answer, No. It is true that in Southern cotton mills, where child labor has always been taken for granted, many owners still feel that their businesses cannot run without the ten-hour day of the loom tenders; and that an occasional factory manager in other parts of the country asks the schools to place with him what he calls the " product " of the schools — those who leave at fourteen. But these conditions are not typical; and there seems no good reason to amend the statement resulting from the investigation of the University of Chicago Settlement:

Aside from parasitic industries, there is no economic necessity for juvenile labor, according to the testimony of employers.[1]

An Iowa investigation led to a similar conclusion.[2] Meanwhile, one state, Minnesota, by a gradual process

[1] Bloomfield, *Youth*, etc., p. 17.
[2] See Comm. of Educ., 1915, p. 223.

extending over ten years, has raised the school age for all children to the sixteenth birthday.

How do Children Obtain Work? — The settlement workers of the United States say that girls should not be required to go about our cities looking for work.[1] Yet in Boston 56 per cent of those girls between fourteen and sixteen who secured work applied in person. The complete table, taken from the same report referred to above, is as follows:

METHODS OF SECURING POSITIONS. BOSTON CHILDREN UNDER
SIXTEEN YEARS OF AGE

In per cents.

	BOYS	GIRLS	BOTH
Applied personally	43.4	56.5	50.0
Through relatives	18.4	14.8	16.6
Through friends	18.7	18.4	18.2
Positions offered unsolicited	5.7	4.6	5.4
Through school or teachers	.5	1.2	.8
Through Placement Bureau	1.8	1.8	1.8
Through business or trade associations . .	—	—	—
Through social or charitable associations .	.6	.1	.4
Through employment agencies	10.8	2.6	6.7
Through competitive examinations . . .	.1	—	.1

If there were jobs enough so that the children could choose something which would lead them to their vocation, we should have no quarrel with what is told by the above table. We know, however, that with many of these children the mere chance of falling into one place rather than another, determines for them the kind

[1] Woods and Kennedy, pp. 17–18.

of work they follow for years to come. The job chooses the vocation. The Richmond *Survey*[1] discloses the fact that continued work in their jobs does not entirely reconcile them to their places, for from three to seven out of every ten of the young men and women at work wish to change to different occupations.

We have been considering the children from fourteen to sixteen. How do the young men and women obtain their places? Certainly in no better ways than do those of younger years. The writer knows of a boy of good scholarship who made thirty futile applications for work during the two or three days after his graduation from high school. He would have taken almost any place offered, regardless of any choice of vocation he had made. In other words, the accidental " boy wanted " would have determined his occupation, for several years, at least. Bloomfield's New York study shows that boys tell each other about places vacant. Mr. Lord's study[2] disclosed the same accidental choices.

It appears, then, that better ways of getting work are needed, and that the school must do what it can to take the matter out of the realm of chance. The vocational counselor must interest himself in placement. What methods may be used we shall discuss in Chapter VIII.

What Kind of Employment does the Young Worker Obtain? — In the 1915 report of the Committee on Industrial Education, National Association of Manufacturers, the chairman of the committee, who is also

---

[1] Pp. 22–24.   [2] *Readings*, p. 29.

the President of the Wisconsin State Board of Industrial
Education, states that " from fourteen to sixteen,
87 per cent of working children are in dead-end, blind-
alley jobs. They are not allowed to work with machinery " (p. 30).

The Boston Continuation School publishes the table
given below, but many children classed as working in
factories are in reality messengers in those establishments.[1]

INDUSTRIES IN WHICH CHILDREN UNDER SIXTEEN YEARS OF AGE
FIND OCCUPATION, BOSTON

	BOYS	GIRLS	BOTH
Factories	18.7	45.4	30.4
Mercantile establishments	40.5	37.4	39.2
Mechanical establishments	11.8	3.4	8.2
Domestic and personal service	1.2	1.8	1.4
Messenger service	10.7	—	5.9
Business offices	10.3	—	5.8
Workshops	3.4	11.8	7.1
Unclassified	3.4	.2	2.

It is to be remembered that these figures include full-
time workers, but do not enumerate the army of part-
time workers : newsboys, peddlers' helpers, market boys,
bootblacks, and the gatherers of coal and wood for
family use.[2]

[1] Probably the same thing is true of Philadelphia figures given by Davis
in *Vocational and Moral Guidance*, p. 155. What kind of work is done is
of more importance than in what kind of an establishment the child
works.

[2] See Davis's *Streetland*, Chapters 6–8; see also Clopper, showing how
seasonal work on the farms cuts down school opportunity, pp. 189–203.

The kind of work open to children in England was made the basis of the report on the poor laws from which Bloomfield quotes in *Youth, School, and Vocation.*[1] It was found that only 18 per cent of the boys went definitely into trades. The rest were errand boys, chore boys, and the like.

All elementary school children and their parents should know about the Chicago investigations reported by Miss Davis at the Richmond meeting. Some of the findings are stated as follows:

It has been found that there are very few positions which offer even a little training to children under sixteen years; that usually the only skill required in any work is speed; that many employers do not want children under sixteen years of age because the law permits them to work only eight hours a day, and because they are so small and unreliable, that it is not worth while to bother with them; that some employers in the very unskilled work prefer children of fourteen because their fingers are more flexible and they can work faster (p. 52).

Bloomfield defines a blind alley as an employment whose possibilities for advancement are exhausted in a short time; an occupation or method of carrying on an occupation in such a way that there is no progress in the direction of increased intelligence and physical development. One of the most common blind alleys for bright boys is the position as errand boy in a high-class establishment such as a broker's office or an engineer's

[1] Pp. 9-13.

laboratory. The higher occupations in such businesses require extensive training, and there is absolutely no ladder reaching up to them from the place of the errand boy, mail boy, or elevator operator. This fact the boy finds out after two to four years' work with some few minor promotions, and leaves the place to begin all over again.

Miss Colleton outlines the work open to elementary school girls in Boston as follows:

There was little or no difference in the occupations open to the girls who graduated and those who left before graduating. The principal places open to them were in the department stores as bundle girls at $2.50 to $3.50; in the factories at $3 to $4; in stores as salesgirls at $5; in tailors' shops at $2.50 to $3.50.[1]

Neither the Richmond nor the Minneapolis Survey is concerned primarily with the occupations of the young worker. Our comment from the Richmond Survey, showing the dissatisfaction among the older brothers and sisters at work, indicates that our former conclusions were correct: the child of fourteen is fitted neither by his own perspective nor by the opportunities open to him to choose his vocation. It is the manifest duty of the schools, therefore, to supervise the employment of those children who are forced to work, so that they may be given the necessary facilities for making a wise choice of vocation, preparation for that occupation through continuation-school opportunity, and some

[1] *Readings*, p. 119.

element of guarantee that they will find work when the time comes for them to change to the better employment.

Opportunites offered by Children's Work. — Children are subjected to all the difficulties characteristic of employment in general, which we shall outline in the next chapter. But added to these are certain special problems which we shall discuss here. If there be need for improving the conditions of adult employment, much more is it the duty of society to supervise and improve, or abolish, child labor.

Miss Davis, of Chicago, from whom we have quoted, continues :

Reports have shown that much of the work open to children under sixteen is seasonal; that the children under sixteen are nearly always the ones who are laid off; that the average child works about one half the time during the two years between fourteen and sixteen, and that the average wage is not more than two dollars a week. [Less than four dollars while at work.] For this paltry sum these children are giving up their right to schooltime and playtime, their right to education and training (p. 52).

The Wisconsin bulletin makes these comments about continuation school girls and boys :

Here in Wisconsin we have a group of about 4000 girls with an average age of fifteen years, in fairly good health, earning approximately an average wage of a little more than $3.00 per week, working either constantly standing or constantly sitting, for forty-eight hours per week, and the majority of them live over a mile from their work, to which they walk. They are employed in candy making, canning and bottling, hand finishing and sewing for tailors and knitters, spinning, spooling, and winding, machine knitting, taping, net weaving, turning gloves and linings, pasting and labeling, cash and messenger service, etc., etc. . . .

Can we say that they are engaged in a recognized, profitable employment? Can we say that they have made a choice of occupation? Can we say that they wish to increase their efficiency in their chosen occupation? . . .

What shall we do with the boys under sixteen who enroll in the Continuation School? Take 4000 of these boys for consideration in Wisconsin. Their average age is fifteen years. They . . . earn on an average a little more than $4.00 per week, and many walk or ride long distances to work. They are employed in making shoes, as messenger and delivery boys, office and errand boys, time keepers, helpers, sorting and assembling, packing and wrapping, folding and filing, tending, and such simple tasks generally. The educational value of their work is very little, if any at all. They shift often from one job to another job, and quite as often from one occupation to another occupation. . . .

It must be said that these boys in general are not in a recognized profitable employment, that they have not already determined their aim to remain in and become efficient in any employment, and that, therefore, general improvement instruction may not wholly miss the mark in serving the group as a whole (pp. 479–480).

The Pennsylvania continuation school law is reviewed by the chairman of the Committee on Industrial Education, National Association of Manufacturers, referred to (p. 189), who makes the following statement:

Heretofore, many children under sixteen worked ten hours a day, and fifty-eight hours a week. Hereafter, they can work only a total of fifty-one hours a week, including the eight hours spent in school, and the maximum may not exceed nine hours in any one day. This last requirement has caused rather bitter complaint, in a few places, where it seemed necessary to work the children either ten hours or not at all, on the ground that some processes now carried on by children require attention constantly so long as the mill runs (p. 28).

The quotation is followed by some plans which are being worked out to make necessary adjustments.

The Boston Continuation School Bulletin, already quoted, gives a table (p. 24) from which it appears that both boys and girls enter upon employment at an average wage slightly below four dollars.[1]

Significant regarding the difficulty of obtaining work is the fact that 19 per cent of the boys and 39 per cent of the girls in the Boston Continuation School (besides the piece workers) obtained promise of work and their employment certificates without knowing what their wages were to be.

Another source of dissatisfaction in the occupations lies in the fact that there is frequently no definite agreement as to the character of the work to be done. It is human nature for the employer to picture conditions in his establishment as attractively as possible, and for the boy or girl to make as good an appearance as he can.

---

[1] Wage figures, of course, were taken before the war increases of 1916 and later. Present wages, and post-war adjustments, will show about the same relation to the cost of living as do these 1914–1915 figures to costs at that time.

When work actually begins, however, difficulties and misunderstandings are common. The younger members of the force must stand ready to run errands for everybody. The writer well remembers how often the work plans in his grocery-store experience were interrupted, and how he was made fun of because he remarked that he wanted a chance to do his " regular work."

The boy or girl who asks for employment brings letters or gives references and fills out an application blank; should not the employer at least be able to show the candidate the specifications of the job? It should not be difficult to tell a boy, in writing, from whom he is to take orders, how far his errands will carry him, what is the latest hour he will reach home, what special tasks he is likely to be assigned, just what he will have to do to obtain promotion, and what kind of clothes he is expected to wear, any more than to tell him what his regular hours are and how long he will be allowed for lunch.

In what manner shall the young worker be taught how to perform his duties? Here is a virgin field for investigation and constructive suggestion. Many employers think that the success or failure of a boy is wholly an individual problem; they do not make it a practice to work out a system of supervision and follow-up. This lack of thoughtful care and helpful suggestion is another cause of difficulty. It often leads to sudden discharge or voluntary leaving without any previous intimation that dissatisfaction existed.

The frequent change of employment is another symptom of an erroneous condition of the youth's working experience. Those who know best about the matter estimate that the average boy of fourteen to sixteen changes jobs from four to six times annually. Boys want to work up, and they are always dreaming that a change will improve the conditions under which they chafe. Since they have no assurance that a job will turn out well, however, under the present chaotic state of employment, the plan of trial and error is the only way open to them.

The reasons for leaving positions given by the Boston Continuation School children (p. 25 of circular) are particularly instructive:

REASONS FOR LEAVING POSITIONS. BOSTON CHILDREN [1]

	BOYS	GIRLS	BOTH
Questions of personal efficiency	11.0	4.8	8.4
Discharged on account of conditions of business or employment	46.5	48.6	47.4
Left, due to employment conditions . . .	34.1	32.8	33.6
School and labor laws	1.4	3.2	2.1
Illness	1.8	3.1	2.4
Home conditions	.4	1.2	.7
Other reasons	4.8	6.3	5.4

Shifting from job to job is a contributing cause to unemployment among children, but by no means the

[1] Figures are for the year ending March 31, 1915; the beginning of the war may have increased the number of discharges. The circular states that the Boston Continuation School seemed to have a steadying influence, — 950 pupils had worked in but one place since entering school, 138 in two, and 47 in three or more. Few of these children, of course, had been a full year in the school.

only cause; the work is unsteady and seasonal, and the youthful efforts crude and inefficient. Some employers make it a practice to engage new hands frequently, discharging them when they grow experienced and wish more pay. Others refuse to break in raw material, but take those trained by other firms.

The Wisconsin Outlines of Lessons, quoted above, has this to say about conditions in that state:

> The people who have dreams that these permit girls should have trade extension courses exclusively, get a shock when they learn that out of the 4000 girls, 500 hold the same job less than one month, 1000 hold the job less than three months, 1000 less than one year, and that barely 25 hold the job for two years (p. 479).

Bloomfield prints a table from an investigation by the Henry Street Settlement, showing the ten jobs held by a girl from her fourteenth to her sixteenth years.[1]

A certain middle-sized New England factory city is said to have more sixteen- to eighteen-year-old boys walking its streets or in its billiard halls than has the city of Boston. These boys have been attracted into the mills at fourteen, have found themselves no better off after two to four years of work, have then quit the mill, and are now without an occupation and with preparation for none.

" Stumbling from one job to another," " job jungle," " vocational anarchy," and " job hoboes," seem to be terms of description which are justified by the facts.

[1] *Youth*, etc., p. 2.

It should be remembered that we have not taken illustrations from unfavorable places in this country, but from states so progressive that continuation schools have been organized to save the wastage.

The schools cannot escape responsibility. A recent speaker states that Boston schools are training not more than 1500 students for industrial careers and approximately 5000 for commercial, in spite of the fact that industrial opportunities are twice as numerous. The school must recast its program of studies, it must give better guidance in the choice of occupation, and it must supervise employment.

What Proposals have been Made to Remedy Existing Evils? — There is no single specific which will cure these evils; developments in the past show the methods for the future, and promise continuous improvement. What has so far been done to make conditions for the young workers better has been the result of coöperative intelligence, expressed in the sincere effort of teachers, workers, and employers. The continuation school, prevocational work, and the part-time plan, as well as many things in the differentiated and enriched school program, have resulted from this effort. Labor unions, manufacturers' associations, and philanthropic organizations have joined the forces of education and the authority of the state in the work of reform.[1] So much

[1] It is futile to ask who did most or who held back. In human nature radical as well as reactionary tendencies usually lie in the accident of economic interest; this is to be reckoned with but is not inevitable. The

o

has been accomplished that there is little doubt as to the future: ten years will beyond all question witness tremendous strides.

We are concerned here with the lines of activity taken by present effort at reform, — with the proposals for improving the plight of the young worker.

Let us first remind the reader that placement[1] (see Chapter IV) is not a satisfactory solution, as is plainly shown by both England's experience and our own. Indeed, placement of children under sixteen — some day we may say eighteen — often aggravates the evil conditions. At any rate let us see if other proposals will not yield better fruit.

Many of the plans for improvement have been touched upon in previous chapters. Thus employment supervision, with school people guiding the working child, would go far to aid the young worker to make a success of his present job, to study his abilities and opportunities, to make a wise choice of vocation, to take steps for definite preparation, and to find work in the chosen occupation when ready for it. The continuation school can do much to save the young worker for better employment. In the Wisconsin Outlines of Lessons Hicks advocates training the boys and girls for certain standard occupations while they are in the continuation school:

point is that coöperation did the work, and that it would not have been done so well and so permanently without that coöperation.

[1] See Mrs. Woolley's statements on placement, Second Conference, p. 29.

The girls, outside of home-making, have at least seven constant occupations for which they may be safely trained, viz., servants, dressmakers, teachers, saleswomen, laundresses, nurses, housekeepers, while with the boys there are twenty or more constant occupations for which they may be safely trained, viz., laborers, retail merchants, clerks, draymen, salesmen, carpenters, steam railroad men, machinists, painters, bookkeepers, waiters, engineers, printers, blacksmiths, masons, barbers, plumbers, street railroad men, shoemakers, bakers (p. 481).

Not only may the continuation school direct the attention of the young worker to these occupations, but the regular school as well, in the lower grades, may warn the pupils that those expecting to go to work early should choose an occupation beyond the errand-boy stage, and should consciously and persistently work toward that occupation. Indeed, the plan we suggested in another place, to have every pupil study several possible occupations, would aid the young worker to get into a better place. Moreover, merchants who use children under sixteen years of age must be taught the duty of providing for the future of their charges, either by offering opportunity for adequate promotion to the higher places within their establishments, or by their willingness to allow the child to leave their employ whenever he can better himself. The job should be recognized as temporary — a mere stepping-stone to a better employment.

Other plans have been carried out or proposed. In Chicago the Vocation Bureau sent letters to parents, embodying the facts presented above and inviting the parents to conferences.

In most cities some effort has been made by private organizations to provide scholarships for worthy children. The Second National Conference on Vocational Guidance devoted a session to Scholarships.[1] It is unthinkable that aid to students should be confined to colleges and universities, or that it should be restricted to the brighter pupils, who need it least.

Another proposal is that a systematic effort be made to open blind alleys — to organize industry so that every job for the young worker will lead to a better one.   This plan involves employment supervision of a highly developed sort, besides a recasting of the plan of operation of many establishments, and a new form of coöperation between different forms of businesses.   Thus the errand boy in a publishing house, if unqualified by potential ability to prepare for a position in the publishing business, must be directed perhaps into learning a trade so that he may be equipped to enter a shop at the age of eighteen or twenty.   We are aware of the difficulties involved in such a plan, — the adjustments of wages, time, schedule of work in the establishment of present employment and in the school, problems of advice and guidance, and the possible changes of plans during any period of the process.   Yet the principle involved here is exactly that of the continuation school, and the continuation school, heralded at first as a fad and an im-

[1] See Proceedings, pp. 59–81.

possibility, has won its way to the approval of all concerned. Part-time schooling has arrived: there remains only the problem of widening the opportunity it offers and of applying it to more workers.

The part-time experiment has proved successful for colleges and high schools; why not for elementary schools, is the argument, in case children find it necessary to earn money? If children are to be the errand runners of industry and commerce, why not have them work in two shifts, one from eight to twelve in the morning, and the other from one to five in the afternoon? If their employment were well supervised, their schooling full of life and play, and their vocational guidance adequate, there seems no reason to suppose that harm would result to themselves or to society from their employment. The half day at work and half day at school would without doubt be better than the plan of alternate weeks, and children's work is so simple that not even the pairing system [1] would be necessary for planning the work in the employing establishments.

Some such plan as the above is mentioned in the Minneapolis Survey as having been suggested to the committee, but is not included in the recommendations of the Survey Committee.[2] Snedden states that the plan of having children work in two shifts of five hours each would probably be less disturbing to business than the present continuation school plan.[3] Thum

[1] See Schneider, *Education*, etc. p. 60.
[2] See Survey Report, pp. 21 and 29; see also Alden.
[3] Mass. Board of Educ., 79th Report, p. 47.

has proposed a plan for part-time in public employment and in high school study.[1]

Before much can be done to reëducate the boys and girls at work, public opinion must be stirred to the necessity for this important piece of conservation. If school people, aided by progressive employers of labor, will continue and extend the experiments now under way, acceptable plans will shortly be developed. Volunteer effort in all the methods we have touched on — supervision of the working child, prevocational and vocational training in the continuation school, scholarships to keep children in school, opening the blind alleys, and half-day work — will provide data for permissive legislation. Indeed, the stage of permissive legislation for continuation schools already has been passed in some states, and the next few years will undoubtedly lead many of the states to make sweeping improvements in the conditions surrounding boys and girls at work.

[1] Thum, William, *A Forward Step for the Democracy of To-morrow.* The Twentieth Century Co., 1910.

CHAPTER VII

THE PROBLEMS OF EMPLOYMENT

OUR purpose in this chapter is to outline the bearing of certain unsolved problems of employment on vocational guidance. Obviously, our worker, at whatever age he begins work, and under whatever circumstances, must be equipped in at least three ways: (1) He must be efficient in his task, (2) He must be imbued with the desire and ability to improve his methods of work and to find development in his vocation, and (3) He must understand something of the economic and social significance of the main problems of employment. It is the third of these fields that we shall explore in this chapter; and we shall assume that the vocational counselor must know something of these problems before he can be effective in aiding boys and girls to choose and prepare for commercial or industrial careers.

Our study will have three main divisions: (1) the problems as seen by the employer; (2) the worker's standpoint; and (3) the signs of improvement in employment conditions.

The Problems of the Employer. Scientific Management. — The sharpness of modern competition has led to studies of management, with the result that Frederick

W. Taylor worked out a comprehensive system of shop operation called scientific management. The boy or girl who goes into any large establishment may find himself under this system, and those who work for small businesses or go into business or manufacture for themselves will of necessity be influenced by some of the many recent ramifications of the movement. We shall here deal first with the aims and methods of scientific management and next with the more general question of personal and social efficiency. In discussing the shortcomings of the methods so far used, we shall not forget the importance to vocational guidance of the movement for efficiency, and that the counselor must have his part in furthering it.

What is Scientific Management? [1] Taylor states its aim and general method as follows:

The principal object of management should be to secure the maximum prosperity for the employer, coupled with the maximum prosperity for each employee. . . .

. . . the development of every branch of the business to its highest state of excellence, so that the prosperity may be permanent.

. . . the development of each man to his state of maximum efficiency, so that he may be able to do, generally speaking, the highest grade of work for which his natural abilities fit him, and . . . giving him, when possible, this class of work to do (*The Principles of Scientific Management*, p. 9).

[1] We are not here discussing the work of the employment manager (see Chapter IV). Until recently the movement for improving the work of the employment manager has had little direct connection with "scientific management."

Taylor's plan calls for detailed instruction cards to be issued to every man, for helpers or teachers who direct and record the work of the men, and for payment by results. It is a distinct departure from mere piece-work, as well as from the " initiative and incentive plan "; these last put the responsibility for success chiefly if not wholly on the men, while scientific management requires highly specialized effort on the part of the superintendents and foremen of the establishment.

The net result to the employer is that the improved method of running his establishment will get more work done, with fewer men. Thus, though the wage per man is higher than before, the labor cost per unit of product is reduced. This principle of lowering labor cost by paying higher wages is perhaps the most striking feature of scientific management.[1]

Taylor antagonized the laboring men at the start by his approach from the side of profits to the employers, by his naïve story of his struggles with the men in the shop, by the use of the stop-watch on the men, by his accusations of loafing and laziness, and by his crude methods of inducing the men to submit to his experiments.[2] Moreover, his critics were not slow to point out certain social and economic implications in the system, which we shall discuss presently.

[1] See Redfield, William C., *The New Industrial Day*, The Century Company, 1913. While in Congress, Redfield opposed the protective tariff on the ground that none would be needed if American manufacturers would improve their methods.

[2] See his conversation with " Schmidt "; *Principles*, p. 44.

Three other writers are well known in connection with the scientific management or efficiency movement: Gilbreth, Gantt, and Emerson (see bibliography). The first two worked in coöperation with Taylor, while Emerson's plan is eclectic. Hoxie, who has recently contributed a study of the subject, states as his judgment that the Taylor system, being the most elaborate and most widely followed, may still be taken as the standard plan.[1]

Scientific management had a bad start in that the men who launched it paid too little attention to certain fundamental social and economic facts. Things not explained, or loosely explained, left opportunity for attack. Thus Gilbreth admits but inadequately explains the fact that with the output increased 300 per cent a man's wages are raised but 25 to 100 per cent (p. 89). Brandeis optimistically talks, in the foreword to Gilbreth's book, of coöperation, square deal, men led, not driven, and a larger share for the working man, but refers the reader to no proof. Taylor (p. 71) shows output increased 269 per cent, wages increased 64 per cent, and cost of production per ton decreased 54 per cent. Again (p. 95) he makes a great point of the fact that 35 girls did the work formerly done by 120, but he gives little inkling of the economic and social problem involved in the cases of the 85 girls discharged.[2]

[1] Hoxie, pp. 7–8.

[2] For a more extended statement of the criticisms of the Taylor plan from the standpoint of organized labor, see John Mitchell, *The Wage Earner and His Problems*, Chap. IV, *The Wage Earner and Industrial Efficiency*.

It has remained for Hoxie[1] to analyze the claims, practices, advantages, and disadvantages of scientific management, as it existed in 1915. Professor Hoxie made his investigations in connection with the work of the federal Commission on Industrial Relations, and had the advantage of expert assistance representing both employers and labor, frequent consultations with Taylor, Gantt, Emerson, and many others, and of visits to establishments operating under scientific management. His general conclusions are that the claims of the plan to benefit labor are not proved.

Some of his conclusions are as follows: The "time-study" men, who hold the key to the system, are neither equipped as a class for their important work nor do they hold an influential place in the managerial staff (p. 57). These time-study men set the tasks for the workers, and

. . . it must not be forgotten that greater knowledge creates also greater opportunities for the unscrupulous and that a method, which in benevolent and intelligent hands makes better dealing possible, may be woefully abused by the ignorant and unscrupulous, and observation proves that time study for task setting is no exception to the rule (p. 53).

Mr. Emerson would not claim with Taylor that scientific management always and of necessity deals out exact justice to the worker (p. 13). Scientific

[1] Note also Thompson, Clarence B. This symposium on scientific management is chiefly descriptive, and planned after the method of the advocate rather than the judge. Labor's point of view is not explicitly given; neither are economic and social considerations elaborated. For studies of the effect of speeding-up work, see Goldmark.

managers express a preference for the one-job man, so that narrow specialization is the result (p. 38). Taylor advocated a complete reorganization of the establishment, so that increased returns would be unlikely for about two years. Hoxie finds, however, that scientfic managers are early pressed for a financial showing, and thus plans are inadequately carried out (p. 29).

Coming more closely now to the problem of vocational guidance, Professor Hoxie finds, in the shops under scientific management, no systematic grappling with the problem of selecting and hiring men. He found that many heads of labor departments were young and inexperienced, that they were unacquainted with the best practices, and that best results were obtained in some shops not under scientific management (p. 33).

Let us quote his statements about the adaptation of the work to the worker:

Nowhere did the writer discover any scientific or adequate methods employed for adapting the worker to the task, that is, for "setting each man to the highest task for which his physical and intellectual capacity fits him." . . . Experimental tests may have been made by scientific management experts, psychological and physiological, for determining special industrial qualifications and aptitudes of workers, but none of them was discovered in the shops. Indeed, the impression of the writer was very strong that the average manager in a scientific management shop is not only quite indifferent to, but profoundly ignorant of, the broader and deeper aspects of the problem of vocational selection and adaptation (p. 35).

It has afforded little opportunity . . . for the discovery and development of special aptitudes among the masses (p. 93).

Considering next the question of industrial peace and rights of the workers, we find these conclusions:

. . . the whole scheme of scientific management, especially the gathering up and systematization of the knowledge formerly in the possession of the workmen, tends enormously to add to the strength of capitalism (p. 134; see also p. 131).[1]

In its extension it is certain that scientific management is a constant menace to industrial peace (p. 135).

[Evidence] in no way justifies the assumption that scientific management offers any effective guarantee against overspeeding and exhaustion of workers (p. 91).

There can be little doubt that scientific management tends, in practice, to weaken the power to the individual worker as against the employer (p. 104).

. . . the democratic possibilities of scientific management, barring the presence of unionism, would seem to be scant (p. 107).

Discussing the question of fundamental harmony of interests between capital and labor, claimed by Taylor, Hoxie finds that some managers agree with the labor unions in finding a conflict of interests between the two. Others, however, lay claim to a belief in industrial democracy, but " the democracy of this class of managers usually turned out to be on analysis a species of benevolent despotism often very worthy indeed, but far removed from the Taylor conception in its scientific purity " (p. 102).

[1] Cf. Schneider, *Education*, etc., p. 7.

On pages 137–139 of Hoxie's book the report as given
to the Commission on Industrial Relations is presented.
It is signed by all three investigators. They find that
scientific management "is to date the latest word
in the sheer mechanics of production and inherently in
line with the march of events." They state, however,
that the social problem created by scientific management does not lie in this field, but rather in the direct
and indirect effects upon labor. Thus, a conflict apparently exists between efficient methods of doing things
and human rights, both of which are good, and both
of which must survive. The Commission is advised
to conduct experiments in the coördination and har-
monizing of these forces.[1]

So much for the problems of scientific management.
It is apparent that the boys and girls who go into occupations to which scientific management is applicable
must be taught neither to glorify mere efficiency nor to
try to turn back the hands of the clock as did the laborers
who broke machinery during the early part of the last
century. They must understand that not even the most
complex mechanical and psychological adjustments can
be substituted for common justice and provision for
the good citizenship of the masses, and, on the other
hand, that the cry "every man should have what he
earns" means nothing unless it takes into consideration

---

[1] We are not here concerned with the vigorous discussion on the valid-
ity of Hoxie's method and conclusions. His book certainly points out
unsolved problems which vitally concern the worker.

the legitimate rights of the management.   The student of vocational guidance must follow the ramifications of this problem, and must contribute to its solution.

What Efficiency Offers Society.—The vocational counselor must approve of and coöperate with the movements for increasing the efficiency of individuals and establishments; he must remember, however, that social safeguards must not be lost sight of.   There is no denying the fact, for example, that in some men's minds efficiency is thought to be the cure for all sorts of business and personal failures, whereas a mere sharpening of the " race for success," without consideration for the successes of the many, might lead to social disaster rather than betterment.   The advertisements of the business magazines must not be allowed to lead our boys and girls to think only of their own personal efficiency.   The school's task is to teach group efficiency as well — the pupils must be shown how the application of social efficiency can save the "waste of unguided ability,"[1] improve methods of distribution[2] and save society the enormous wastes in various forms of preventable friction.

The responsibility for these new forms of efficiency is being widely recognized.   Efforts to extend educational opportunity, to provide industrial education, to establish settlements, to bring about coöperative schooling, to seek the aid of advisory committees, and

[1] See Woods in *Readings*, p. 19; and Ward.
[2] See Roman, N. E. A., p. 1173.

to supplement in various ways the work of the schools — all show that the social aim is not being lost sight of.

Personal efficiency must be cultivated by the schools, and the child must be taught that his own efforts to improve his abilities are indispensable to his success. He must also be shown, however, that lasting and satisfactory rewards come only to those who use their abilities in performing useful service. Efficiency, in other words, must be used for producing commodities useful to the social whole, and not for mere personal aggrandizement in a struggle to rise above competitors. These considerations must be understood by the counselor, and must form part of the educational and vocational guidance of the child.

The Employer's Problem in the " Turnover " of Employees. — Investigations show that employers are forced to put up with the aimless migration of workers from one establishment to another. This requires constant effort spent in teaching duties to new men. Recent computations by Alexander (see bibliography) of the General Electric Company set the costs for training men as follows: highly skilled worker, $48; next grade, $38–50; unskilled worker, $8.50; clerk, $29; pieceworker, $65.50. In a study of twelve factories, he found that at the beginning of 1912 the number of employees was 38,668; at the end, 46,796, and that during the year there were 44,365 persons hired, an apparently unnecessary engagement of 22,225 workers, after all allowances are made, who were hired and " broken in " at a total cost of $774,139.

Investigations show that establishments engage each year a number of new workers which is from twenty to three hundred per cent of their regular force, and that the cost of replacing a worker is ordinarily from thirty to one hundred dollars.[1] Mr. A. Lincoln Filene states that it is the experience of his business " that the percentage of college men who fail to stick to the first job that they try on leaving college is as large, if not larger, than the boy who hasn't been through college." [2]

The vocational counselor, then, must cope with these facts: that there is a well-established habit among workers to change from job to job, of their own accord; that this causes a very large waste of time and money; that part of these changes are educative, in that the trial and success method is the only one open to most individuals; that both school and employer must study the problem, with the hope of providing for experimentation in the school, specifying in advance the requirements of the job, and supervising the entrance into the occupation.[3]

Other Problems of the Employer. — Complexities hedge the employer about, in the modern systems of business and industry, so that it is not surprising that mistakes are made. The professional attitude is only

[1] See Gruenberg; Bloomfield, *Nation's Business.*
[2] Nat. Conference, p. 174.
[3] See Willits and Hopkins, Philadelphia report, pp. 86–90, 162–168.

P

gradually being developed; men in business have heretofore had no ready way to find out about the failures and successes of plans tried by their rivals.

One of the mooted points is in regard to health advice and help. The Clothcraft Shops in Cleveland have frequent medical examinations of their workers,[1] and treatment is furnished both in the shops and in the homes. William Filene's Sons Company of Boston have equipped a hospital in the store, and offer but do not compel medical examination, advice, and treatment. Many establishments handling foodstuffs safeguard cleanliness by means of physical examinations. Many firms give examinations such as eyesight tests upon entering employment. Variety of practice prevails. Workers do not always welcome examinations, for they fear that they are aimed at discovering defects which will cost them their positions and perhaps make it difficult to secure other employment. It would seem that a solution to the problem of health guidance might be found in a simple test, when obviously needed, on entering employment, and frequent inspection to safeguard the workers and the product. Then medical examination, advice, and treatment might be left wholly in the hands of the workers, through mutual benefit associations or labor unions.

Health examination and advice relating to occupations prior to employment, may be given by the school authorities, with the chief purpose of keeping children

[1] See Feiss.

out of places which might injure them.[1] Note what has been said (pp. 165–168) on the dangers of guidance through over-attention to physical characteristics. Such advice would certainly have erred in the cases of Stevenson, Beethoven, and Dalton.

The movement for " Safety First " has interested employers, especially in view of recent compensation laws. The best progress has been achieved when the workers themselves have had a part in the movement. The California Bureau of Labor Statistics in a recent report (p. 97) gives the plan of a lumber company, which formed a committee of five, three of whom were employees, to confer about safety and to recommend precautions against accidents.

Another pressing problem is that concerned with social work, formerly called " welfare work." When large bodies of workers are in one establishment there is an obvious necessity to provide for lunchrooms, rest rooms, opportunity for noon-time recreation, and for other facilities for unifying the force. Feiss holds that the spirit of the worker, shown in his loyalty to the management, is a much more important requirement than initial skill.

How shall these activities be instituted and maintained? William Filene's Sons Company puts them entirely in the hands of the employees, while the Larkin Company directs them through the employment manager. Both companies have extensive facilities for

[1] See Bloomfield, *Readings*, pp. 704–711; *Youth*, etc., pp. 148–157.

social activities, and in the case of each the company pays the expense.

The issues involved in social work are complex. On the one hand, some establishments have a shifting force largely composed of unskilled workers, who live a sordid life in their homes, have little initiative for coöperation, and work and act like automata in the shop. On the other hand, if anything is done to brighten their lives in the recesses of shop work, they complain that they would " rather have the money in wages." The lot of the director of social work is often a hard one, dependent as he is on the good graces both of the management and of the workers.[1]

Against these discouraging experiences, however, there are being set many hopeful experiments in coöperative endeavor. If the cigar makers in New York City shops will unite to hire somebody to read to them while they work, it becomes likely that factory workers will find it advisable to raise no complaint against innovations which make the hours of labor happier ones. It is true that the managers who have had success with social work find that it means increased returns through better work on the part of the employees. Then the owners need only acknowledge this fact, and raise wages correspondingly, as many of them have done. The workers do not really object to social work as such, but they wish opportunity to work out their own self-direc-

---

[1] See Valentine's statement from the side of the management, Davis, *Field of Social Service*, p. 133.

tion in things which have to do with leisure time. This desire is commendable, and should be encouraged.

Another problem of the employer — and this the student of vocational guidance must especially consider — is the ever-recurring question of legislation affecting his business. These are the days of many laws, and no merchant can be sure, from one session of the legislature to another, that his business will not be put in jeopardy. The congress fixes tariffs and interstate commerce laws, and the city council taxes and licenses him. Hours of labor, minimum wages, safety laws, fire escapes, air shafts, elevator rules, windows and lighting, building laws, and a hundred other subjects may be altered by state statute which subject him to fine or imprisonment. Armies of inspectors visit him, besides many kindly social workers who will shortly press the legislators for more reforms, when the present ones are enforced. In helping to rationalize industrial and commercial legislation the vocational-guidance student will render great service to society. If employment supervision becomes an actuality, the vocation bureau will be better equipped to perform this service of guiding legislation than perhaps any other agency. More even than the legislator the counselor will represent the social interests of the public, besides which he will have intimate and authoritative contact with employer, worker, factory, home, and school.

So much for the problems of the employer. Our theses are two: that the student of vocational guidance must understand and contribute to the solution of these problems, and, second, that he must see that the future employers and employees understand them too, and that they go out of the school ready to improve upon the attempted solutions made by the present generation.

The Problems of the Employed. — Many of the problems of the workers are the same as those of the employers, though the viewpoint is the opposite. In discussing scientific management above, we touched on the question of some present conflicting interests between the two parties, and on the necessity for reconciling efficient management with human rights. It should be noted at this point, however, that the complaint of labor is not always against machinery, or efficiency as such, but rather at the unfair advantages which these institutions give to management. Put in its most intelligent form, it is not a protest against any set of men or any particular way of doing business, but rather an objection to the continuance of conditions which may be corrected with benefit to all concerned.

The Need for Guidance in Obtaining Work. — The growth of the factory system has almost eliminated the industrial laborer who works for himself and employs no help. We have been unable to find data on the subject, but it is very likely true that the small shop keepers, the small farmers, and certain professional people would represent the greater part of this remnant of an individualistic system of occupations. Moreover, since these

occupations require capital or highly-specialized training, we may say, broadly speaking, that it is impossible
nowadays for the average man to work without first
seeking the opportunity.

Without guidance, the natural results of this condition would be, for the unskilled, at least, unemployment,
poverty, exploitation, low wages, lack of adaptation
to the work obtained, and loss of self-respect. To seek
for work the laborer goes to an employment agency, or
answers a "want ad." The California Bureau of
Labor Statistics reports 923 complaints against employment agencies for misrepresentation, for the year
ending June 30, 1914, 632 of which were decided for the
petitioners and over $2300 ordered returned (pp. 10–11).
The Manly report[1] for the Commission on Industrial
Relations states:

A study of newspaper want advertisements made a few
years ago revealed that when times are good one fourth or
more are "fake ads," while in hard times more than one
half are in this class (p. 171).

The existence of these conditions shows the need of
guidance, both for adults and for children.

Unemployment. — Bound up with the necessity for
seeking work is the problem of unemployment. Dearle
shows how wastefully trades are recruited with workers,
there being always a list of hangers-on for every large

---

[1] This report has been labeled unfair — biased toward the side of
labor. Nevertheless, it remains a challenge to all those who refuse to
be satisfied that the *status quo* does not need improvement.

establishment, waiting to be employed.[1] The Manly report for the Commission on Industrial Relations devotes twenty-two pages to the subject of unemployment, every word of which is worthy of quotation here, had we the space available. The student of vocational guidance must use this report as one of his textbooks. The studies on which these findings are based were conducted in all parts of the country, and justify the summary statement that:

A careful analysis of all available statistics shows that in our great basic industries the workers are unemployed for an average of at least one fifth of the year, and that at all times during any normal year there is an army of men, who can be numbered only by hundreds of thousands, who are unable to find work or who have so far degenerated that they cannot or will not work. Can any nation boast of industrial efficiency when the workers, the source of her productive wealth, are employed to so small a fraction of their productive capacity?[2]

These conclusions are borne out by a recent study of employment in Philadelphia, conducted under the direction of the Department of Public Works by Joseph H. Willits, Instructor in Industry, Warton School of the University of Pennsylvania. Textile mills and garment factories operate from twenty to eighty per cent of full

[1] Bloomfield, *Readings*, p. 34.

[2] P. 34; see also pp. 161, 162, 23, 34, 163, 164, 170–183. Even should the war solve the unemployment problem for years to come, yet, if the causes of unemployment are untouched, the evil will ultimately reappear.

time.[1] Published charts show great fluctuation in number of workers employed (pp. 24, 39, 41, 44, 45). The effect of unemployment on poverty, family life, and crime is discussed on pages 49–57. Particularly interesting is the diary of a man's experience in one day's hunt for work, with the accompanying map (pp. 115–116).

To the student of vocational guidance, one of the most interesting conclusions of this Philadelphia report is that unemployment forces men to take up work for which they are not fitted : to take anything that offers, with the common result that the worker is never able to return to his own trade.

During the winter of 1913–1914 Arthur Evans Wood of Reed College conducted an intensive study of the unemployed in Portland, Oregon. His findings are similar to the data already quoted. He concludes :

These facts constitute a grave social problem, the solution of which devolves upon the state and city and national authorities, inasmuch as the welfare of the state is dependent upon the welfare of its industrial workers (p. 32).

Various remedies for unemployment have been proposed and partially tried. The Dennison Manufacturing Company of Framingham made a systematic effort to eliminate the seasonal rush, by seeking early orders for Christmas trade, by making containers and other cheaper products far in advance of need, and by developing a trade for and manufacturing new goods used

[1] Willits, *The Unemployed in Philadelphia*, p. 5.

throughout the dull seasons. Such companies recognize the value of a steady force of workers, and see that a highly seasonal business may become a menace rather than a benefit to the community.

Insurance against unemployment has been proposed, but the contributory feature seems impracticable in view of the attitude of labor and the shifting of men from place to place. Nevertheless, some of the states may confidently be expected to experiment with such legislation, based on European experience.

Another remedy which seems eminently desirable is the adjustment of public work so that it will become greatest at times of most unemployment. The argument behind this plan is that legislation now protects the individual in his life, health, safety from fire and accident, property, morals, and education; but offers very inadequate protection against poverty. It is fully as necessary for society to protect itself against the results of unemployment, as brought about by idleness, discouragement, and crime. If, therefore, the city, state, and nation should offer any person out of employment opportunity to work, at a figure which need not compete with present and well-established businesses and industries, no one would have the present excuses for idleness, begging, charity, wife-desertion, burglary and other evils against society.

The most common proposal for the cure of unemployment is one that has been tried in many American cities and states — the public employment bureau. It is now recognized that interstate or national federation is necessary for the success of public employment bureaus, and even then the problem will hardly be solved without concurrent application of some of the other remedies noted above. But the widespread establishment of state and municipal employment agencies, with a central bureau issuing bulletins such as emanate from the Weather Bureau, would go far toward relieving the present pressure on the unskilled.

What has the vocational counselor to do with the unemployment problem? He must first of all see that it cannot completely be solved inside the schoolroom by equipping each prospective worker with skill in business or industry. " The causes of unemployment are not merely individual, — physical incapacity, lack of training, inefficiency, and unwillingness to work, — they are usually general and quite beyond the control of the individual workman." [1] On this account the counselor must help in the effort to solve the problem by collective action, and he must warn the future workers concerning the conditions which they will meet.

Wages are often Inadequate. — Another difficulty, from the viewpoint of the employed, lies in the question of wages. A few years ago Professor Nearing found that the average man in the United States received less than $600 yearly, and the female worker less than $400. Even then there is difficulty; the California Bureau of Labor Statistics reports that in three years' time

[1] Coman, p. 667.

12,802 complaints were registered with the bureau against employers for non-payment of wages. " The Bureau succeeded in collecting 8409 of the claims amounting to $171,808.21 " (p. 15).

The Worker's Right to Satisfaction and Development in his Work. — Lack of individual development and satisfaction in the occupation, even when the worker is steadily employed, is the consequence of certain characteristics of industry and commerce already noted.

The need for supervision and the demand that should be made for the job to give an account of itself is forcefully stated by Bloomfield in *Youth, School, and Vocation*, p. 26. The worker has the right to ask what the job will do for him — where he will be after five or ten years of work.

Every manufacturer, as well as every student of vocational guidance, should read Dean Schneider's "*Laws of the Two Kinds of Work,*" on pages 10–11 of *Education for Industrial Workers*. It is a graphic description of the development of a modern factory town, and clearly shows what must be alleviated, cured, or prevented.

What the cure may be no one knows, but that some of the many plans being tried or being proposed will relieve conditions no one can doubt. And there can be no possibility of anything but hopefulness when one considers the tremendous progress that twenty years has brought.

Labor Organizations. — Few students of the subject openly advocate the abandonment of labor organizations, but many have grave doubts and important qualifications regarding them. Thus, while Hoxie (p. 138) and Manly (p. 183) claim that in no other way than by the development of labor union strength and collective bargaining can the problems of industry and commerce be met, some of the members of the Commission on Industrial Relations direct their attention solely to the mistakes of these organizations (pp. 414–442). Regardless of such terms as " autocracy of wealth," " class struggle," and " mob rule," however, the fact is patent that both sides to the controversy have sinned against society, and the further fact that somehow they must be made to serve society. The better statements and better policies of either, rather than the worst, must be accepted at the fullest value possible, and their good intentions capitalized.[1] The vocational counselor, knowing the needs and the problems of each, can materialy assist in the work.

The Value of Constructive Discontent in Solving Labor Problems. — The spread of education is sure to be accompanied by certain forms of discontent among the workers, and it is the business of the vocational counselor to see that this discontent becomes construc-

---

[1] John Mitchell, in a recent New York City speech, declared these points to constitute the program of labor: a minimum wage conformable to American standards; the eight-hour day; abolition of child labor; safety in work and compensation for injuries; better housing conditions; preservation of the guarantees of trial by jury, free speech, and a free press. The student of vocational guidance can surely go with the unions thus far, reserving the right to part company on other points, if necessary.

tive and helpful to society. Whether or not we outline these problems to the children in school, the brighter among them will later read and study on their own account, and will become intelligent in the solutions attempted if our vocational guidance is directed to that end.

Constructive discontent must see that " democracy means something more than the right to vote. Democracy means the abolition of special privilege and the securing of equal opportunity for all." Without economic and social knowledge of a protective sort the individual worker would be as helpless as a farmer without means of transportation, and the school must give the pupil this knowledge and aid him to secure the rightful protection. We may claim not that the world owes each man a living, but that the world should yield each worker a foothold — an opportunity to work and to advance.[1]

We cannot here discuss the problem of how much or how little the children in our schools should be led to consider these things. That is a matter of many factors particular to each time and situation. But that the child should be equipped to grapple with them is not to be doubted, if we are educating him for a democracy.[2]

[1] Veblen shows that, even with dynasties destroyed and a league to enforce peace established, autocracy of wealth will breed world war (*The Nature of Peace*, Chapter VII).

[2] The narrow viewpoint of those arguing for a narrow form of education is shown by Shorey's assumption that democracy is expressed by " equality before the law " (*The Assault on Humanism*, p. 36). If this attitude be " humanism," obviously a scholar and an idiot could be equal before the law, and thereby " democracy " would be achieved.

May we not even go so far as to say that every child should be broadly educated for an " energizing " occupation, and then if he cannot find that kind of employment we may at least be sure that an intelligent and constructive discontent will be at work to better conditions about him. In reference to wrongs existing in the occupations, the future worker must be taught that mere submission means individual atrophy and social stagnation, and that mere strife is no more efficacious than would be running against a wall; but that intelligent and constructive adjustment and coöperation is best.

We should derive our optimism by considering the blessings already gained. A talk with one who has lived under long-passed conditions of work may well be made an exercise of the class for the study of occupations. Thus, some women still live who worked in textile mills from 4 : 45 in the morning till 7 : 30 at night. Such progress as we have already made assures us of the future.

The Many Signs of Improvement. — But our hope for the future is not based entirely on contrast with the past. There are some sharp contrasts in the present — some experiments being conducted, and succeeding, which are pointing the way to the solution of vexing questions. Many of these have been touched upon already: the reduction of the labor turnover; the opportunity to transfer from one department of an establishment to another; the " blue-printing " of a job; the employment supervision exercised by certain schools and placement agencies; the Birmingham voluntary committees; improved legislation in regard to child labor; the decision of certain firms to employ no child under sixteen; the establishment of new kinds of schools and courses; the promotion of recreation both for children and for adults.

In addition to these signs of improvement we cannot fail to note the new spirit of coöperation possessing the employer and the school. The four recent industrial surveys — those in Richmond, Minneapolis, Cleveland, and Indiana — were made possible only by such joint action. The development of this spirit marks a new era in vocational guidance, if not in the whole employment problem. The Minneapolis Survey [1] was able to work out a series of trade agreements to include the school, the industry, and the worker. Such agreements bid fair to bring back an apprentice system, revised to fit modern conditions and very greatly improved (let us hope) because the school has a place in them.

Another hopeful indication is the spread of the idea of arbitration for labor differences, and the judicial settlement of claims and disputes. The California Bureau of Labor Statistics (pp. 15–48) deals with the laws and their operation in that state, and the Manly report for the Commission of Industrial Relations (pp. 133–139 and 191–202) outlines what may be expected shortly.

[1] Chap. XXIII, and App. C.

Coöperation in industry, profit sharing, and all movements in the direction of industrial democracy are of special significance to the student of vocational guidance. Methods of approach are rapidly being worked out, and evidence to prove the wisdom of the experiments is growing in volume.

The coöperation being practiced in the store of William Filene's Sons Company in Boston is typical of what may soon come to pass in many other establishments. The extent of the plan, the success of its operation, and the spirit of the clubrooms, remind one strongly of the student-government activities of the large Los Angeles High Schools. It gives renewed hope for the ordering of work so that educative values may be conserved.

It is more than likely that some such coöperative schemes, developed as fast as solid experience and the growing intelligence of the workers will allow, may point the way to a form of industrialism appropriate to a democracy.

The Lessons for Vocational Guidance. — During the progress of this chapter we have repeatedly indicated the duty of the counselor to study the problems of employment, to coöperate with both employer and worker in the solution of these problems, to represent the educational forces of society in the effort to conserve youth and hopefulness, and to equip the future worker for effective grappling with these complex problems.

It should now be apparent that the student of vocational guidance should take an active interest in legis-

Q

lation which concerns school and labor, and should aid in the effort for better laws. It should further be clear that school pupils must be taught the principles and practice of coöperation, for only by joint action can certain difficulties be overcome. Schools must provide a measure of self-government, with the direction of student activities more or less in the hands of the pupils. By such methods young people will learn the true meanings of both obedience and leadership, and we may confidently expect that the workers themselves will join in bringing to fruition the " hope that the near future will see our schools unite with the best employers to further, during its decisive years, youth's promise of service and growth." [1]

[1] Bloomfield, *Youth*, etc., p. 26.

CHAPTER VIII

A PROGRAM FOR VOCATIONAL GUIDANCE

OUR study so far has included (1) A statement of the problems of vocational guidance; (2) A review of present attempts to provide guidance in schools and in occupations; (3) A study of educational as related to vocational guidance; (4) An examination of the work of the counselor; (5) A criticism of some questionable methods in guidance; (6) A study of the young worker in industry and commerce; and (7) A survey of the problems of employment. It will be the purpose of this chapter to summarize the conclusions reached in the foregoing studies, and therewith to outline a proposed program for effective vocational guidance.

A Working Definition of Vocational Guidance. — In the first chapter we noted the propriety of proceeding on the assumption that the ordinary meanings of the two words "vocational" and "guidance" should hold valid. In spite of disagreements as to the exact meaning of the word "vocational," differences in applying the guidance, and attempts of classifiers to mark off the divisions of the subject,[1]

[1] See the definition in the Massachusetts law and Professor Moore's Criticism in *What is Education*, p. 164. Notice also the ordinary use of the term on page 316 of the same book.

A recent writer separates our subject into (1) Educational guidance;

the common, dictionary definitions give us the most light. We may therefore propose the following as a workable statement:

Vocational guidance is a systematic effort, based on knowledge of the occupations and on acquaintance with and study of the individual, to inform, advise, or coöperate with him in choosing, preparing for, entering upon, or making progress in his occupation.

With this definition in mind, we shall divide our study of an appropriate program for vocational guidance into the following topics, which will form the subject matter of this chapter: (1) The types of schools needed; (2) The function of the school people; (3) Coöperative effort for vocational guidance; (4) The improvement of the conditions of employment; (5) Methods of guidance; (6) Training in vocational guidance; (7) Some appropriate next steps.

The Types of Schools Needed for Vocational Guidance. — In order that vocational guidance may find its most efficient expression, the schools must be organized in a manner conformable with the best educational theory and practice. It is now generally recognized that the

(2) Vocational guidance; (3) Avocational guidance (see Jacobs). For convenient treatment, there is some justification for this classification, but not for logical division. As we have seen in Chapter I, the first two of these classes greatly overlap. "Avocational" is hardly the word. It is questionable to call duties of citizenship avocational; this is Moore's objection. Again, Jesse Davis shows that moral and civic duties do not "call away" from the vocation, but aid it and are aided by it. Finally, the word "avocational" has indefinite and contradictory meanings, as a reference to the dictionary will show.

education of the children should be under state control, with authority delegated to local boards and committees except in those matters where centralization seems advisable, as for example, certification of teachers ; apportionment of the school tax ; special aid for rural, agricultural, and vocational education ; and minimum requirements in school term, buildings, salaries, and programs of studies.   State boards as well as local boards or committees may call to their assistance groups of men from all walks of life to act as advisory committees.

Turning to the actual schools, we have seen that the movement for vocational guidance is interested in the progress of the child from his earliest years.   The value of early play in the home has been noted.   The kindergarten gives opportunity for a social contact that should form a good foundation for later training, aids the children to develop the dramatic sense, and gives them, through the songs, games, sand-box, and other exercises, the beginnings of their acquaintance with occupations. However rudimentary these gains are, from a vocational point of view, the child with the kindergarten training should be better off than one without it.   Kindergartens should therefore form a part of the school system which aims to provide vocational guidance, and their methods should largely be followed in the earlier grades of the elementary school.[1]

The elementary school should equip its pupils with an interest in the basic fields of knowledge and experience.

[1] See Bartlett, *Vocational Guidance in Pomona City Schools.*

We have called attention in Chapter III to the vocational values in the various studies, and in a later portion of the present chapter we shall discuss the plan for a class in the study of occupations, the life-career class, for each grade beginning with the fourth.

Class work is adapted to the great majority of children, but there must be provision for special classes and individual instruction paralleling the entire school system. Such classes should handle all those children who need the personal attention available for special groups. For the normal children, it may be safe to have class work with uniform curricula up to and including the sixth grade. Here the elementary school course may properly end.

The intermediate or junior high school should include the seventh, eighth, and ninth grades. Here differentiation of a positive sort should begin. Here, too, provision for vocational guidance must be clear and adequate. Three courses are often provided: the General Course, the Industrial Course, and the Business or Commercial Course, and each entering pupil must make his choice. Here is important opportunity to prevent wrong choice, and the counselor, in the person of the principal, vice-principal, or special advisor, should interview each child far enough in advance of his entrance to make the choice as deliberate as possible.

But children at the age of thirteen are too young for making such momentous decisions. It may prove to be a better policy, therefore, to turn the intermediate school into a prevocational school, with a great variety of offerings, and with each child put into contact with many different kinds of activities. Consider, for example, the following list:

PROPOSED ACTIVITIES FOR CHILDREN 12 TO 16 YEARS OF AGE

INTERMEDIATE OR JUNIOR HIGH SCHOOL

NOTE. — It is proposed that all the studies of Group I be required, and that each pupil be required, during the three years' course, to take at least two courses from each of the other groups. The remainder of the work should be selected, under educational and vocational guidance.

Group I
  Life-career class
  Commercial and Industrial
    geography
  Elementary economics and
    sociology
  Community civics
Group II
  English literature
  Composition
  Oral English
  Work on school paper
  Dramatics
  Debating
Group III
  History
  General science
  Modern language
  Shop arithmetic
  Household arithmetic
  Algebra and geometry

Group IV
  Music
  Glee clubs
  Choruses
  Orchestras
  Bands
Group V
  Typewriting
  School clerical work
  Commercial arithmetic
  Penmanship
  Bookkeeping
  Management of lunch-
    room, bookstore, etc.
  Library work
Group VI
  Freehand drawing
  Mechanical drawing
Group VII
  Physical training
  Athletic games

Group VIII
  Student self-government
  Social meetings
  Reception committee
  Auditorium meetings
  Literary societies
  Entertainments
  Summer camps
Group IX
  (*a*) Janitor work
     Fire department
     Sanitation committee
  (*b*) Cooking
     Sewing
     Millinery
     Laundry
  (*c*) Gardening
     Agriculture

  Care of animals
  Dairying
  Competition in corn
     and other clubs
(*d*) Woodshop
  Machine shop
  Sheet-metal shop
  Brick, plaster, and
     stone
  Cement work
  Elementary electricity
  Painting and finishing
  Leather and cobbling
  Jewelry
  Bookbinding
  Printing
  Textiles
  Modeling

It is conceivable that a modern school system might offer most of these activities in the intermediate grades (or at least in the high school), and that a wide choice should be open to every child. Some subjects may be given in alternate years, and in a large city types of schools may offer different programs. Transportation facilities should be arranged for, however, so that no child will necessarily be limited to the work of the school nearest him.[1] In planning his curriculum for the three years of the intermediate school, each child might

[1] The custom of attending two schools at once seems not to be common among pupils. Hence it may be best to have every school maintain a large variety of activities, even if each study is carried on in miniature.

be required to take certain prescribed studies, to take at least two subjects in every group, and to choose one group for comparative specialization. (Cf. the "concentration and distribution plan" of Harvard College.) For illustration, a given student might take all of the studies of Group I and the first three of Group II as required subjects; might elect general science and music in Groups III and IV, typewriting and school clerical work in V, freehand and mechanical drawing in VI, and athletic games and participation in auditorium meetings in Groups VII and VIII, and might specialize in Group IX, taking agriculture, care of animals, dairying, competition in a dairy contest, and cement work. The amount of each subject, and the order of studies, would still remain to be determined.

The justification for this plan of choice and trial is that the intermediate age is an experimental and a finding period, and a smattering of several things is better for its purposes than thoroughness in a few.[1] Versatility is important here, at least as a first step toward discovery of powers and tastes. We do not mean that a child should be forced into versatility against his positive desire to specialize: the rules for required

The general shop is a perfectly feasible plan for small schools of intermediate grade. A prevocational school is limited to an unwarranted degree if it has but one or two kinds of manual work. Suburban schools for urban children may in time offer a solution; here the schools of different types could be grouped within convenient reach of each other.

[1] In schools of Rochester, Arlington, and other cities brief trial courses of six weeks or less have been provided.

and elected studies should be subject to change to suit individual needs.

A lesson in method may be learned from the project idea of the Boy Scouts organization. Credits are given for definite tasks performed. To apply this plan to our list above, we should require our pupil, rather than to pass in certain studies, to give a talk before the school, to write a paper about the factories of his city, to typewrite that paper, to make the pattern for a simple casting, to make the casting, to bind a book, to raise a sheep, to wash ten school windows under the direction of the janitor.

The plan here proposed is not so simple in its operation as is the Los Angeles Intermediate school plan, in which the entering pupil chooses one of the five courses and proceeds through that course to graduation, with the presumption against the facility of his transfer to another course. The latter plan assumes that a wise choice can be made at the thirteenth year: there seems, however, to be little evidence to justify the assumption. The plan here proposed allows the pupil to make a choice of the activities which seem now to attract him, but insists that under usual circumstances he shall experiment with many other activities as well, so that at graduation he would have come into contact with a large number of the occupational experiences of life.

If some of the children must earn money during the intermediate age, they should have half-time schooling as proposed in a former chapter (p. 197).

With the entrance into high school we shall find that many of our pupils feel ready to specialize for definite callings, while others need a continuation of the broad experimentation described above. If we may judge by some observations already made, however, even those who have decided on their occupations are subject to change of mind. Our school courses, therefore, must be strongly interlocked, so that boys and girls may make needed transfers without loss of time.

Vocational guidance is very much concerned with the question whether high schools should be general in character or whether they should each center their attention on preparing for a restricted set of occupations. If efficiency in the occupation were the only consideration, the matter would not be a difficult one to settle. But there is the fact that pupils change their minds, and the further consideration that undemocratic ideals may be fostered by breaking up the high-school pupils into the " classical " group and the " technical " group. Further experiment will be needed before a sufficiently clear answer can be given to the question. .On the one hand, present experience seems to show specialization in the aim of the high school makes for efficiency in instruction and economy of expense ; on the other hand the high school of varied program furnishes an opportunity for broad experimentation, and makes allowances for changes in the choice of occupation. It may be found that the specialized high school is best for those who have definitely chosen their occupations, while the general school is best for those who have not. If this be the fact it would seem that both types of school are needed. The vocational counselor must contribute to the solution of these questions.[1]

We may be sure, in any case, that our high schools should provide broad curricula for those students who have not yet decided on their life-careers and for those who have chosen professions and plan to go to college, and should provide as well for those who wish specific vocational education and for those who are forced to work. Part-time work may finally be found the most practicable plan for all kinds of vocational education.[2]

The relation of these questions to vocational guidance must be clear. Long before the pupil enters high school, he should have the benefit of counsel in regard to the different paths open to him. During the entire three or four years of his course he should have coöperation in making the important decisions which affect his future so profoundly.

What college education should be, in view of vocational guidance, is rather too big a question for treatment here. We may protest in passing, however, against the assumption that the college course should be merely " liberal " and thereby indefinite, and that all specialization of a vocational sort should be deferred till the professional

---

[1] One student of vocational guidance has recently shown that the pupils in his high school — a commercial high school — are not by any means sure that they will enter the occupations for which this vocational school prepares. (E. A. Post, in an unpublished study.)

[2] See Schneider, *Education for*, etc., and Stimson.

school. This policy takes no account of the many students who never go on to the professional school or who drop out before completing the college course. These students often leave college unfitted for vocational choice or for adaptation to the exigencies of actual work.

All high schools should have evening sessions, and should maintain vacation schools as well. Further, the time may soon come when summer camps may be held under school auspices, and when trips of pupils may be a part of the school's program.[1] We may hope, too, that a parent-teacher association be a part of each school's plan, and that the teachers will coöperate with many social, civic, political, professional, commercial, and industrial organizations. Each school, too, should have a growing and changing museum, or at least should habitually coöperate with such institutions in the vicinity.

So much for the types of schools needed for vocational guidance. We shall next consider the part played in guidance by various school officers.

The Function of the School People, in Vocational Guidance. — The teacher of whatever subject should be on the alert to find and use the vocational values in every lesson. His chief task is to act as educational guide, and he must make the educational guidance function as vocational guidance whenever this seems desirable. To do this he will need to widen the scope of classroom activity. Play, competition, and various

---

[1] Camps and trips are common in private schools and boys' clubs; fees may be charged to help defray expenses.

forms of self-direction, group effort[1] and individual instruction should be utilized whenever possible. Debates in the history lessons, contests in arithmetic, dramatics in the language class, excursions for geography, original work in music, and competitions in drawing — all these show what may be done to open the way for discovery of talents. Johnson shows the need for competition in games[2]; much of the same spirit, if carefully supervised, can be profitably developed in other studies.

How far in vocational guidance can the regular teachers go? No doubt all of them can make their studies count for guidance, and can systematically study their pupils. Many of them can offer occasional counsel, and a few can do efficient work based on knowledge of occupational opportunities. All of the teachers should be prepared to furnish significant information about each child to the counselors who specialize in the work.

In many if not most schools for several years the teacher will be the only counselor the child has. Hence the need for our normal schools and colleges to give the prospective teachers the viewpoint of vocational guidance. As we remarked in a former place, the child's teacher is most favorably situated to guide him; it would be desirable if every teacher could be a counselor.

If the school has one or more teachers who are allowed part of their time for vocational guidance, these teachers

---

[1] Scott, *Social Education.*
[2] *Education through Recreation*, pp. 29–32.

may begin their work, as we have suggested in Chapter IV, by investigating the causes of elimination from school, and by following the children's careers as they enter upon work. These investigations will lead the teacher into contact with the occupations, and will thus give him valuable information to use in advising pupils. Other work which may profitably be undertaken is the employment supervision of the graduates of the school. This of course should be done in coöperation with the employers. If some of the graduates are in business for themselves, they can be greatly assisted by friendly, intelligent advice, given by the counselor himself, or by men and women of experience who will coöperate with the schools.

The part-time counselor may also make home visits, and may collect composite information about the child and his progress. He should be prepared to counsel children as to courses and change of curricula, and to furnish aid to any teacher in connection with vocational guidance. He should collect literature on vocations, and should have charge of the life-career classes of the school.

The school principal, if he cannot have a part-time counselor in his staff, should do all or most of this work himself, or should apportion it among his teachers. He should see that cumulative record cards are kept, so that the successes of the child may be continued as he advances in the school. These records may be frequently renewed or revised, and should register changes of viewpoint on the part of the child, his school marks, the preferences of his parents, and his interests outside the school studies. Except in the case of grave necessity, nothing derogatory should be recorded.

The principal's leadership among the pupils largely determines the spirit of the school. The lessons of coöperation learned through the varied manifestations of a good school spirit are so valuable that no principal should fail to take advantage of the opportunity. Personal contact with the pupils, and an active sympathy with their problems in studies, athletics, and student activities, will go far toward preparing the ground for effective vocational guidance.

Leadership of the teachers is not less in importance. If the principal can somehow make the teachers feel that they are really helping in determining the policies of the school, this cannot fail to make them consider more carefully the aims of the school and the means of realizing these aims.

We come now to the question of an expert counselor and a central office. It is possible that the early writers on vocational guidance gave the impression that one's becoming " expert " gave him an occult power that others could not understand or approach. Between the teacher who is unconscious of vocational guidance, and a person of experience in counseling there is no gulf fixed ; the fact is merely that one teacher has studied and practiced more than the other in the particular occupation of vocational guidance. Such a person may well begin as we have explained above; his ability will develop as his experience grows.

How should the bureau be organized? In the first place it cannot be organized *de novo;* it must grow out of investigations and guidance activities in the different schools.[1] When these investigations have become so extensive that a clearing house is needed, then the bureau becomes a necessity. Until that time, school money had best be spent in allowing teachers in the individual schools time to do investigating and counseling.

What relation should the bureau bear to other departments of the school system? It may sometimes be necessary to have as its general director a head of department who has charge also of compulsory attendance, work certificates, placement, industrial work, and night schools; but none of these activities should be set above vocational guidance. Consolidation of departments may frequently be necessary, but absorption and amalgamation should be prevented. The work of vocational guidance will most likely have vital connection with all the departments of the system, but it must be free to formulate its policies in the light of its own independent needs and investigations. As Miss Davis and Miss Lathrop have pointed out, guidance forced to serve present economic needs of children, with no outlook beyond, fails of its opportunity.[2] The

[1] See Bloomfield, *Youth*, etc., p. 51.
[2] Nat. V. G. Assn., 1914, pp. 49-52.

R

bureau may profitably begin its work by interviewing those who apply to the school officers for work permits. It should be recognized that these studies are pathological, however, for as Hanus says, " vocational guidance cannot be safely deferred until the pupil is on the threshold of the world's work." [1]

We shall not go into detail here on the many activities which a central bureau may profitably undertake. In brief it may collect, publish, and disseminate vocational information; aid in equipping teachers for the work of counseling; collect funds for scholarships for needy children; enlist the aid of college students in making investigations, business men for part-time work, advice, and coöperation, and civic, labor, commercial, industrial, and legislative organizations in improving conditions of labor; aid teachers in the solution of difficult problems; and stand ready to offer help in whatever direction will count for the better guidance of pupil or worker. The bureau should have a select library on vocational guidance and vocations, and should coöperate with public libraries. It should hold frequent conferences, at which are brought together the various interests concerned with work and guidance. It should strive unceasingly for opening new avenues of child-help, through all such plans as public employment bureaus, volunteer committees to give advice to children, and school officers in all parts of the city ready to be consulted by any worker, young or old. Finally, its chief concerns

[1] Bloomfield, *Readings*, p. 94.

should be two : aiding in the work of improving the school program, and helping to bring about a system of employment supervision which will extend the care of the school over all children.

The work of the bureau may be subdivided, some assistants doing actual counseling, and others making studies of occupations.

The superintendent of schools should first of all chart his educational opportunities, or, better, join forces with civic organizations which will do the work in such a way as to include all educational institutions.[1] He may actively assist the work in vocational guidance by lending his support to the meetings, by attending conferences with employers and others, by showing pupils his interest in their life-careers, and by taking active part in the civic, commercial, industrial, and professional life of the community.   In most cases, too, for the present, at least, he will need to impress on taxpayers, voters, and board members the necessity for using school money to stop the waste of unguided ability.

The state officers of education can act with the state and federal officers who collect information about occupations (see p. 135), and can aid in the distribution of printed matter.   The state officers of education may aid in rousing dormant energy to be used for counseling.   They may help in the inspection of industries, so that the welfare of the workers will be better conserved.

[1] See Harper.

The Bureau of Education at Washington should continue and extend the expressions of its recent strong interest in vocational guidance. The bureau aids in issuing the *Vocational-Guidance Bulletin;* has published *The School and the Start in Life,* and the proceedings of the third national conference; and has under way at least two other studies for early publication. There are needed many more studies of occupations, a manual for students' use in life-career classes, a classified index to the literature on the subject, and a comprehensive survey of the present attempts to provide vocational guidance. The Bureau at Washington is in a particularly good position to become a national and international clearing house of information on aims, plans, methods, and results in vocational guidance.

We have so far briefly surveyed the function of the school people in vocational guidance. We hold that the schools should lead in the work, and in most cases direct whatever coöperative effort shall be called forth. Guidance must not be considered an affair of fees, exploitation, advertising, or promotion of any sort, except educational. Those engaged in the work will have need of the highest ideals in education, both to keep their own activities in the correct channels, and to free the vocational guidance movement from tendencies which would seriously handicap its usefulness.

Coöperative Effort on the Part of Those Interested in Guidance. — We have constantly taken the position that no strides forward can be taken in the vocational-guidance movement without the joint action of the forces interested. Coöperation will be required for almost all the processes connected with guidance; let us here consider that needed for the following: obtaining vocational information; choosing the occupation; preparing for the vocation; instituting and managing part-time work; placement; employment supervision; improving conditions of employment; legislation.

Coöperation for obtaining Vocational Information. — Vocational information can best be obtained as it was in Richmond and Minneapolis, — by the cordial joint action of employer, worker, and school. The teacher must be welcomed when he goes into the office, store, shop, or factory to ask questions, and he must be privileged to ask the questions both of the managers and of the workers. The coöperation must be so genuine that the investigator can be reasonably sure that the avenues of information are all open to him, and that the replies he gets to his questions are truthful, with nothing held back. Much yet remains to be done before these ideals are fully realized, but the progress during the past five years has been so astonishing that there is no doubt about the final outcome.

On pages 128–137 we have outlined a plan for gathering the necessary information, and have indicated that clubs, associations, unions, and organizations of many other kinds can profitably join in the work. The school people should lead, because if equipped for the work they will be the best judges regarding what knowledge is of most worth. The viewpoint of the school people in this particular should be determined by the researches and mature conclusions of the vocational-guidance department. In the work of gathering information the children in the schools can help; the knowledge most useful to them is that which they create for themselves through their work in geography, arithmetic, and the life-career class.

Extensive coöperation between school and employer is likely to be the rule, because of the great returns which are bound to flow from it. The employer will find a better class of workers coming to him, and will note that his business has less of its speculative and disappointing features, and offers more real satisfaction.[1] The benefits to the worker flowing from joint action with school and manager will be increased intelligence, better provision for education, and improved conditions of employment. Finally, to the school the advantages of work with these other agencies are patent; the educational system derives from them the points of view necessary to make it of real service to the public.

Coöperation in choosing the Occupation. — The child's choice of occupation should involve, besides the use of vocational information already noted, the possibility for him to meet and talk with workers already engaged in the occupations under consideration. The vocational

[1] This satisfaction is expressed in the title of a recent book, *Where Garments and Americans are Made.* (MacCarthy.)

guide, therefore, should arrange for conferences in which
the pupils in the life-career classes may question experienced adults; he should organize volunteer committees
after the Birmingham plan.

The choice of occupation should be the concern of
the parent almost as much as it is that of the child, and
the work of the counselor will include many conferences
with fathers and mothers. At least one large high school,
that at Pomona, California, has organized a course of
talks and discussions for the parents, in order that
their function in guidance may be more intelligently
understood and performed. Such meetings furnish
excellent opportunity to interest citizens in the efforts
of the school to give effective training to the children,
and to obtain helpful criticism. Besides, such gatherings
are certain to lead to conferences with individual parents,
in which the plans for each child may receive the discussion, criticism, coöperation, and support so necessary
for the wise choice of a life-career. In some cases the
vocational counselor must protect the child from
decisions arbitrarily made and insisted on by the home.
In many cases the value of more education must be
clearly shown. In a large number, hopes and ambitions
may be encouraged, and means and methods found for
their realization. In all cases the parents may be
shown the advantage of keeping the educational opportunity for the child broad, and for prolonging his
vocational infancy. In all cases, too, the school and
the home may coöperate in making the most of the

daily opportunities for broadening the child's knowledge and experience.[1]

Coöperation in Preparing for the Vocation. — Preparation for the vocation, too, will require that the child have access to persons of experience, success, and good judgment, so that he may be able to get first-hand information and advice about the proper method of preparation.[2]

[1] In view of occasional writings on vocational guidance it cannot be too strongly insisted upon that no child should be hurried into the choice of an occupation. If coöperation aims to find the child his calling before he is ready to choose for himself, then that coöperation is ill-advised. The forces of school, home, and community should be used rather to fit the child, by means of knowledge and concrete experience, so that he shall be able to make his own decisions wisely. We have advocated a life-career class in the fourth grade; it must not be understood, however, that such a class is to be concerned with anything more than laying the foundation for wise choices later. It is true that leakages from school begin to be serious shortly after the fourth grade, and on this account the teacher may find it necessary to give rather definite vocational information to those children who threaten to leave school soon. Such cases, however, must not be allowed to determine the subject-matter of the class; it is better in the long run for the teacher to combat this state of affairs (leaving school in the early grades), than to seem to acquiesce in it. Future generations of school children must be considered, and while for the present some fifth grade children may be forced to take what work they can get, the great majority cannot be expected to decide wisely until they are close to the twenties, and some not until much later. The life-career class in the fourth grade is concerned with laying broad foundations for the choice of career, and this actual choice should be deferred until the child is fully ready to make it. (Cf. the proposed plan for tentative choices of three to five occupations for special study.)

[2] The work of supervising this personal advice is a very important duty of the counselor. Some successful men and women are not very efficient in helping others to succeed. The advisors should frequently be called into conference, and, so far as seems appropriate, the scope of their work and their methods as well should be planned by the vocational counselor and put into printed form.

In connection with prevocational and vocational education of whatever sort, the school department should organize advisory committees of employers and workers, and these committees, each for a particular occupation or group of occupations, should aid the school in making the training efficient.

Coöperation in Instituting and Managing Part-time Work. — If the vocational training is to take the form of part-time work, as no doubt it will in many cases, the school authorities will have to make agreements with the stores, shops, offices, and factories in which the students work. The plans used in Cincinnati and Dayton [1] seem to give satisfaction. In the words of Schneider:

It has been conclusively demonstrated that the school and shop can work together if the one common ground will be the mutually safe ground of the mental, physical, and the moral advancement of those who work. . . . The thing is being done and is being done satisfactorily (p. 76).

Good reports come, too, from those in charge of the Boston experiments. It is but just that the workers already in an industry should also be a party to part-time agreements, in order that sudden surpluses of workers may be avoided. The school must gather together all interested parties, — parents, youth, teachers, employers, and representatives of the workers, — and must aid them all in formulating agreements which shall

[1] See Schneider, *Education for,* etc., p. 55–57; also Rochester and Dayton leaflets.

center their attention on the welfare of the worker, and at the same time protect the legitimate interests of all concerned. After the part-time work is instituted the " coördinators " must represent and put into effect the coöperation between school and occupation. It is not difficult to see that if the school can succeed in these undertakings, the social effect in the direction of solving labor problems will be very great indeed.

Coöperation in Placement. — In Chapter IV, and in other places as well, we have discussed the necessity for beginning guidance before the child is obliged to leave school for work. If a system of vocational guidance begins in the school, and early enough to give the child some insight and outlook regarding occupations before he needs to leave, there can be nothing but approval if placement and supervision of employment also form parts of the system. As we stated before, however, among some people placement has been taken to mean the chief if not the whole function of vocational guidance. It is undoubtedly an important part, but it is likely that more fruitful results in vocational guidance will be accomplished in the period of the child's life before he leaves school for work than can be accomplished thereafter. Placement has always been a disquieting problem, and the entrance of educational and philanthropic agencies into the field has not been altogether a happy one. Just when the merchants and manufacturers have about concluded that the fourteen-to sixteen-year-old working child is useless to himself and to the occupation, the placement people come, study the child and the job, watch over his entrance into work, advise and admonish him, and make of him a tolerable success. Thus the merchant or manufacturer is convinced that his diagnosis was wrong, and becomes satisfied to employ children again. It is such considerations that lead thoughtful social workers to look with concern on the vocational guidance which interests itself merely in placement and employment supervision.

In spite of these dangers, however, there is no question but that better methods of finding work are needed. What can be done? In the first place, the school should coöperate with the employers in finding out about the number of persons engaged in each kind of work, and the approximate number hired each year. Second, the school can ascertain and publish the list of actual present vacancies. Third, the counselor can use his influence in systematizing and rationalizing the hiring of workers — he can coöperate with employment managers' associations, and can aid in writing the specifications of jobs and in formulating application blanks and preliminary tests.

We cannot yet state that the school department should maintain an employment agency for minors. No doubt public employment agencies will extend their operations, until finally the private agency, with all its abuses, will be no more. But it may seem best for the municipal or state bureau to confine its attention to persons over twenty-one years of age, and to leave to the school department the employment and supervision of those under twenty-one. (At the least the juvenile labor exchange should be a separate department from that for the adults.) Legislation must soon bring under the school's supervision the working conditions of minors, for an aroused public will not long be complaisant with all care devoted to the few and with those most exposed to danger allowed to shift for themselves. What the nature of the legislation should be seems impossible to say; but we do know that there are certain logical next steps which will aid us in developing a satisfactory system. For example, the work certificate, already required in many cities, is a great step in advance. Cincinnati, Boston, and other cities now require a new certificate for each new job. The first certificate is issued only after the child already has the promise of a job. Right here a new step seems practicable. Why should not the work certificate office have a written copy of the agreement between the child and the employer? With this step taken the school authorities would be in a much better position to propose and finally enforce certain minimum requirements in the conditions of employment.

In the next place, why might not the employer be asked to refrain from advertising for persons under twenty-one and from sending for them to the private employment agencies? If we grant the propriety of asking the child to come to the office for a new working certificate, why should not we grant the propriety of the employer's being required to notify a school placement bureau whenever he has a vacancy to be filled by a minor? If this plan seems to be too far-reaching, or if it must be introduced gradually, the requirement may be modified to the rule that the employer must notify the school placement bureau *before* advertising or sending word to other agencies. Through some such plan as this proposed, the vocational-guidance bureau could better working conditions without on the one hand interfering to an unwarranted degree with the business affairs of the employer, or on the other hand imposing a paternalistic system of job-assignment upon the worker. The employer would still be able to select his help, and the worker to select his job. But the information about the vacancy would be available at the central office, the specifications of the job would be known, and the present haphazard method of job hunting would be partly broken up. Further, the plan proposed would very likely prevent much of the " job-hoboism " now caused by the habit of boys and girls of going to another job with the blind hope that it may by good luck prove better than the one they now have.

Coöperation in Employment Supervision. — Coöperation in employment supervision is essential. Legislation or no legislation, the school people can do little without the cordial support of the workers and the employers. Here are two great tasks to be worked out by joint action : the job must be made to serve the highest purposes of the boy or girl ; and the accessions to industry should be made in such a way as to serve rather than to interfere with the interests of all concerned. No service the school can render is of greater moment.

How can the teacher single-handed begin the solution of these problems, without waiting for the inauguration of a system? He may start at any time by following the children whom he knows, finding out from them how they are getting on in the occupation, and talking with their employers and co-workers. Later, if he feels prepared to extend the work, he may confer with representatives of labor and with employers, may aid them in writing the specifications of certain jobs, may find out and advise in regard to ways of promotion, may secure advice about the work offered in the school, may ask coöperation in providing extension courses for children at work, and may make an effort to establish and extend part-time work. Such coöperation should serve to improve the vocational guidance both in the school and in the occupation, and should pave the way for better understanding and efficient joint action beneficial to all concerned.

It is to be noted that we must still provide, in our system of employment supervision, for keeping individual contact with the worker. This may be done by means of volunteer helpers, or in the cities through officers stationed in the individual schools in various parts of the city. These supervisors or helpers should frequently be called into conference to exchange experiences and formulate policies.

Coöperation in Improving Conditions of Labor. — All that we have proposed should operate to improve the conditions of labor. But what about the larger questions of industry: unions, steady employment, scientific management, adequate wages, opportunity for career, industrial democracy? Can the school coöperate in the solution of these perplexing questions? The answer is that it has so coöperated and is doing so at the present time. The Minneapolis, Milwaukee, and Rochester trade agreements, the interest of educational people in the employment managers' associations, the joint action in the industrial and commercial surveys, the participation in the activities of Chambers of Commerce — all testify to the effectiveness of the school's new-found interest in the world for which the children are being prepared. Further, the young people are being taught something about the problems of employment, and no doubt, when all else is said and done, the training of a new generation of workers, prepared to cope intelligently with these problems, is the most sane and effective way of getting them solved.

Coöperation in Legislation. — Laws which run far ahead of public desire or public intelligence are apt to give more trouble than they are worth. Hence the need for the kind of teaching of which we have just spoken — that about the problems of employment. When the time is ripe for new steps in legislation, however, the school must coöperate in bringing these laws to pass. In order that the contribution of the school may be intelligent and effective, vocational counselors must make many connections which give them information and influence respected by the lawmakers. Thus, the man in charge of the vocational-guidance movement in Grand Rapids, Jesse B. Davis, has recently been chosen a director of the Grand Rapids Chamber of Commerce; this position gives the movement an excellent opportunity both to gather information about the practicability of desired legislation, and to express and support effectively its proposals. Bloomfield has always kept in touch with organizations of employers and employed. The counselor should keep himself in touch with many kinds of organizations, and should gain their confidence and support.

When legislation is under consideration, the committees on education and on industry in the legislature must be aided in their work; this should be an important duty of the vocational guide. Information should be furnished the members of the committee about practices in other cities and states, the results of investigations should be given them in summary fashion, and the counselor should be ready to speak before the committee effectively. As a preparation for such work wide reading and some knowledge of laws will be necessary, and it would be well for the vocational-guidance department to have facilities for preparing sample laws as suggestions to interested members of the legislature.

It should go without saying that in the preparation of bills the counselor needs to coöperate with all persons in the state interested in the active work of vocational guidance, and, most important, that he should whenever possible secure the point of view, advice, and active support of all the organizations of employers, workers, teachers, and other interested persons.

We have here attempted to show the main avenues of coöperation open to the vocational-guidance movement in furthering its work, and to show that without this joint action the work would be greatly handicapped. We shall now discuss more specifically the conditions within the occupations themselves, and shall try to find a basis for determining what the relation of the movement for vocational guidance should be toward them.

The Improvement of the Conditions of Employment. Opportunity for Part-time Work. — The experience already furnished by the continuation school indicates the values in such training to worker and to employer. It is already evident that the continuation-school principle might with profit be extended to include much more time devoted to school work, and to apply to many more workers. We have already proposed a plan for errand boys and girls to work at the occupation four hours daily and spend four other hours in the work and play of school (p. 197). Again, the work of many department stores in organizing short courses for adult workers indicates what may be done with profit by the schools, for workers of all ages. The Boston Continuation School maintains such voluntary classes, and devotes a section of the report to them (Circular, pp. 34–44).

In instituting continuation classes or part-time work great care is needed to make adjustments satisfactory in view of the time schedule of the establishments served,

s

and to supervise the work of the employees. If the half-time plan be used for children up to sixteen or seventeen years of age, the employer will be forced to deal with double the number of individuals he did before, and should be aided by the school in every legitimate way. Thus, the school may arrange after-hours conferences with the children from each establishment, in this way doing part of the work of teaching the rules and duties of the tasks. Again, a person about to enter a given establishment may be put under the preliminary tutelage of another person in that establishment. Finally, the school may make itself a clearing house for information about writing the specifications of jobs, and may aid the employment managers of establishments to plan their working tasks so carefully that the initiation of a beginner and the supervision of a regular worker will not present such difficulties as they do now.

The opportunity for part-time work seems eminently desirable; it should serve to free the child from the sudden plunge into the occupation, which frequently means for him mistakes, misunderstandings, discouragement, temptations, and failures. Part-time work would also make possible a better correlation between the school program and the occupational needs of the pupils; this advantage alone seems so promising that it would not be surprising to see the part-time plan extend itself till it applies to many workers over twenty-one years of age.[1]

[1] See article on National Association of Corporation Schools, *World's Work*, vol. 31, No. 4, Feb. 1916, pp. 417-420. See also Thum.

Again, as we have indicated above, it would inevitably make possible a better system of employment supervision. Its manifold advantages should commend to the counselor the effort to arrange for a part-time agreement whenever it seems necessary for a child to leave school.

School systems on their part should not be backward in readjusting their programs. Boston high schools already make it a practice to allow senior girls to spend Mondays in the stores. No plea that " the work of the school is interfered with " should stand in the way of the more important duty of holding children under the school influence a little longer and preparing them adequately for the tasks ahead of them.

Extending the Work of the Employment Manager. — The employment manager of the establishment deals with the occupational problems with which the school is most concerned. The vocational guide, therefore, whether acting as teacher, placement officer, or employment supervisor, must do whatever he can (1) to induce firms to put the solution of the employment problems in charge of some one agent; (2) to help to make the position of the employment manager so important that this officer will have real influence in determining the policies of the establishment; (3) to coöperate with the manager in connection with the work of employment supervision on behalf of the schools; (4) to induce and aid the employment managers of a city or metropolitan area to study their problems and to improve their methods through conferences, visits, and joint action; (5) to further the professional training of employment managers, whether through college courses, business-school courses, or private study.

The Opportunity for a Career in the Occupation. — We have shown that Professor Hoxie's investigations led him to the conclusion that scientific management in practice has not so far succeeded in choosing for the men the tasks best suited to their abilities or in adapting the tasks to the workers. We have also seen how one progressive plant, under the system of transferring workers to tasks better adapted to them, as worked out by its employment manager, has been able to secure better work and a more contented force. The thing most needed in the occupational world, apparently, in order to satisfy the desire for advancement, is a mapping out of all the jobs in an establishment in such a way that paths will lead successively from one to the other in an orderly series of promotions. The school exemplifies the promotion idea; no doubt the worker wishes it to follow him into the occupation.

To the average factory manager, perhaps this problem would seem insoluble. The machinery of the factory — the actual machines, we mean — gets in the way of a solution. It is difficult and expensive for the management to teach the profitable operation of many machines to any one individual.[1] There never has been, therefore,

---

[1] Automatic machinery makes this versatility less difficult. In any case it must be done, and is done, in many establishments, with profit to all concerned.

generally speaking, any line of promotion throughout the factory. That would involve teaching, and it has usually been assumed that there were two separate compartments — *teaching*, all in the school, and *doing*, all in the occupation.

Yet some hints of a better policy have been noted. The messenger boys of the London post office are being trained to pass examinations for letter carriers.[1] The jobs in the Dennison factory have been put into three classes so that the members of the force can prepare themselves for higher kinds of work. And the effort to write down the specifications of jobs facilitates comparison: the advantages and disadvantages of each job may be more readily seen. The system of transfers then aids the worker in securing the proper task.

It is the school's further duty and right to teach the children that they are to take their part in the continuous process of improving the vocations. It will be agreed, in spite of the apparent difficulties in the way, that in time the occupation must relieve the worker of the monotony of machine-like labor by change of work and rotation of tasks; must have a comprehensive plan of promotions whereby vacancies in the higher positions can be filled by persons occupying those below; must make it easy to register complaints and suggestions from the workers; must in many cases progressively shorten the hours of labor and raise the wages; must offer opportunities for advanced study; must conserve the productive element

[1] Dearle, pp. 377, 378.

as against the mere mechanical in the work-tasks of the unskilled [1] and must somehow make progress toward giving the workers a share in determining the rules and conditions under which they shall work. Without these improvements a " job " can hardly be said to offer a " career." Hence the vocational counselor, whose ideal must be an opportunity for a career for every worker, is very much concerned with all efforts to carry out these proposals.

Opportunity to use the Land. — The real seriousness of the land question in the United States is shown in the Manly report for the Commission on Industrial Relations, a report whose conclusions have been questioned, but whose facts speak for themselves. On pages 127–132 he treats of " The Land Question and the Condition of Agricultural Labor," showing the alarming growth of tenancy farming, with its wastefulness, extortion, debt, discouragement, irresponsibility, concentration of wealth, and poverty. In eighty-two Texas counties tenants operate on an average sixty per cent of the farms.

Manly recommends the exemption from taxation of all improvements and the taxation at full value of unused land. Whether or not the land tax or single-tax plan would help to solve the problem, the vocational counselor must realize that here is work for him to do, in the study of this question and in coöperating for its solution. Furthermore, the school pupils, especially those who are

[1] See Woods in Bloomfield's *Readings*, p. 31.

considering farming as a vocation, must be informed concerning this acute problem.

The amelioration of conditions of labor must go on
under the patronage of enlightened employers, and at
the same time the workers must be awakened to deserve
and require better things. Many forces work for social
reform, and the vocational-guidance movement must
coöperate with all of them.

**Methods of Guidance. Arousing the Child's Interest
in his Career.** — It is one thing to guide a child who wants
help in choosing his career, and quite another to arouse
a person who shows no interest in the question of his
vocation. The logic of the recent studies of elimination
from school is that the child must begin to think about
his vocation at the fifth grade or earlier. This does not
mean that he must at once choose a vocation, but rather
that he should begin thinking about the purposes of
his schooling and the occupations of his environment.
We have shown that from earliest years, both in play
and in studies, he may profitably think much in terms of
occupations. This should arouse his interest in considering the part he himself will play in the world. Davis
says that pupils who take part in student activities are
the most desirable when it comes to filling positions in
the commercial or industrial world;[1] the counselor
should foster these organizations of students as a means
of arousing interest in the life-career.

Even in the actual life-career class the teacher may

[1] *Vocational and Moral Guidance*, p. 125.

find pupils little interested in analyzing occupations or discovering aptitudes. Bloomfield has suggested then that the teacher of a group of city boys might begin with an occupation such as that of a professional baseball player. Thus, the members of the class might be led to draw up the specifications of the job of catcher on a big league team: the kind of man wanted, the pay, the season, the traveling, the lack of home life, the excitement, the notoriety, the period of usefulness, the preparation necessary, the way of entering the occupation, and the dozens of other things which the boys will think out. The work of the school janitor may be analyzed, and then that of the teacher, the conductor, the motorman, the policeman, the actor, and the banker. This method follows the interest and common knowledge of the children, and it imposes no fixed subject matter and outline upon them. What if they do not cover certain standard occupations? Better than that, they will have a method and an interest which they can apply to any situation; these will outlast any amount of mere information.

Having developed the interest of the children, we shall need to guide them through the successive steps which each individual takes. For convenience we have listed these steps as follows: surveying opportunities; choosing the occupation; preparing for the occupation; entering on work; progress and promotion; change and readjustment. Between the treatments of the first two, as contributing to both if not all of the steps, we shall interpolate a discussion of the life-career class. We turn now to a brief survey of each of these fields.

Guidance in Surveying Opportunities. — Opportunities may be considered as being of two kinds: those without, as expressed in the offerings which the vocations make; and those within, as expressed by the inclinations and abilities of the individual. It has been said that vocational guidance consists in the harmonious adjustment and coöperation of these two factors. Let us consider first the discovery of one's own powers and interests.

The burden of Chapter III is that the best vocational guidance is that accomplished by means of educational guidance. Thus the prevocational plan, or the junior high school with a program which includes manual work of a practical sort, enables the child to measure himself by several kinds of tests, and thereby aids him in finding out what his powers and inclinations are. Much of the academic work of these schools may be closely related to the manual work, the tasks may be set within the powers of the child, and he may be given a wide variety of experiences. Again, student and club activities should be encouraged, for through them many pupils find themselves. Every child may be asked the questions: To what organizations do you belong? What do you do in them? What activities do you like best? How do you spend your leisure time? Summer camps, corn clubs, junior associations, dramatics, student self-government, school papers, debating, bands, and orchestras, — all should be a part of the educational guidance of school children.

Outside relationships not only show the child something about the occupations; they show him his own powers besides. Thus, if men and women from the occupations, workers and employers, come to the school to talk to the classes, especially if the groups are small and questions are asked, and if travel trips and visits to establishments form part of the school's activities, the vocational imagination will be stirred and clews to interests and abilities may be found.

The child will need more than mere educational advantages in order to discover his interests and abilities: he will need to have the benefit of personal conferences about his problems. The teacher should investigate the choices which children make, — their choices of studies, courses, companions, and schools. Enrollment blanks should be filled out anew at least twice each year, and on them the child should be asked to fill in his choices of occupations, if he has developed any preferences. Records of examinations or grades in school studies should be put upon cards, together with the other questions suggested by the plans outlined above. A record of the child's successes should go with him through the grades.

The Life-career Class. — The class for the study of life careers serves to aid the child to survey his opportunities, to decide on his career, and to prepare for his vocation. We shall therefore treat it here.

Should the life-career class be a part of the English

work? We have discussed in Chapter III the relation of this work to literature, written composition, and Oral English. All of them can be of use in vocational guidance. But the subject of the vocation is of such moment that there are the same objections to making it subordinate to any other study that there are to making the vocational-guidance department of the city schools a subordinate branch of another department.

What then should be the plan and substance of the life-career class in the elementary grades? As low as the fourth grade the children can begin to discuss the work tasks of the people about them, to bring to the class information they have gathered from outside the schoolroom, to read and think about simple biographies, to analyze the tasks of a few typical occupations, to make out as a class exercise the qualities needed in certain kinds of work, and each to start a scrapbook of information about a group of occupations in which he expresses most interest.

In default of a textbook the teacher may bring out by questions and discussions the meaning of the education the children are obtaining, the opportunities ahead of them, and the value of definite preparation for life. The work in the fifth and sixth grades may follow the same general plan, the children building up their own knowledge, and being taught more and more to use outside sources of information, and to bring to class and give to the others interesting data about occupations. Here the collecting interest can be utilized, and a school museum started, made up of both ephemeral and permanent material. Business circulars, time-tables, mail-order catalogues, newspaper clippings, and magazine articles can be used, and a notebook devoted to written material, clippings, and pictures may be constructed by each pupil. The members of the class should have access to books on occupations, handy books for boys and girls, and simple written biographies, and the teacher should guide the children in their reading.

In the seventh, eighth, and ninth grades more systematic work can be done, though substantially the same methods may be followed. The teacher here may lead the children into wider experiences, if they are interested in the work, and may make a general survey of the field of occupations. Further, the children in these intermediate grades can begin to consider two things more seriously: the value of continuing with their education through the high-school age, and the systematic and wise choice of a vocation. In connection with the question of high school, visits may be arranged, and every effort should be made to give whatever personal counsel seems appropriate. There should in time be prepared a simple textbook for the life-career class of the intermediate grades, with its material well within the comprehension of the children, but serving as substance for solid study.

With the high school age a good textbook would be of great help, and there is need for definiteness of outline in the work of the class.

There are three kinds of books about occupations which the teacher should avoid in choosing texts for the life-career class: (1) many of those written by successful men and women about their own occupations; (2) those which substitute for solid facts irrelevant pictures and claptrap; (3) those hurriedly and carelessly gotten together. Successful men and women of the past generation are frequently disqualified for two reasons from telling the next generation how to succeed. First, the methods in business and industry, and in many professions, and the ethical standards as well, have changed and are now changing so radically that the boy or girl who copies these methods has little guarantee that satisfactory results will follow. Second, the successful man or woman is likely to treat his subject in a personal, restricted way, to emphasize too strongly the obstacles overcome, and to paint in too bright colors the heights of attainment reached. In regard to the second and third classes of textbooks noted above, those which are overenthusiastic and those which are hurriedly put together, we need not point out the dangers in their use.

The class in vocations should be as serious in its subject-matter, methods, and requirements as any other class, and nothing but the best should be used as text and reference books.

The textbook should be supplied with exercises and suggestive questions, and should provide for the study of printed matter, visits, interviews, original investigations, reports, discussions, and debates. It should candidly state the difficulties and problems in the occupations, and should touch upon the social and economic questions necessary to be understood. It should be free from sentimentalism and other objectionable subject-matter. Three or four good books to cover the commercial, industrial, and professional occupations should be used as supplementary texts, and the books selected should have been written with the modern vocational-guidance point of view in mind.

In the high school age the pupils will be able to profit by detailed analyses of the occupations, and by analyses and examinations of their own characteristics as measured by concrete requirements.

The college also should maintain a life-career class, for college students do much thinking on the perplexing question, What shall I do?[1]

In all the life-career classes, whether in elementary school or college, the teacher should keep a personal record card for each student. On this card should be noted all facts and opinions which indicate strong interests and definite forms of ability.

Guidance in Choosing the Occupation. — On pages 125–128 we have indicated some of the principles that should govern the choice of a vocation. We shall here note some additional observations to be considered in making choices.

Too much emphasis should not be put upon the matter

[1] See Elliff; and also Jennings, who shows the need for a college vocational bureau, and outlines a plan.

of choice. Like the overemphasis placed on securing
the first job, this tends to obscure the real problems —
what the child is doing to succeed in his present tasks,
what he is going to do after choice, and whether the choice
turns out to be a wise one. Neither should the child be
asked to decide too soon; if he is occupying his time in
ways profitable to himself and those about him he may
well be allowed to take his time. It would be a perfectly
feasible proposition for a student to spend time preparing
for several related occupations, and to continue while
actually working the study of the one finally chosen.

Another matter for careful consideration of the
counselor is the temptation upon him to encourage the
brighter boys and girls to go into the professions, or at
least to prepare themselves for a " clean-collar job."
Are not these aims and ambitions often based on a false
ideal of labor, honor, and position? Should not working
conditions and our conceptions of labor be reorganized
to give as good a basis for usefulness and happiness on
the farm and in the shop as at the bar and in the pulpit?
It would seem to be a far safer thing to do to train
every person to a trade than to train every one to a profession. It has often been remarked that some men do
not consider themselves quite respectable until they
have at least failed at a profession. The counselor
can combat these notions by telling about the struggles
for success and the low average earnings in the professions,
and the attractive opportunities in other fields, provided
one will thoroughly prepare himself for the work. What-

ever be the future revision of thought and practice in these directions, the shop work of the prevocational school, where all the boys meet in overalls and join in productive labor, should have its influence for good. The teacher, too, can aid the spread of a better attitude toward labor, particularly, perhaps, by joining with the boys in the work of caring for the athletic field and the running track. If the teacher of Latin will occasionally take off his coat and help rake the track or dig up the jumping pit, the boys and girls of the school may be set to thinking some thoughts they might otherwise miss.[1]

In the whole problem of the choice of an occupation, breadth of education and of experience is the main thing to look out for. The nearer the school can come to the concrete situations of life, especially in the upper grades of the elementary school and in the high school, the better.

The child should be encouraged to aim at the position which will give most satisfaction to his interests and use most effectively his powers. At the same time, however, he should be trained to self-reliant usefulness at his present stage of preparation, so that he could take care of himself whenever the necessity should arise.

Guidance in Preparing for the Occupation. — On pages 90–92 we have sketched the main principles one may follow in preparing for his vocation. Our plan involves

---

[1] Women in apartment houses are sometimes quite thoughtless of the rights and feelings of the janitor or of tradespeople who serve them. The reason seems to be that they have never done any of that kind of work themselves and cannot put themselves in the other person's place.

breadth of preparation, so that avenues to other possible vocations will not be closed; the study of schools, to select wisely; study of the occupation; part-time experience, if advisable; and the related preparation for civic, social, political, and domestic duties.[1]

Sometimes vocational education will have to be obtained while the boy or girl is working at a blind-alley job, and here the continuation school is important. School systems apparently will have to require continuation school opportunities far beyond the age of sixteen, for it has been found that the sixteen-year-old child is frequently not ready to decide on his vocation. Day schooling, whenever possible, should be allowed the worker; and night vocational training should be offered to those who cannot attend the day classes. The continuation hours may be extended until they are sufficient to make the work correspond to what we now call part-time schooling, with approximately half of each school day spent in school. If the worker is in a blind-alley job, our effort must be to make his present work efficient and to prepare him to leave it for something better; if he is in promising work, we may make the schooling supplement the occupational experiences and prepare the worker for advancement.

The school, too, should arrange for systematic vocational guidance, so that each boy or girl will have the

---

[1] It should be more widely recognized that just as the girl has to make a double preparation, for vocation and for home-making, so the boy has certain things to learn about his duty as a successful life-partner.

T

benefit of a lasting acquaintance and friendship with an experienced counselor, and, if possible, also with some person of experience and good judgment who has already succeeded in the vocation chosen by the student. The counselor or coördinator should supervise the employment of the children he is guiding, so that he may follow their progress outside the school.

No part of the training for the vocation is of greater importance than the study of industrial and commercial conditions. This study is likely to be much more concrete and valuable after the boy or girl has chosen his occupation than before. With his vocation decided upon, sociology, economics, commercial geography, business organization, industrial history, and community civics take on definite applications. The teacher must keep himself informed on current events and bring them into his classes and his vocational guidance in a way to interest the pupils. Thrift should be discussed, as affording opportunity for advanced study, travel, and business on one's own account.[1] Some of the perplexing questions of our industrial and commercial life may profitably be brought to the attention of the students, and they may try their powers at answering them.

The same concreteness may be given other studies after the vocation is chosen; it is for this reason that Eliot favors tentative choices at early ages.[2] Children should be shown the importance of ability to talk well,

[1] See Prichard and Turkington, *Stories of Thrift.*
[2] See *Readings,* p. 9.

and to make freehand drawings. History, literature, chemistry, physics, languages, music, and art may be taught as aiding the vocation and as helping to make a well-rounded life. The study of family budgets may give both boys and girls good training in domestic economy.

Finally, the student and club activities, the summer camps, and the recreations will give the young people practice in coöperation, leadership, and the solution of concrete problems of adjustment to each other and to the environment. Without such training the preparation for the vocation would be incomplete.

Guidance in Entering upon Work. — We have proposed (p. 252) that the school authorities supervise the employment of all workers under the age of twenty-one, and that employers be required to notify the vocational-guidance department whenever a vacancy is to be filled. There is no doubt but that an adequate system of guidance must make some provision for the perplexing problem of getting work. Yet the unsatisfactory features of placement are many (pp. 109–114, 250). It seems possible that more good would be done if the money now spent in placing children were expended in an effort to keep them in school longer. If the school age can be raised, and if children can be given adequate training before the time for placement comes, — in knowledge of occupations, information about the problems with which they will have to cope, and training in effective speaking, — it seems possible that the young people might find their own places. With the registration of vacancies advocated above, this would not mean wandering the streets looking for work, but rather calling at certain listed establishments.

At some time the worker must learn to stand on his own feet in the occupational world, — to make his own adjustments. No system of vocational guidance should delay the coming of independent action, provided the child is capable. Until the child is better equipped for seeking work, and until his sources of information are better, it may be necessary for the school system to maintain a placement bureau or to make placement work incidental to vocational guidance.

Guidance in Progress and Promotion. — Our plan for employment supervision (or for coördinators in part-time work) would furnish each child with an experienced friend as a volunteer helper, and with close contact with a vocational counselor as well. From these persons, as well as from his employer, he may obtain advice and guidance about his progress and promotion in the occupation.

The school department must maintain many kinds of classes for advanced training: evening classes, short courses, part-time work, extension courses, continuation-school work, factory and store schools, and summer and dull-season courses, and these classes must cover a wide range of subjects, both academic and vocational. The Minneapolis Survey report discusses the unsatisfactory nature of correspondence courses (pp. 116–121), and the schools must find a substitute. In Richmond, classes of workers were gathered together first, and the studies which were to be offered were determined afterward.[1]

Guidance in Change and Readjustment. — In Myer's monograph on the *Problems of Vocational Education in Germany* (p. 11) are pointed out the evils of a system in which there is no possibility of transfer from an unskilled to a skilled occupation. Ambition and hope are cut off, and even the continuation-school work becomes sordid and inefficient. Obviously, such a state of affairs should have no place in a democratic commonwealth. Aside from the bad effect on the individual, it would be a source of danger to the state.

Pending the time when industry and commerce are organized to provide for a system of promotions throughout the establishment, the vocational guide or his agents, the volunteer helper or employment supervisor, must aid the worker in making whatever changes and readjustments seem beneficial. The worker must have access to these disinterested sources of advice. If the job is a " blind " one, the public and the employer must be taught to look upon it as a temporary place, and must learn to encourage and facilitate change. During the probation period at the unskilled trade, the employment supervisor should study the boy or girl, making inquiries of his employers, parents, and co-workers, and should keep a record of all available significant informa-

[1] See 1915 *Bureau of Educ. Report*, Part. I, p. 260.

tion. The worker, on his part, must be taught to give satisfaction in whatever position he finds himself, to make himself worthy of a change, to aid the counselor and respond to his help, to be on the lookout for a better place, and to be patient till a better opportunity comes. He must be taught that he should not leave one place until he has another in view, unless for good cause, and that in all his business dealings he should apply the Golden Rule.

What shall the vocational counselor do with the worker who wants none of his help or advice? Obviously, let him alone. Vocational guidance should never be compulsory; if it ever becomes so its chief value to society and to the individual is gone. Of course, there are certain minimum requirements for the child's schooling, working age, hours of work, wages, and other laws, both civil and criminal; these must be enforced. Aside from these the worker should be free to solve his own problems. In this complex world, however, no one lives to himself, and no person can make progress in his occupation without the aid and coöperation of others. The purpose of vocational guidance is but to systematize and direct this aid and coöperation. The worker who wishes to be independent of this organized help should be allowed to have his way. Independence may profitably be encouraged; a better way may be developed, or, if not, helpful lessons will be learned, even through hard experiences, — lessons which might not be learned in any other manner.

Summary of Methods of Guidance. — The means at the disposal of the vocational-guidance movement are, then, as follows: the teacher; the trained counselor; the volunteer helper; the coördinator; the employment supervisor; the librarian; the employer; the employment manager; civic associations; labor unions; employers' organizations; the " vocationalized " school program; the prevocational school; the continuation and part-time plan; the life-career class; the student activities.

The method of vocational guidance concerns itself with a school program rich and varied enough to aid in discovering the interests and powers of the child; surveys of occupations; the child's study of occupations and employment problems; and the advice and guidance of a trained counselor.

Training for Vocational Guidance. Normal School Classes. — If these methods are to be followed by teachers and others, and if the efficient means are to be provided, the work must be undertaken by men and women who are trained for it, and normal school and college courses must be provided for aiding in the training.

In the normal school two courses may profitably be given, to be required during the last two years of the school program. The first course should give the vocational-guidance point of view, by centering the attention on a study of the vocational possibilities in the studies and other activities of the elementary school.

One after another each of the various studies of the program may be considered, and its content and appropriate method examined in relation to the children from the kindergarten through the eighth grade. This examination should direct the attention of the normal school students to the occupations to which the elementary school studies should be related. Next the pupils' activities should be examined — athletics, dramatics, excursions, music, scouting, clubs, camps, vacation work, pleasures, and play — for the purpose of determining what vocational utility they possess. Finally, the elements in the choice of high schools and the reasons for further training should be considered, so that the prospective teacher may aid the pupil in continuing his education.

The work of the second or advanced course should take up as its central study the problem of the life-career class in the elementary school, — its content, aims, and methods. In connection with the work there should be a consideration of occupational study and of the problems of employment (with as much concrete observation as seems possible), a study of the means of actually preparing for the vocation, and an opportunity for experience in conducting life-career classes in the practice school, and in counseling individuals, all under supervision and instruction.

College Classes in Vocational Guidance. — The college courses in vocational guidance should provide at least for three classes of persons: (1) those who expect to become high school teachers of ordinary subjects, and wish to obtain the vocational-guidance point of view; (2) those who have had school experience, and wish to lead life-career classes and become vocational counselors; (3) those who are or expect to be supervisors or administrators, and wish to learn how to foster the vocational-guidance movement in their schools or school systems.

The first group — prospective teachers of the various high school subjects — may follow a plan similar to that outlined above for the beginning class in the normal school, dealing now, of course, with high school subjects. Since this group will ordinarily consist largely of college seniors and graduate students, there may be some consideration of the problem of the life-career class in high-school education for the vocation, problems of employment, and plans for coöperation between school and occupation.

The second group, prospective counselors, may profitably take the work as outlined above for the first group, and, in an advanced course, may consider in more detail the various problems with which vocational guidance must deal. Here each student should select a question for his own investigation on which he will report from time to time, and the class work should supplement these topics so that the members of the group will gain a view of most of the important problems in the field. Observation visits should be arranged, and, if possible, actual participation in guidance.

For the third group, supervisors and administrators, there should be provided a general course which will consider many of the topics of the other two courses but will especially take up the question of organizing the work of guidance.   Thus, the question of educational guidance should be discussed, together with a general survey of the methods used in various school systems for arranging for and financing vocational guidance, and the methods of counseling used.   Observational visits, participation in guidance, and the individual study of problems may form part of the work of the course.

The Equipment of the Vocational Counselor. — Students in any of these normal-school or college courses who manifest a purpose to choose vocational counseling or related work in guidance as their life-careers, should of course be given special attention by the instructor. Early in the course a study should be made of the present equipment of each of such students: his schooling; the breadth of his experience in teaching; his knowledge of the various studies of the school program; his interest in and connection with the play and games of pupils; the scope and intensity of his experience in the occupations; his knowledge of ways and means of finding points of contact with commerce and industry; his grasp of sociology and economics; his ability to use statistical methods; his power to make investigations on his own account; his ability to coöperate with people; his purposes in going into the work of vocational guidance; and his conceptions of the duties and opportunities of the work.   The study in the university course should then be made to supplement this preliminary equipment.

Breadth of equipment is important, for the counselor must meet, understand, be understood by, and confer successfully with the employment manager, the merchant, the manufacturer, the shop superintendent, the labor union agent, the worker, the legislator, the superintendent of schools, the principal, the teacher, the parent, and, very likely, groups of any or all of these persons assembled in meetings.   It is particularly important, therefore, that the training course should somehow bring the student into contact with the kinds of persons with whom he will have to deal in his work.

Summary of the Program of Vocational Guidance. — We may here set forth in summary form the requirements in an adequate program of vocational guidance somewhat as follows :

1. A school organization and program broad, varied, and flexible enough to be fairly representative of all the activities of life, and intensive enough to test the powers of the pupil and discover to himself and to others his special inclinations and abilities.

2. A course of study, in every subject, which relates itself whenever possible to the vocational needs of the pupils.

3. A life-career class in every school grade (from the fourth up) and in college, studying the opportunity furnished by education, the requirements and opportunities of the occupations, and the economic and social problems of employment.

4. Individual counsel for every child, as often as may seem appropriate.[1] Record cards and conferences with parents and others would make the work of counseling more efficient.

5. The organization, under one officer responsible directly to the superintendent of schools, of all the vocational-guidance activities of the schools.

6. Coöperation of school and other agencies, local, state, and national, for the collection and dissemination of occupational information.

7. The supervision, by school authorities, and under the direction of the vocational-guidance department, of the employment of all workers under twenty-one years of age, with liberal opportunity for part-time work.

8. Adequate vocational training, both for pupils in school and for persons at work.

9. The progressive improvement of commerce and industry, by

(a) The elimination of young workers from full-time employment.

(b) Employment supervision, through employment managers coöperating with school agents.

(c) Better methods of obtaining work.

(d) Graded systems of promotion, all furnishing prospect of satisfactory careers in the occupations.

(e) Relief from long hours, enervating tasks, dangerous work, and low wages.

(f) Opportunity to obtain the use of idle land and unused or exploited natural resources.

(g) Well-considered progress toward a more democratic administration of those affairs in industry and commerce which

---

[1] It is difficult to set up a rule here, but it would seem that a friendly conversation each half-year, to discuss plans, progress, schooling, play, and vocational hopes, might be proposed as a minimum for counseling each child in the upper grades.

concern the welfare of the workers, with preliminary training of the workers for assuming such responsibilities.

10. Preparation of men and women for the work of vocational guidance.

11. A legislative program, permissive at first, if it seems best, to bring into effect the above requirements, whenever better laws will aid.

Some Appropriate Next Steps. — The above program may seem rather formidable; therefore we shall consider here some lesser steps which may be taken to further the work of vocational guidance, — steps which seem appropriate, practicable, and every way desirable. For convenience we shall set these also in summary form:

1. A systematic attempt, through reading circles, talks, lectures, discussions, and extension courses, to interest the teachers in developing the vocational values in the school studies, and in counseling individuals about their vocational opportunities.

2. Differentiation of school program in the seventh and eighth grades, by the introduction of a variety of prevocational work.

3. The further development of the many present plans and practices for vocational education.

4. Coöperation between school and employers for the extension of the half-time or part-time principle.

5. The appointment and training of selected teachers for special work in investigation and counseling, and the assignment to them of time to do the work.

6. In lieu of a full course in life-careers, the undertaking of such work in the classes in composition, oral English, geography, civics, etc.

7. The organization of a committee of counselors, with an elected or appointed chairman, to supervise and systematize the work, and to collect and disseminate information.

8. An investigation of the causes of leaving school, and of the working experiences of those who have recently left.

9. An attempt, in normal school and college courses, either in general education classes or in vocational-guidance classes, to show to all prospective teachers the vocational possibilities in the school program, and to offer training for vocational guidance.

10. The study, on the part of teachers, of the problems and conditions of employment.

11. Experiments, by city, state, and federal departments, in preparing workers for democratic management of such institutions as the post office, the forestry service, and schools, for the purpose of stimulating similar experiments in industry and commerce.

12. Legislation to cover the following points:

(a) The setting aside of definite funds for extending the work of vocational guidance.

(b) Raising the school age for full-time schooling, and for part-time schooling for wage earners.

(c) Giving to the school the responsibility for the supervision of all children up to the age of eighteen, whether working or not.

(d) Establishment of public employment agencies and labor exchanges.

Conclusion. — If we consider the progress that has been made in school and in occupation during the past decade, during the life of the modern vocational-guidance movement, it will not seem much to set ourselves to the accomplishment of this program. Enlightenment almost of itself brings progress, and the critical knowledge of school and occupation which has recently come to teachers and others through this movement for the conservation of the careers of the children is certain to lead to the greater usefulness of the school and to more satisfactory conditions in employment.

The teacher and the counselor are directly concerned, of course, with making the best attempt they can to guide the individual boy or girl through the school and into his chosen occupation. In this process, however, we see that our work is not as effective as it might be if schools and industrial and commercial conditions were improved. Vocational guidance is indeed occupied with aiding the individual to make the most of his powers; but this we find we cannot do without better schools and better work. The welfare of the individual citizen and of the state demands the progressive realization of these hopes.

APPENDIX I

SPECIAL GLOSSARY

Blind Alley: A job or occupation which offers little opportunity for growth in skill or knowledge, advancement, or extension of usefulness with consequent increase of earning power and which does not usually lead to a better occupation.

Commercial Occupation: A calling which is concerned with business or mercantile affairs. Usually includes clerical occupations as well, and sometimes the callings connected with transportation.

Continuation School: A school for adolescents or others at work, in which they may have day instruction, during working hours, either upon the work they are doing or upon matters of general value. See Schneider, p. 57; also coöperative schooling, below.

Coöperative Schooling: A plan in which the time of the individual pupil is divided between shop or store and school; *e.g.* workers paired so that they alternate, one having a week in school while the other is at work. School and employer coöperate in the agreements. Same as part-time schooling. See Schneider, p. 55.

Coördinators: Officers in the coöperative system, who see that the school work is related to the shop work, and that the instruction and progress in the shop are satisfactory.

Democratic Management: Yet to be defined. Progress toward a more democratic management is made whenever the knowledge and point of view of the employees is used in helping to determine the policies or management of the establishment.

Dexterity: Skill of a simple kind; an ability to perform a process which may be learned in a relatively short time.

Differentiation: Variety of curricula for different pupils.

U

Educational Guidance: Information, advice, or coöperation relating to growth and mental development. When it concerns the occupations it is vocational guidance as well.

Employment Manager: An officer in an establishment who has charge of the hiring, training, transfer, discharge, and (often) general welfare of employees.

Employment Supervision: The oversight, with or without authority, of the occupational experiences of workers. As used in vocational guidance, employment supervision is taken to mean supervision and advice by school officers.

Follow-Up: An investigation of the employment experiences of those who have left school to go to work. Follow-up is the first step toward employment supervision by the school.

Industrial Education: Training for an industrial occupation. See below.

Industrial Occupation: A calling which requires, among other things, manual or mechanical exercise, dexterity, or skill. Often used to include farming. Should not be used to include commercial or professional occupations.

Industrial Survey: An occupational survey (see below), restricted to the industrial callings. (Often loosely used to include all occupations.)

Intermediate School: See junior high school.

Job: The particular position held by a worker at any given time; the set of duties assigned to him by the establishment for which he works.

Junior High School: Usually a separate school comprising the 7th, 8th, and 9th (first year of high school) grades, with differentiated courses, high school methods, and varied activities. The junior high school will ordinarily offer prevocational work (see below).

Life-Career: The occupation of a person; that which offers him opportunity for progress and satisfaction in his work.

Life-Career Class: A school group for the study of occupational opportunities and problems.

Occupation: The kind of work one is engaged in doing; the vocation; the calling.

Occupational Survey: A systematic investigation to determine the kinds of work and the conditions of work in a given community. Usually for the purpose of determining what kind of vocational education should be offered. A vocational survey.

Part-Time School: Continuation or coöperative schooling.

Placement: Finding employment for an individual.

Prevocational Work: School work which is designed to precede actual training for an occupation. Usually applied to manual or mechanical exercises in the school program, though all the school program of a junior high school may properly be called prevocational. Good prevocational work provides for experimentation with many kinds of activities. See Schneider, p. 49.

Profession: An occupation requiring long preparation, involving a high degree of education, and having certain aims or standards of ability and of conduct.

Program of Studies: The entire range of subjects offered by a school or school system.

Skilled Occupation: A mechanical calling requiring a more or less extended training in preparation.

Technical School: A school which trains for an industrial occupation.

Trade School: A school preparing for industrial occupations, in which the mechanical processes are taught in the school instead of in the commercial shop.

Vocation: A calling or occupation.

Vocational Education: Training which prepares for the calling.

Vocational Guidance: A systematic effort, based on knowledge of the occupations and on personal acquaintance with and study of the individual, to inform, advise, or coöperate with a person in choosing, preparing for, entering upon, or making progress in his occupation.

Vocational-Guidance Class: A group of persons engaged in a study of the principles, methods, or problems of vocational guidance.

Vocational-Guidance Survey: An investigation for the purpose of recommending plans for adequate vocational guidance.

Vocational Survey: An occupational survey.

APPENDIX II

BIBLIOGRAPHY

NOTE. — This list includes only the list of works consulted or used for reference. For a review of the important literature see *A Selected Critical Bibliography of Vocational Guidance*. Brewer, John M., and Kelly, Roy Willmarth. Harvard University Press, 1917.

Alden, George I. *A Plan for Better Education of Boys and Girls who Leave the Grammar School to Seek Employment in the Unskilled Industries*. Read before the Worcester (Mass.) Education Association, 1913.

Alderman, L. R. *School Credit for Home Work*. Houghton Mifflin Co., 1915.

Alexander, Magnus W. *Waste in Hiring and Discharging Employees*. Scientific American Supplement, No. 2041, Feb. 13, 1915, pp. 102–103. Also in American Academy; see below.

Allen, Frederick J. *Business Employments*. Ginn and Company, 1916.

——. *The Law as a Vocation*. The Vocation Bureau of Boston, 1913.

——. *The Shoe Industry*. The Vocation Bureau of Boston, 1916.

American Academy of Political and Social Science. *Personnel and Employment Problems in Industrial Management*. Annals of the Academy, Vol. LXV, No. 154, 1916. Editors, Meyer Bloomfield and Joseph H. Willits.

Angell, James R. *The Doctrine of Formal Discipline in the Light of the Principles of General Psychology*. Educational Review, Vol. 36, No. 1, June, 1908, pp. 1–14.

Ayres, Leonard P. *Constant and Variable Occupations and their Bearing on Problems of Vocational Education*. The Division of Education of the Russell Sage Foundation, No. E136, 1914. Bloomfield's *Readings*, pp. 141–149.

Ayres, Leonard P. *Laggards in Our Schools.* The Charities Publication Committee, 1909.

———. *Psychological Tests in Vocational Guidance.* In Bureau of Education Bulletin, 1914, No. 14, Vocational Guidance, pp. 33–37. Also Bulletin No. E128 of the Russell Sage Foundation. Also Journal of Educational Psychology, Vol. IV, No. 4, April, 1913, pp. 232–237.

———. *Some Conditions Affecting Problems of Vocational Education in 78 American School Systems.* Bulletin No. E135 of Russell Sage Foundation, 1914. Bloomfield's *Readings*, pp. 150–171.

Bagley, W. C. *The Educative Process.* The Macmillan Company, 1912.

Barnard, J. Lynn, and others. *The Teaching of Community Civics.* Bureau of Education, Bulletin, 1915, No. 23.

Bartlett, L. W. *Vocational Guidance in Pomona City Schools.* Pomona (Cal.) School District, 1917.

Bate, William G. *An Experiment in Teaching a Course in Elementary Sociology.* The School Review, Vol. 23, No. 5, May, 1915, pp. 331–340.

———. *Vocational Guidance in a Small City.* American School Board Journal, Vol. 51, No. 2, Aug. 1915, pp. 11–12.

Bawden, William T. *Vocational Education.* Being Chapter IX of the Report of the Commissioner of Education of the United States, 1915, Vol. I, pp. 221–278.

Bloomfield, Meyer. *The New Profession of Handling Men.* Annals of the American Academy of Political and Social Science, 1915, Publication No. 928, p. 6.

——— (ed.). *Readings in Vocational Guidance.* Ginn and Company, 1915.

———. *The School and the Start in Life.* Bureau of Education Bulletin, 1914, No. 4.

———. *Training Men in the Art of Employing Others.* The Nation's Business, Vol. III, No. 8, Aug. 15, 1915, p. 6. (Reviewed in The Literary Digest, Oct. 9, 1915.)

———. *Vocational Guidance of Youth.* Houghton Mifflin Company, 1911. Introduction by Paul H. Hanus.

Bloomfield, Meyer. *Youth, School, and Vocation.* Houghton Mifflin Company, 1915. Introduction by Henry Suzzallo.

Blumenthal, Gustave A. *Vocational Analysis.* In *Some Aspects of Vocational Guidance*, Central Committee on Vocational Guidance, New York City, 1912, pp. 14–18.

Bolton, Frederick E. *Curricula in University Departments of Education.* School and Society, Vol. II, No. 50, Dec. 11, 1915, pp. 829–841.

Bonser, Frederick G. *Is "Prevocational" a Needed or Desirable Term?* Manual Training and Vocational Education, Vol. XVII, No. 8, April, 1916, pp. 585–588.

——. *Necessity of Professional Training for Vocational Counseling.* In Vocational Guidance, Bureau of Education, Bulletin, 1914, No. 14, pp. 37–42. Also in Bloomfield's *Readings*, pp. 109–116.

——.. *The Curriculum as a Means of Revealing Vocational Aptitudes.* Education, Vol. XXXVII, No. 3, Nov. 1916, pp. 145–159.

Boston School Committee. *Annual Report.* School Document No. 10, 1912.

——. *Circular of Information Relating to the Continuation Schools*, No. 26, 1915.

Boston Masters' Association. *Brief of Papers on Vocational Guidance*, 1912. In Bloomfield's *Readings*, pp. 117–128.

Boy Scouts of America. *Handbook for Boys.* New York City, Doubleday, Page and Company.

Breckenridge, Sophonisba P. *Guidance by the Development of Placement and Follow-up Work.* In Vocational Guidance, Bureau of Education Bulletin, 1914, No. 14, pp. 59–64.

——. and Abbott, Edith. *The School and the Working Child.* Report to Woman's Club, Association of Collegiate Alumnæ and Woman's City Club, of Chicago, 1913. In Bloomfield's *Readings*, pp. 485–503.

Breese, B. B. *Vocational Guidance.* Unpopular Review, Vol. V, No. 8, Oct.–Dec. 1915, pp. 343–357.

Brewer, John M. *A Broader View of Vocational Guidance.* School and Society, Vol. V, No. 128, June 9, 1917, pp. 661–668.

Brewer, John M. *Vocational Guidance in School and Occupation.* Am. Acad. of Political and Social Science, Annals, *New Possibilities in Education,* Vol. LXVII, No. 156, Sept. 1916, pp. 54–63.

Briggs, Thomas H. *Secondary Education.* In Commissioner of Education, U. S., Report, 1914, Part I, pp. 127–157.

Brooks, Stratton D. *Vocational Guidance in the Boston Schools.* The School Review, Vol. 19, No. 1, Jan. 1911, pp. 42–50. Also in Bloomfield's *Readings,* pp. 83–91.

Bureau of the Census. *Index to Occupations.* 1915.

Bureau of Education. *Commissioner of Education, U. S., Annual Reports* 1914 *and* 1915.

——. *Vocational Guidance.* Bulletin, 1914, No. 14. The Papers Presented at the Organization Meeting of The Vocational Guidance Association, Grand Rapids, Oct. 1913. (See Ayres, Bonser, Breckenridge, Fletcher, Giles, Leavitt, Lovejoy, Martin, Mead, Richards, Roberts, Woolley.)

Bureau of Labor Statistics. *Vocational Education Survey of Richmond, Va.* Bulletin Whole No. 162, Misc. Series No. 7, 1916.

Burk, Frederic. *In Re Everychild, a Minor, vs. Lockstep Schooling.* Monograph C, San Francisco State Normal School, 1915.

Burris, William P. *The Public School System of Gary, Indiana.* U. S. Bureau of Education, Bulletin, 1914, No. 18.

Cabot, Ella Lyman. *Volunteer Help to the Schools.* Houghton Mifflin Company, 1914.

California Bureau of Labor Statistics. *Sixteenth Biennial Report.* 1913–1914, State Printing Office, 1914.

Campfire Girls' National Headquarters. *The Book of the Campfire Girls.*

Central Committee on Vocational Guidance. *Some Aspects of Vocational Guidance.* 1912, New York City.

Chamberlain, Jas. F. *The Occupations of Man.* New York Teachers' Monograph, June, 1903.

Chicago Board of Education. *Sixtieth Annual Report,* for the year ending June 30, 1914.

Civil Service Commission of the United States. *Manual of Examinations, for the Spring of* 1916.

Claxton, Philander P. *Part-time Secondary Schooling and Vocational Guidance.* Nat. Voc. Guidance Assn., Proc. 1914, pp. 44–48.

Cleveland Educational Survey. Nine volumes on vocational education. Division of Education, Russell Sage Foundation, Auspices The Survey Committee of the Cleveland Foundation, 1916.

    The following volumes relate to vocational education, and thus, indirectly, to vocational guidance:

    Bryner, Edna. *Dressmaking and Millinery.*

    ——. *The Garment Trades.*

    Fleming, Ralph D. *Railroad and Street Transportation.*

    Lutz, R. R. *The Metal Trades.*

    ——. *Wage Earning and Education.*

    O'Leary, Iris P. *Department Store Occupations.*

    Shaw, Frank P. *The Building Trades.*

    ——. *The Printing Trades.*

    Stevens, Bertha. *Boys and Girls in Commercial Work.*

Clopper, Edward N., and Hine, Lewis W. *Child Labor in the Sugar-Beet Fields of Colorado.* The Child Labor Bulletin, Vol. 4, No. 4, Feb. 1916, Part I, pp. 176–206.

Cole, Percival R. *Industrial Education in the Elementary School.* Houghton Mifflin Company, 1914.

Collet, Miss. Two reports on juvenile labor in London, — ready-made women's clothing, and bookbinding and stationery trades, 1911 and 1912. See Bloomfield's *Readings*, pp. 647–665 and 666–678.

Colleton. See Boston Masters' Association.

Coman, Katherine. *Unemployment, a World Problem, and the Congress at Ghent.* The Survey, Vol. XXXI, No. 22, Feb. 28, 1914, pp. 667–669.

Commission on Industrial Relations, United States. *Final Report.* 1915.

Davis, Anne S. *A Brief Statement of the Work of the Vocational Bureau and the Joint Committee for Vocational Supervision.* Nat. Voc. Guid. Assn., Proc. 1914, pp. 51–56.

Davis, Anne S. *Occupations and Industries Open to Children between Fourteen and Sixteen Years of Age.* Pamphlet published by the Board of Education, Chicago, 1914. Also in Bloomfield's *Readings*, pp. 542–556.

——. See Bureau of Education, Vocational Guidance, Bulletin 1914, No. 14, pp. 86–88.

Davis, Jesse B. *Vocational and Moral Guidance.* Ginn and Company, 1914.

Davis, Philip (ed.). *The Field of Social Service.* Small, Maynard and Company, 1915.

——. *The Street and the Start in Life.* Nat. Voc. Guid. Assn., Proc. 1914, pp. 8–9.

——. *Streetland.* Small, Maynard and Company, 1915.

Dearborn, Walter F. *Experimental Education.* The School Review Monographs, No. 1, 1911, pp. 6–13.

Dearle, N. B. *Industrial Training.* P. S. King and Son, London, 1914.

Denison, Elsa. *Helping School Children.* Harper and Bros., 1912.

Devine, Edward T. Remarks as Chairman of the Conference on Placement. Nat. Conference on Voc. Guid., Second, 1912, Proc., pp. 1–2.

——. *Education and Social Economy.* N. E. A. Proc., 1914, pp. 142–150.

Dewey, John. *The Need of an Industrial Education in an Industrial Democracy.* Manual Training and Vocational Education, Vol. XVII, No. 6, Feb. 1916, pp. 409–414.

—— and Dewey, Evelyn. *Schools of To-morrow.* E. P. Dutton and Co., 1915.

Dodge, Harriet Hazel. *Survey of Occupations Open to the Girl of Fourteen to Sixteen Years.* Girls' Trade Education League, Boston, 1912. Also in Bloomfield's *Readings*, pp. 571–601.

Dopp, Katherine E. *The Place of Industries in Elementary Education.* University of Chicago Press, 1909.

Dunn, Arthur W. *Civic Education in Elementary Schools as Illustrated in Indianapolis.* United States Bureau of Education, Bulletin, 1915, No. 17.

Eaton, Jeanette, and Stevens, Bertha M. *Commercial Work and Training for Girls.* The Macmillan Company, 1915.

Eliot, Charles W. *The Value, during Education, of the Life-Career Motive.* Nat. Educ. Assn., Proc. 1910, pp. 133–141. Also in Bloomfield's *Readings*, pp. 1–12.

Elliff, J. D. *Vocational Guidance — A Function of the University.* Nat. Voc. Guid. Assn., Proc. 1914, pp. 12–16.

Emerson, Harrington. *Efficiency as a Basis for Operation and Wages.* The Engineering Magazine, publishers, 1909.

Feiss, Richard A. *Personal Relationship as a Basis of Scientific Management.* Society to Promote the Science of Management, Vol. I, No. 6, Nov. 1915, pp. 5–25. Also in Annals.

——. *Scientific Management Applied to the Steadying of Employment, and its Effect in an Industrial Establishment.* American Academy of Political and Social Science, Annals, Sept. 1915, Publication No. 926.

Filene, A. Lincoln. *The Relation of Vocational Guidance to the Employer.* Nat. Conference on Voc. Guid., Proc., 1912, pp. 173–177.

Filene Coöperative Association. *A Thumbnail Sketch of the Filene Coöperative Association,* 1915. (Wm. Filene's Sons Co., Boston.)

Fitch, John A. *A Method for Industrial Surveys.* Nat. Conference on Voc. Guid., Proc. 1912, pp. 44–53.

Fletcher, Alfred P. *Guidance by Means of a System of Differentiated Courses.* In Vocational Guidance, United States Bureau of Educ. Bulletin, 1914, No. 14, pp. 48–52.

Fullerton, Hugh S. *Getting and Holding a Job.* American Magazine, Vol. 83, No. 3, Mar. 11, 1916.

Gantt, H. L. *Industrial Leadership.* Yale Press, 1916.

Garnett, J. C. Maxwell. *Education and Industry.* School and Society, Vol. II, No. 46, Nov. 13, 1915, pp. 685–694.

Gayler, G. W. *Vocational Direction of Pupils in the Elementary Grades.* Illinois State Teachers' Assoc., Proc. 1914, pp. 99–101.

——. *Vocational Guidance in the High School.* Psychological Clinic, Vol. IX, No. 6, Nov. 15, 1915, pp. 161–166.

Giddings, Franklin H. *The Child as a Member of Society.* Teachers College Record, Vol. 16, No. 5, Nov. 1915, pp. 21–30.

Gilbreth, Frank B. *Primer of Scientific Management.* D. Van Nostrand Company, 1912.

Giles, F. M. *Guidance by Systematic Courses of Instruction in Vocational Opportunities and Personal Characteristics.* In Vocational Guidance, United States Bureau of Education Bulletin, 1914, No. 14, pp. 52–59.

Gillette, John M. *Vocational Education.* American Book Co., 1910.

Girls' Trade Education League, of Boston. Several bulletins, "Vocations for Boston Girls," 1913.

Goldmark, Josephine. *Fatigue and Efficiency.* Charities Publication Committee, 1912.

Goodwin, Frank P. See Bloomfield's *Readings*, pp. 129–140.

Gowin, Enoch B., and Wheatley, William A. *Occupations.* Ginn and Company, 1916.

Greany, Ellen M. *A Study of the Vocational Guidance of Grammar School Pupils.* Educational Administration and Supervision, Vol. I, No. 3, March, 1915, pp. 173–194. Also in Bloomfield's *Readings*, pp. 267–287.

Gruenberg, Benjamin C. *Vocational Guidance and Efficiency.* Pamphlet by the Vocational Guidance Association of New York, taken from the Scientific American, Vol. 110, pp. 312–318, April 11, 1914.

——. *Why is Vocational Guidance?* Reprint for the Vocational Guidance Association of New York, 1914.

Hamburgischen Gesellschaft zur Beförderung der Künste und nützlichen Gewerbe. *Ratgeber für Berufswahl.* I. Teil, Meiszners, Hamburg, 1907.

Hancock, Harris. *What Course of Study should be Taken by a Boy who is Entering High School?* School and Society, Vol. I, No. 25, June 19, 1915, pp. 893–900.

Haney, James Parton. *Art Education in the Public Schools of the United States.* American Art Annual, New York, 1908.

Hanus, Paul H. *Beginnings in Industrial Education,* and other educational discussions. Houghton Mifflin Company, 1908.

Hanus, Paul H. *School Efficiency, a Constructive Study Applied to New York City.* World Book Company, 1913.

——. *Vocational Guidance and Public Education.* The School Review, Vol. 19, No. 1, Jan. 1911, pp. 51–56. Also in Bloomfield's *Readings*, pp. 92–95.

Harper, Jane R. *A Survey of Opportunities for Vocational Education in and near Philadelphia.* Public Education Association, Philadelphia, 1915.

Haynes, John. *Economics in the High School.* Houghton Mifflin Company, 1914.

Healy, William. *The Individual Delinquent.* Little, Brown and Co., 1915.

Heck, W. H. *Mental Discipline and Educational Values.* John Lane Company, 1909.

Hicks, Warren E. See Wisconsin.

Hill, David Spence. *Facts about the Public Schools of New Orleans in Relation to Vocation.* Commission Council, New Orleans, 1914.

——. *The Problem of Vocational Guidance in the South.* Nat. Voc. Guid. Assn., Proc., 1914, pp. 36–44.

——. *Survey of the Industries and Mechanical Operations in New Orleans by the Division of Research.* School and Society, Vol. II, Nos. 38 and 39, pp. 421–427 and 461–466.

Hollingworth, H. L. *Specialized Vocational Tests and Methods.* School and Society, Vol. I, No. 26, June 26, 1915, pp. 918–922.

——. *Vocational Psychology.* D. Appleton and Co., 1916.

Hopkins, Ernest M. See Willits, The Unemployed, etc.

Horton, D. W. *A Plan for Vocational Guidance.* The School Review, Vol. 23, No. 4, April, 1915, pp. 236–243.

Hoxie, Robert F. *Scientific Management and Labor.* D. Appleton and Company, 1915.

Hyde, William DeWitt. *Self-Measurement.* B. W. Huebsch, 1908.

Intercollegiate Bureau of Occupations. *Opportunities in Occupations other than Teaching.* Published by the Bureau, 1915.

Jacobs, Charles L. *An Experiment in High School Vocational Guidance.* Manual Training and Vocational Education, Vol. XVII, No. 2, Oct. 1915, pp. 81–85.

James, William. *The Moral Equivalent of War.* American Association for International Conciliation, 1910.

——. *Principles of Psychology.* 1893.

Jennings, Irwin G. *Vocational Guidance in Colleges and Universities.* Educational Review, Vol. 51, No. 4, April, 1916, 331–341.

Jevons, W. Stanley. *Political Economy.* American Book Company, 1878.

Johnson, George E. *Education by Plays and Games.* Ginn and Company, 1907.

——. *Education through Recreation.* The Survey Committee of the Cleveland Foundation, 1916.

——. *The Place of Play in a Liberal Education.* Harvard Teachers' Association Leaflet, Vol. I, No. 3, Dec. 1915.

Judd, Charles H. *Psychology of High-School Subjects.* Ginn and Company, 1915.

——. *The Relation of Special Training to General Intelligence.* Educational Review, Vol. 36, No. 1, June, 1908, pp. 28–42.

Kelley, Truman L. *Educational Guidance.* Teachers College, Columbia University, Contributions to Education, No. 71, 1914.

Kelly, Roy Willmarth. *Hiring the Worker.* The Engineering Magazine Company, 1917.

Kitson, H. D. *Suggestions toward a Tenable Theory of Vocational Guidance.* Manual Training and Vocational Education, Vol. XV, No. 5, Jan. 1915, pp. 265–270. Also in Bloomfield's *Readings,* pp. 103–108.

——. *Psychological Tests and Vocational Guidance.* The School Review, Vol. 24, No. 3, March, 1916, pp. 207–214.

Lapp, John A., and Mote, Carl H. *Learning to Earn.* Bobbs-Merrill Company, 1915.

Laselle, Mary A., and Wiley, Katherine E. *Vocations for Girls.* Houghton Mifflin Company, 1913.

Lathrop, Julia C. *Some Items to be Considered in a Vocational Guidance Program.* Nat. Voc. Guid. Assn., Proc. 1914, pp. 49–50.

Leavitt, Frank M. *Examples of Industrial Education.* Ginn and Company, 1912.

——. *President's Address,* Nat. Voc. Guid. Assn., Proc. 1914, pp. 5–7.

——. *The School Phases of Vocational Guidance.* The School Review, Vol. 23, No. 10, Dec. 1915, pp. 687–696.

——. *Some Sociological Phases of the Movement for Industrial Education.* Nat. Educ. Assn., Proc. 1912, pp. 921–926. Also, American Journal of Sociology, Vol. XVIII, No. 3, Nov. 1912, pp. 352–360.

—— and Brown, Edith. *Prevocational Education in the Public Schools.* Houghton Mifflin Company, 1915.

Lee, Joseph. *Play in Education.* The Macmillan Company, 1915.

Lord, Everett W. *Vocational Direction or the Boy and his Job.* In Nat. Child Labor Comm., Proc., 1910, pp. 73–85.

Los Angeles. *Report of Superintendent of Schools,* year ending June 30, 1914.

——. *Vocational Bulletin No. 1.* Los Angeles School Department, 1914.

Lough, James E. *Experimental Psychology in Vocational Guidance.* Nat. Conference on Voc. Guid., 1912, Proc. pp. 89–96.

Lovejoy, Owen R. *Vocational Guidance and Child Labor.* United States Bureau of Education Bulletin, 1914, No. 14, Vocational Guidance, pp. 9–16.

Lull, Herbert G. *Vocational Instruction in the High School.* Manual Training and Vocational Education, Vol. XVI, No. 9, May, 1915, pp. 529–536.

MacCarthy, Jessie Howell. *Where Garments and Americans are Made.* (The Sicher System.) Writers' Publishing Co., 1917.

Manly. See Commission on Industrial Relations.

Martin, Charles. *Developing Placement and Follow-up Work.* United States Bureau of Education Bulletin, 1914, No. 14, pp. 64–66.

Massachusetts Board of Education. *Annual Report, 79th.* 1916.

——. *The Needs and Possibilities of Part-Time Education.* A special report submitted to the legislature, 1913.

——. *Revised Laws Relating to Public Instruction,* 1915.

Massachusetts Committee on Unemployment. *Why Labor Exchanges?* Bulletin No. 1, 1915.

McCann, Mathew R. *The Fitchburg Plan of Coöperative Industrial Education.* United States Bureau of Education Bulletin, 1913, No. 50.

Mead, A. D. *Orientation Courses for Freshmen at Brown University.* School and Society, Vol. III, No. 64, March 18, 1916, p. 428.

Mead, George Herbert. *The Larger Educational Bearings of Vocational Guidance.* United States Bureau of Education Bulletin, 1914, No. 14, pp. 16–26. Also in Bloomfield's *Readings*, pp. 43–55.

Miles. See Nat. Assn. of Manufacturers.

Minneapolis Survey. See Nat. Soc. for Prom. of Indust. Educ.

Mitchell, John. *The Wage Earner and His Problems.* P. S. Ridsdale, Washington, D. C., 1913.

Moore, Ernest Carroll. *What is Education?* Ginn and Company, 1915.

Münsterberg, Hugo. *Psychology and Industrial Efficiency.* Houghton Mifflin Company, 1913.

Myers, George E. *Bibliography of Surveys Bearing on Vocational Education.* Manual Training and Vocational Education, Vol. XVII, No. 5, Jan. 1916, pp. 372–377.

——. *Problems of Vocational Education in Germany*, with special application to conditions in the United States. United States Bureau of Education, Bulletin, 1915, No. 33.

National Association of Corporation Schools. *Third Annual Convention*, Papers and Reports, 1915.

National Association of Manufacturers. *Industrial Education.* Report of a committee, H. E. Miles, chairman, 1915. Reprinted by Bureau of Education, Washington.

National Conference on Vocational Guidance, Proceedings of the Second, New York City, 1912; auspices The Central Committee on Vocational Guidance, New York City.

National Society for the Promotion of Industrial Education. *Report of the Minneapolis Survey for Vocational Education.* Published by the society, Bulletin No. 21, 1916.

National Society for the Study of Education. *The Fourteenth Yearbook.* Part I, Minimum Essentials in Elementary-School subjects. The University of Chicago Press, 1915.

National Vocational Guidance Association. Proceedings of the 1913 meeting at Grand Rapids. Published as Vocational Guidance, United States Bureau of Education Bulletin, 1914, No. 14. See Bureau of Education, above, with names quoted.

——. Proceedings of the Richmond meeting, 1914. Published by the association, 1915.

——. Vocational Guidance Bulletin, beginning 1915.

Nearing, Scott. *Wages in the United States.* The Macmillan Company, 1911.

New York City Board of Education. Committee on High Schools and Training Schools. Report on *Vocational Guidance,* 1914. Reprinted in Bloomfield's *Readings,* pp. 288–345.

——. Superintendent of Schools, 16th annual report, year ending July 31, 1914.

New York City Central Committee on Vocational Guidance. *Some Aspects of Vocational Guidance.* 1912.

Odencrantz, Louise C. *Placement Work for Women and Girls in New York City.* Manual Training and Vocational Education, Vol. XVII, No. 3, Nov. 1915, pp. 169–177.

Overstreet, H. *The Community Brain.* The New Republic, Vol. VI, No. 70, March 4, 1916, pp. 128–129.

Parsons, Belle Ragnor. *Plays and Games for Indoors and Outdoors.* A. S. Barnes and Company, 1909.

Parsons, Frank. *Choosing a Vocation.* Houghton Mifflin Company, 1909.

Perkins, Frances. Summary of the discussion on occupations. Second National Conference, Proceedings, pp. 56–58.

Pillsbury, W. B. *The Effects of Training on Memory.* Educational Review, Vol. 36, No. 1, June, 1908, pp. 15–27.

—— and others. *Latin and Greek in American Education.* The Macmillan Company, 1911.

Pritchard, Myron T., and Turkington, Grace A. *Stories of Thrift for Young Americans.* Charles Scribner's Sons, 1915.

Prosser, Charles A. *Practical Arts and Vocational Guidance.* Manual Training Magazine, Vol. XIV, No. 6, Feb. 1913, pp. 209-221. Also in Bloomfield's *Readings*, pp. 235-367.

Puffer, J. Adams. *Vocational Guidance.* Rand McNally and Company, 1913.

Rathmann, Carl G. *The Educational Museum of the St. Louis Public Schools.* United States Bureau of Education Bulletin, 1914, No. 48.

Readings. See Bloomfield, *Readings in Vocational Guidance.*

Redfield, William C. *The New Industrial Day.* The Century Company, 1913.

Reed, Anna Y. *Vocational Guidance Report, 1913-1916.* Board of School Directors, Seattle, Wash., 1916.

Reed College Record. Catalog. 1914-1915. Reed College, Portland, Oregon.

Richards, Charles R. *What We Need to Know about Occupations.* Nat. Conference on Vocational Guidance, Proc. of Second, 1912, pp. 35-44. Also in *Readings*, Bloomfield, pp. 405-514.

——. *How Shall we Study the Industries for the Purposes of Vocational Education?* United States Bureau of Education Bulletin, 1914, No. 14, pp. 73-79.

Richards, Lysander S. *Vocophy.* Pratt Bros., Marlboro, 1881.

Richmond Survey. See Bureau of Labor Statistics.

Righter, Leonard. *The Curriculum and Vocational Guidance.* The Elementary School Journal, Vol. XVI, No. 7, March, 1916, pp. 369-380.

Rochester Bulletins. Pamphlets issued by the Department of Public Instruction, Rochester, New York, N. Y., 1915.

Roman, Frederick W. *Vocational Education — Its Dependence upon Elementary Cultural Training.* N. E. A. Addresses and Proc. 1915, pp. 1173-1177.

Schneider, Herman. *Education for Industrial Workers.* World Book Company, 1915. School Efficiency Series.

——. *Selecting Young Men for Particular Jobs.* American Machinist, April 10, 1913. Also in Bloomfield's *Readings*, pp. 368-378.

Scott, Colin A. *Social Education.* Ginn and Company, 1908.

x

Scott, Walter Dill. *Influencing Men in Business.* Roland Press Company, 1911.

———. *The Scientific Selection of Salesmen.* Advertising and Selling Magazine, Vol. 25, Nos. 5, 6, and 7, Oct., Nov., and Dec., 1915. See also American Academy.

Sears, J. B. *Occupations of Fathers and Occupational Choices of 1039 Boys in Grades Seven and Eight of the Oakland Schools.* School and Society, Vol. I, No. 21, May 22, 1915, pp. 752–756.

Seashore, Carl Emile. *The Measurement of Pitch Discrimination.* Psychological Review Monographs, Vol. 13, No. 1, (Whole No. 53), 1910, pp. 21–60.

Second National Conference on Vocational Guidance. See National Conference.

Shorey, Paul. *The Assault on Humanism.* Atlantic Monographs. Atlantic Monthly Company, 1917.

Somerville, Mass., School Committee. Report of Committee on Vocational Guidance. In annual report, 1910, p. 23.

Spaulding, F. E. *Problems of Vocational Guidance.* N. E. A., Dept. of Superintendence, 1915 Proc., pp. 83–86. N. E. A. Addresses and Proc., 1915, pp. 331–334. Also in Bloomfield's *Readings*, pp. 69–74.

Stimson, R. W. *The Massachusetts Home Project Plan of Vocational Agricultural Education.* United States Bureau of Education, Bulletin, 1914, No. 8.

Taylor, Frederick Winslow. *The Principles of Scientific Management.* Harper and Brothers, 1911.

Thompson, Clarence B. (ed.). *Scientific Management.* Harvard University Press, 1914.

Thompson, Frank V. *Commercial Education.* Being Chapter X in United States Commissioner of Education, Report, 1915, Part I, pp. 279–283.

———. *Commercial Education in Public Secondary Schools.* World Book Company, 1915. School Efficiency Series.

———. *Vocational Guidance in Boston.* Nat. Voc. Guid. Assn., Proc. 1914, pp. 17–24. Also The School Review, Vol. 23, No. 2, Feb. 1915, pp. 105–112.

Thorndike, Edward L. *Educational Psychology.* Teachers College, Columbia University, 1914. In three volumes: *The Original Nature of Man, The Psychology of Learning and Work, and Fatigue and Individual Differences.*

——. *Educational Psychology.* Briefer Course, Teachers College, Columbia University, 1914.

——. *The Permanence of Interests and their Relation to Abilities.* Popular Science Monthly, Vol. LXXXI, No. 5, Nov. 1912, pp. 449–456. Also in Bloomfield's *Readings,* pp. 386–395.

Thum, William. *A Forward Step.* The Twentieth Century Company, 1910.

Todd, Arthur J. *Old Age and the Industrial Scrap Heap.* Quarterly Publication of the American Statistical Assn., Vol. XIV, New Series, No. 110, June, 1915, pp. 550–566.

Unpopular Review. See Breese.

Van Denburg, Joseph K. *Causes of the Elimination of Students in Public Secondary Schools of New York City.* Teachers College, Columbia University, Contributions to Education, No. 47, 1911.

Van Sickle, James H. *Education in the Larger Cities.* Being Chapter II in United States Commissioner of Education, Report, 1915, Part I, pp. 27–46.

——. *The Vocational Trend in Education.* Editorial in Educational Administration and Supervision, Vol. I, No. 1, Jan. 1915, pp. 67–68.

Veblen, Thorstein. *The Nature of Peace.* The Macmillan Company, 1917.

The Vocation Bureau of Boston. *Vocational Guidance and the Work of the Vocation Bureau of Boston.* 1915 report.

Vocational Guidance Bulletin. See Nat. Voc. Guid. Assn.

Ward, Lester F. *Applied Sociology.* Ginn and Company, 1906.

——. *Eugenics, Euthenics, and Eudemics.* American Journal of Sociology, Vol. 18, No. 6, May, 1913, pp. 737–757.

Weaver, E. W. *Vocations for Girls.* The A. S. Barnes Company, 1913.

—— and Byler, J. Frank. *Profitable Vocations for Boys.* The A. S. Barnes Company, 1915.

Wells, Ralph G. See American Academy. Personnel, etc.

Westgate, C. E. *Vocational Guidance in the Stadium High School.* Tacoma, Wash. Manual Training and Vocational Education, Vol. XVII, No. 7, March, 1916, pp. 511–514.

Wheatley, William A. *Some Suggestions for Presenting a Course in Vocational Information to Pupils in our Smaller Schools.* Nat. Voc. Guid. Assn., Proc. 1914, pp. 24–29.

——. *Vocational Information for Pupils in a Small City High School.* The School Review, Vol. 23, No. 3, March, 1915, pp. 175–180.

Wile, Ira S. *Vocational Guidance and the Curriculum.* Nat. Voc. Guid. Assn., Proc., 1914, pp. 29–35.

Willits, Joseph H. *The Labor Turnover and the Humanizing of Industry.* American Academy of Political and Social Science, Annals, Sept. 1915, Publication No. 929.

——. *The Unemployed in Philadelphia.* Dept. of Public Works, Philadelphia, 1915. Also in Supp. to Annals, May, 1916.

Winch, W. H. *Further Experimental Researches on Learning to Spell.* The Journal of Educational Psychology, Vol. V, No. 8, Oct. 1914, pp. 449–460.

Wisconsin State Board of Industrial Education. *Outlines of Lessons.* No. 10, Second Edition, 1914.

Women's Educational and Industrial Union. *The Public Schools and Women in Office Service.* Boston, 1914.

Women's Municipal League of Boston. *Opportunities for Vocational Training in Boston,* 1913.

Wood, Arthur Evans. *A Study of the Unemployed.* Reed College Record, No. 18, Dec. 1914.

Woods, Erville B. *The Social Waste of Unguided Personal Ability.* American Journal of Sociology, Vol. XIX, No. 3, Nov. 1913, pp. 358–369. Also in Bloomfield's *Readings,* pp. 19–31.

Woods, Robert A., and Kennedy, Albert J. *Young Working Girls.* Houghton Mifflin Company, 1913.

Woolley, Helen Thompson. *Charting Children in Cincinnati.* The Survey, Vol. 30, No. 19, Aug. 9, 1913, pp. 601–606. Also in Bloomfield's *Readings,* pp. 220–233.

Woolley, Helen Thompson. *The Legal Registration of Certificates as an Aid to Follow-up Work.* Nat. Conference on Voc. Guid., 1912, Proc., pp. 27–30.

——. *A New Scale of Mental and Physical Measurements for Adolescents, and Some of its Uses.* The Journal of Educational Psychology, Vol. VI, No. 9, Nov. 1915, pp. 521–550.

——. *The Present Trend of Vocational Guidance in the United States.* United States Bureau of Education, Bulletin, 1914, No. 14, Vocational Guidance, pp. 43–47.

——. *The Psychological Laboratory as an Adjunct to a Vocational Bureau.* Nat. Conference of Voc. Guid., Proc., 1912, pp. 84–88.

Woolman, Mrs. Mary Schenck. *Investigations, the Need and Value.* Nat. Conference on Voc. Guid., Proc., 1912, pp. 53–56.

Wright, F. W. *Bridging the Gap — The Transfer Class.* The Harvard-Newton Bulletins, Harvard University Press, 1915.

APPENDIX III

PROBLEMS AND QUESTIONS

Chapter I: Problems of Vocational Guidance

1. Do you think that cultural or moral ideals are likely to be neglected if the child begins to think about his vocational future? Give reasons.

2. Justify or refute the statement of a recent commencement orator, that the purpose of the high school is to keep boys and girls from thinking about making a living.

3. Criticise the statement, attributed to a college dean, that when a student begins to select courses with his future occupation in mind, at that moment his education ends.

4. Discuss the difference between education and training, with illustrations. Do they work together, or separately?

5. If vocational guidance is so much needed, how do you account for the indifference of teachers, principals, and superintendents?

6. Draw up a statement to show the need for vocational guidance in your community. Make it concrete and comprehensive. Direct it at one of the following: your principal; your superintendent of schools; the board of education; a teachers' association; a women's club; a chamber of commerce or board of trade; a labor union; a legislative body.

7. What methods can you propose for doing away with the erroneous guidance of magazine advertisements?

8. Interview a person of educational, industrial, or commercial importance, for the purpose of finding out his attitude toward vocational guidance. Report the result to the class.

9. How do you think it has happened that the act of placement seems to some persons to express the chief function of the vocational-guidance movement?

10. Show how placement, if well done, would inevitably lead to other activities in guidance.

11. Can you see any objection to the statement that the kernel of truth in the vocational-guidance movement is vocational education? What would be the dangers involved in vocational education without vocational guidance?

12. Do you indorse Van Sickle's statement on page 14? Would vocational guidance in a school endanger the cultural studies? If so, how may this difficulty be avoided?

13. Certain other names have been suggested, to take the place of vocational guidance. Study the expressions here given, using the dictionary, and reach a conclusion which satisfies you. Be prepared to criticise each suggested name, and to defend your preference.

> Occupational guidance.
> Occupational direction.
> Vocational direction.
> Vocational enlightenment.
> Vocational help.
> Educational and vocational guidance.
> Vocational and moral guidance.
> Life-career direction.
> Occupational information.

Have you other names to propose?

Chapter II: Beginnings

1. Why is it that so many attempts are made to choose vocations by occult and short-cut methods? Do you see any hope in such methods? Why?

2. Study Parsons' book to find his references to psychology. Are his statements justified? Have the hopes he expresses been realized? Has progress been made?

3. Study the "cases" described by Parsons. What do you think are the advantages and disadvantages of this method? Propose amendments to the plan, to make it more satisfactory.

4. In view of the activities of the Vocation Bureau of Boston, what other lines of work might be undertaken by such an institution?

5. Do you think the Boston plan is best, the high schools being more or less independent from the central office in their vocational-guidance work? Write a defense of the Boston plan, or propose a plan for coöperation.

6. In view of the plans outlined in this chapter, draw up a brief set of specifications for starting systematic work in guidance in your school or school system.

7. If it were necessary to concentrate time, energy, and money on one phase of vocational-guidance work, what do you think should be the kind of work selected?

8. Write to one of the cities or institutions mentioned as carrying on activity in guidance, for the purpose of finding out about the latest developments in the work.

9. What are the advantages of voluntary as against paid work in vocational guidance, on the part of teachers?

10. Make a statement giving the advantages and disadvantages of vocational guidance offered by Christian Associations and churches.

11. Interview secretaries of associations or pastors of churches, to find out what work in vocational guidance they are doing. Find out if they have any criticisms of the school's effort to guide pupils. Give your report in class.

12. Investigate and report to class on the readjustments and guidance made necessary on account of the European War.

Chapter III: Guidance through Education

1. Give instances to show the superior importance of educational guidance. Is this true for all children, or only for those likely to go into the professions?

2. What moral qualities does the child develop through play and in the kindergarten? Give concrete examples.

3. Visit a museum in your vicinity and note whether it appeals merely to the sense of the curious, or whether it also aids in the interpretation of the common problems of life.

4. Draw up a program of studies for the fifth or sixth grade, with vocational guidance in mind.

5. Show how geography, reading, or drawing can be used to give vocational enlightenment.

6. Make out a tentative scheme for the studies of the junior high school age.

7. Discuss the dangers, so far as effective vocational guidance is concerned, in the plan of having separate courses of study for different groups of pupils in the intermediate school (or high school).

8. Find out the vocational aims of pupils in one of the technical or vocational courses in the high school. For example, find out whether or not boys and girls in the commercial course are going into commercial occupations. What result do you find and what conclusions do you draw?

9. Outline plans for boys and girls to earn money while attending school. What cautions must be exercised?

10. Is there danger that vocational guidance will tempt children out of school? If so, how can this difficulty be obviated?

11. Examine the list of literary masterpieces used in the English work of your school, to see if they furnish any opportunity for discussing occupational problems. Report your findings, showing how opportunities may be utilized.

12. Discuss with a high school class the proposition of using for outside reading such books as Allen's *Business Employments*, Gowin and Wheatley's *Occupations*, and Weaver and Byler's *Profitable Vocations for Girls*. Find out how many would like to use such books; or report upon actual use.

13. Investigate the need for and use of parliamentary law in occupations, asking a number of persons to give their testimony on these points. In view of your findings, do you think parliamentary law should be taught in the high school?

14. Examine a standard textbook in arithmetic. Do you think it aims to furnish problems related to occupational life? Give to the class a criticism of the book, in the light of vocational guidance.

15. Prepare plans for using history for vocational guidance purposes. Outline your proposals before the class, giving illustrations.

16. Show how the ability to draw is necessary in many kinds of occupations.

17. Discuss the proposition: The ability to talk well is a necessity in many occupations and an asset in all, therefore the school should do systematic work in oral English.

18. Examine several textbooks in algebra, arithmetic, or geometry, to find out which ones have most reference to problems met in actual life. Report to the class.

19. Examine several books used as readers (or foreign language textbooks). Are they filled merely with stories and appeals to curiosity, or are they supplied with some material helpful for vocational guidance?

20. Investigate the books in a library. Are enough of them related to occupational life?

21. How can public libraries aid in vocational guidance, aside from having the necessary books?

22. Outline a plan for your school to utilize the student affairs and outside activities of the pupils for the development of qualities useful for vocational guidance.

23. What arguments are there for having separate schools for the prevocational and continuation school work?

24. What arguments are there for having the intermediate or junior high school do prevocational and continuation work?

25. What unsatisfactory conditions are likely to arise in a system of vocational education without vocational guidance?

26. Do you think that good traits of character are more easily developed in a school offering only instruction in academic subjects, or in one offering a variety of subjects and other activities? Give reasons.

Chapter IV: Counseling

1. How do you explain the desire to devise "psychological tests" for vocational guidance? Why are school examinations unsatisfactory for testing vocational aptitudes? How could they be made more effective for this purpose?

2. Prepare a blank form for securing teachers' opinions on qualities manifested by pupils.

3. Secure an application blank from a firm of good reputation. What qualities does their card take into consideration? Do you think the schools aid in the development of these good qualities? Would the teachers be able to state whether or not a boy or girl possesses these qualities?

4. Give illustrations to show the difficulties encountered in talking about qualities in the abstract, without relation to specific situations.

5. Propose plans for determining whether or not children will develop a high degree of each of several good qualities.

6. Prepare a record card for the purposes of vocational guidance in your school, the card to be used for data about individual pupils.

7. Interview some of the persons who find jobs for children in your community. Can you say that they offer these children adequate vocational guidance?

8. Secure the names and address (1) of those who graduated from your school during the last school year, and (2) of those who left school during the same time. Find out what they are now doing and report your information. (Aid of other teachers and of pupils may be secured, and the investigation may be indefinitely elaborated.)

9. Outline a plan by which you might do part-time teaching and part-time employment supervision.

10. Interview the employment manager of a factory, store, or other business. What aims has he, and what methods does he use?

11. What is the significance, for the vocational guidance of workers, in the movement to have managers in charge of employment?

12. In what ways could the school coöperate with the employment managers?

13. Talk with some of your friends in various occupations, in regard to the plan of having occupational advisors to whom advanced pupils might go for counsel. In view of your conversations, do you think such a plan would be feasible?

14. Prepare a circular letter which might be sent out to men and women in all walks of life, asking if they will join in the work of advising parents and children about occupations.

15. Find out from some persons in professional occupations, and from some in industrial or commercial pursuits, what decisions and changes of decisions they made, in their vocational progress. Try to analyze the causes of their changes of mind, and to determine whether or not these changes were detrimental to success.

16. Draw up a brief list of questions to be investigated in determining the characteristics and requirements of an occupation. Make the list an appropriate one for the use of high-school students, so that they may obtain the answers by visits and interviews.

17. Outline a plan for a vocational-guidance survey of your community, to be made either (1) by the advanced pupils of your school, or (2) by the faculty, or (3) by persons experienced in vocational guidance.

18. Do you think that brief pamphlets on occupations can be used in the schoolroom? How would you use such printed matter, and what do you think would be the results?

19. Is it necessary that a vocational counselor should at the same time be a teacher? Should he have had teaching experience? Should he have had experience in several occupations?

20. Is there any justification for the statement, "The counselor for boys should always be a man, and for girls a woman"?

21. Discuss the present policy of a city in paying certain vocational counselors in the high schools less salary than is paid to "regular" teachers of academic subjects.

Chapter V: Pseudo-Guidance

1. Look up the records of several pupils in "abstract" studies and in "concrete" subjects. Do you find that those good in one kind of studies are poor in the other kind? Is there a positive or negative relationship between school marks in "abstract" and "concrete" studies? If possible, work out some correlation formulas to show the facts.

2. Show how a boy who says he dislikes books may be treated.

3. How would you help order the educational work of a boy or girl who professes to dislike all handwork?

4. Give instances to show the need for *every person*, no matter how high or low his position, to be upon occasion a leader, and upon other occasions a follower.

5. Show how the school can develop for every pupil the ability to lead and to follow.

6. Examine the book "Vocational Psychology," by Hollingworth (Appleton), and review its conclusions for the class.

7. Visit two or three progressive businesses and inquire what tests they apply to find out the aptitudes and abilities of those who apply to them for work. What results do they claim for these tests?

8. Propose many different plans for securing a pupil's dependability (or any other good quality).

9. Propose plans for testing a pupil's ability to "concentrate his mind."

10. Propose a valid test to determine a pupil's "ability to follow directions."

11. Cite instances of men and women who have overcome apparent physical handicaps in their occupational progress. If convenient, bring direct testimony and opinion in these matters to class.

12. Have you ever heard of any way to determine "native ability" as differentiated from "acquired ability"? Do you think there is justification for using either adjective? Would it be useful to speak of latent and actual ability? Do you think of any methods to measure latent ability?

13. What vocational advice might you give to a very small young man who wishes to be a policeman, or to a girl who fails to study but wishes to become an actress?

14. What reply would you make to this proposition: "It would be a serious mistake to engage as a maker of lace a person with skin and hair of coarse texture"?

15. In spite of its dangers, has not self-analysis a great value, at least for mature persons? Outline these values and propose a "safe and sane" method.

16. Discuss this problem in connection with "over-guidance": Has anybody ever the right or duty to tell a person exactly what

he should or should not do in the matter of a pending vocational decision? Give reasons and illustrations.

17. Suppose there is a commercial agency in your town, run by a well-meaning person, for giving vocational advice. How would you go about putting the work completely on an educational basis?

18. At the vocational-guidance convention at Philadelphia, one of the members proposed that the federal government should be asked to deny the use of the mails to magazines printing advertisements which are questionable from the standpoint of good vocational guidance. What are your comments on this proposition?

19. Interview the persons in your community who are interested in offering courses in salesmanship. Do you find that these persons have an approvable social understanding of the relationship of their work to the welfare of society? What cautions do they exercise to prevent unsocial practices?

20. State the advantages that might come from assigning the work in vocational guidance to another department of educational endeavor.

Chapter VI: The Young Worker

1. Explain the difficulties which meet the investigator who tries to find out why children leave school. What precautions must be taken?

2. Make a study of a limited number of cases of pupils who have left school during the past year. What results do you find, and what remedies do you propose?

3. Investigate the use of child labor during war time. Was it necessary and profitable to lower the standards?

4. Investigate and report upon the work of the National Child Labor Committee.

5. Look up and report upon the laws governing the labor of minors in your city and state.

6. Make an appraisement of the ways open to children in your community for obtaining work. Discuss the advantages and disadvantages of the present facilities, and suggest possible improvements.

7. In view of the fact that children can rarely obtain really good jobs, do you feel that this is an argument for keeping them out of all employment, or for organizing a plan to make these first jobs stepping stones to better positions?

8. Outline a good plan for helping a boy or girl to understand the duties of a position. Do you think business firms are definite enough in instructions to beginners? Is the indefiniteness which exists due to mere neglect, or to other reasons?

9. Consult an employment manager of a progressive firm, and report what he has to say on the problem of juvenile labor.

10. Schneider says that school people claim that employers would be unwilling to organize their juvenile help on a part-time plan; he says, too, that employers claim that the school people would be the obstructors. What is your opinion in this matter? If possible, gather some evidence.

Chapter VII: Problems of Employment

1. Is it necessary that the present school pupils understand labor problems? Give reasons and instances.

2. Why is it necessary for counselors to understand scientific management?

3. One of the writers on scientific management or "positive management" states that under the plan advocated matters would rest on a "fact basis," and thus disputes would be avoided or easily settled. Criticise this statement.

4. What is the difficulty with the statements, "a fair day's pay for a fair day's work," "labor should have what it earns," "the product of labor should go to the laborer"?

5. Make a list of the things that you think a store or factory could do to steady its force; i.e. to decrease turnover; to keep its help.

6. Discuss the relative advantages to the child in filling several positions during the course of a year as against sticking to one job.

7. Investigate one or more of these problems in a store or factory: Americanization; safety-first; recreation; profit-sharing; breaking in new workmen; tendencies toward a more democratic management.

8. It is often said that the *interests* of the employer and the worker are identical. Even if this be so, are the *problems* of each the same? Discuss these questions.

9. What kind of guidance do you think is necessary for persons seeking work? What is the difference between an employment bureau and a labor exchange? Should the problem of juvenile help be kept separate from adult employment? What part in the process of securing employment should the worker himself take? How should young girls secure employment?

10. During active periods of labor what steps need to be taken to provide against unemployment in dull times?

11. In dull times should city, state, and nation employ more men than usual? Outline a plan for government action to prevent or alleviate unemployment.

12. What has the problem of unemployment to do with the question of versatility as against specialization in vocational education?

13. Investigate the subject of collective bargaining, in encyclopedias or other sources, and in actual practice if you can interview persons who have been parties to such agreements. Report your findings and conclusions.

14. Make out a list of five or more problems upon which the schools and the labor organizations can coöperate. Outline plans for such coöperation.

15. Make an investigation and report on one of the following topics: labor turnover; duties and opportunities of the foreman or overseer; the kinds of labor organizations and their aims and methods; the American Federation of Labor; the Industrial Workers of the World; the land tax or single tax; land tenure and the farmer; farm mortgages; attitude of various political parties toward labor problems; workingmen's compensation; old age pensions; conciliation and arbitration; profit-sharing; welfare work.

16. Suppose a boy of sixteen to eighteen years is about to become an operative in a large factory which is run on the scientific-management plan. Write him a brief statement concerning things he needs to know or the problems he will meet.

17. Suppose a young man asks you whether or not he should join the union. What reply would you give him?

18. A man interested in employment problems states that no one should be employed unless he can earn a living wage. He says that in that case the education, training, or care of the unemployed would become a social problem, "as it should be," and that "poverty would be driven out into the open" where it can be cured. Discuss this point of view.

19. Do you think that a firm profits most from a given sum invested in cheap labor or in expensive? Give illustrations and reasons.

20. Discuss the aims and methods of corporation schools.

21. Discuss the general question: How can the vocational counselor aid in the work of improving labor conditions?

22. Outline plans which you intend to try to carry out, as your contribution to the cause of industrial betterment.

23. Discuss this proposition: A high-school course in elementary social and economic problems is of greater importance to the welfare of the individual (or the community) than the course in occupations.

Chapter VIII: A Constructive Program

1. Examine some modern geography textbooks for the purpose of finding out what contribution they make to occupational enlightenment. Report your findings, with plans for improving such books.

2. Study the proposed list of subjects for children twelve to sixteen years of age, given on page 231, and revise it in the light of your own experience and educational ideas. Be prepared to defend your proposals.

3. What reply would you make to a principal who says, "Difficulties connected with drawing up the school program make it impossible to provide so many studies or to have courses shorter than a half year"?

4. Investigate the availability and the limitations of the "project method" for teaching in the intermediate or high school.

x

5. Is there any educational justification for the practice of organizing specialized high schools? Should Greek and blacksmithing be under one roof, or is it best to separate them in different types of schools?

6. Outline the arguments, in relation to vocational guidance, for one of the following: summer camps; scouting activities; student self-government.

7. Do you see any objections to the plan of having every teacher alert to find and utilize the vocational-guidance implications in every lesson? Is there danger of overdoing the matter?

8. Discuss the proposition that the vocational counselor should at the same time carry on teaching and investigating as well as counseling.

9. Draw up a plan for the organization of a vocational-guidance bureau in your city.

10. Find out the attitude toward vocational guidance on the part of one of the following: your school superintendent; the state board of education or commissioner of education; the federal Bureau of Education. Do you know of other officials or persons in high positions who are interested? Give a report of your findings, with suggestions for utilizing their interest and help.

11. Outline a plan for collecting information about occupations, and draw up an appropriate list of topics under which to classify the data obtained.

12. Prepare a list of topics in vocational guidance for the consideration of parents' meetings.

13. What attitude should the counselor take toward a parent who insists that his son or daughter ought to decide on an occupation at once? Draw up a letter or statement for such a parent.

14. Study some plans for issuing work certificates, and outline a plan for your city.

15. Prepare a blank card to be signed by the employer before a working certificate is issued.

16. Cincinnati data seem to show that those young workers who finally secure best positions are those who have changed their jobs one or more times during the year. Is there an educative value in changing jobs? Why? How should it be safeguarded?

17. Prepare a blank and outline a method for a follow-up investigation.

18. What kind of an employer is "Uncle Sam"? Investigate conditions of labor in some department of federal service, and report your findings, with recommendations.

19. Are there any tendencies toward democratic management in city or state service? In the teaching profession?

20. What reply should be made to a principal's statement, "Pupils must not allow outside work to interfere with school duties"?

21. What is meant by the statement, "Blind alleys must be opened"? Outline a plan for doing it.

22. Discuss the truth or falsity of one of the following proverbs, from the standpoint of vocational guidance, giving illustrations:

> A rolling stone gathers no moss.
> There is always room at the top.
> Opportunity knocks but once.
> All things come to him who waits.

23. Secure a rating sheet or record blank from a commercial or industrial establishment, and note how it may be used to analyze both the job and the individual. Make out a sample rating of some person you know, and of an appropriate job. Be prepared to discuss the method and the results.

24. Prepare a brief but thought-stimulating list of questions for pupils of the intermediate (or high school) age.

25. Discuss the question whether the vocational counseling should be done by each "home-room" teacher for his pupils, or by one teacher for the whole school.

26. Prepare an outline for a year class in occupations for one of the following groups: fourth grade; fifth or sixth grade; seventh grade; eighth grade; first high school year; second or third high school year; high school seniors; boys or girls in any of these groups; a settlement class; an extension class for working boys or girls; a class for adults; a "vocational" school; a technical college.

27. Examine several possible textbooks available for life-career (occupations) classes. Select one for review, and discuss its advantages and limitations and how to use it.

28. In an avowedly vocational school could not the occupations class be dispensed with? Outline an adequate plan of guidance for a technical high school.

29. Discuss the relative importance of the various possible activities in vocational guidance. If one had to invest a limited amount of money and time in vocational guidance, with what activities should he begin? (This problem may best be related to a concrete situation.)

30. Outline a proposed course or group of courses, in the principles and practice of vocational guidance, for a normal school.

31. Outline a course for teachers already in service.

32. Write a brief statement to show the need for vocational guidance in your school or in an institution about which you know.

33. What are the *advantages* of the plan of having separate schools for continuation school work, prevocational work, and intermediate school work?

34. What ideas of your own can you contribute to the subject matter or the method of the life-career class?

35. Make a list of five interesting and valuable problems which might be investigated by individual teachers or by committees of teachers or pupils.

36. List in brief form a few practicable plans by which the school may coöperate with commerce and industry.

37. Can you make a general characterization of the articles on vocational guidance which you have read?

38. How do you intend to apply what you have learned to your work in the future?

INDEX OF NAMES

Abbott, Edith, 132, 294.
Alden, George I., 197, 292.
Alderman, L. R., 84, 292.
Alexander, Magnus W., 208, 292.
Allen, Frederick J., 31, 292.
Angell, James R., 292.
Ayres, Leonard P., 99, 132, 156, 179, 292, 293.

Bagley, W. C., 162, 293.
Barnard, J. L., 72, 293.
Bartlett, L. W., 229, 293.
Bate, William G., 72, 293.
Bawden, William T., 87, 293.
Bloomfield, Meyer, 2, 4, 6, 13, 21, 25, 41, 48, 50, 58, 78, 100, 106, 117, 123, 127, 130, 134, 138, 140, 141, 156, 158, 162, 179, 181, 183, 185, 186, 192, 209, 211, 216, 220, 226, 241, 242, 256, 262, 264, 274, 293, 294.
Blumenthal, Gustave A., 153, 294.
Bolton, Frederick E., 45, 294.
Bonser, Frederick G., 70, 87, 141, 294.
Brandeis, Louis, 202.
Breckenridge, Sophonisba, 116, 132, 294.
Breese, B. B., 123, 156, 159, 294.
Brewer, John M., 292, 294, 295.
Briggs, Thomas H., 60, 295.
Brooks, Stratton D., 32, 35.
Brown, Edith, 85, 302.
Bryner, Edna, 132, 296.
Burk, Frederic, 57, 295.
Burris, William T., 65, 295.

Cabot, Ella Lyman, 295.
Chamberlain, James F., 70, 295.
Claxton, Philander P., 81, 296.
Clopper, Edward N., 184, 296.
Cole, Percival R., 75, 296.
Collet, Miss, 296.
Colleton, Eleanor M., 180, 186, 296.
Coman, Katherine, 219, 296.

Davis, Anne S., 185, 187, 241, 296, 297.
Davis, Jesse B., 3, 47, 48, 67, 81, 84, 103, 106, 110, 132, 137, 141, 179, 184, 228, 256, 263, 297.
Davis, Philip, 4, 80, 184, 212, 297.
Dearborn, Walter F., 297.
Dearle, N. B., 132, 215, 261, 297.
Denison, Elsa, 84, 297.
Devine, Edward T., 9, 91, 113, 297.
Dewey, Evelyn, 297.
Dewey, John, 57, 65, 297.
Dodge, Harriet Hazel, 297.
Dopp, Katherine E., 59, 297.
Dunn, Arthur W., 72, 297.

Eaton, Jeanette, 91, 133, 298.
Eaton, Mary N., 67.
Eliot, Charles W., 2, 58, 274, 298.
Elliff, J. D., 270, 298.
Emerson, Harrington, 292, 298.

Feiss, Richard A., 160, 210, 211, 298.
Filene, A. Lincoln, 209, 298.
Filene, E. A., 120.
Fitch, John A., 132, 298.
Fleming, Ralph D., 132, 296.
Fletcher, Alfred P., 298.
Fullerton, Hugh S., 166, 298.

Gantt, H. L., 202, 298.
Garnett, J. C. Maxwell, 139, 298.
Gayler, G. W., 298.
Giddings, Franklin H., 152, 153, 299.
Gilbreth, Frank B., 202, 299.
Giles, F. W., 124, 132, 299.
Gillette, John M., 72, 91, 299.
Ginn, Susan B., 33, 164.
Goldmark, Josephine, 203, 299.
Goodwin, Frank P., 85, 299.
Gowin, Enoch B., 44, 133, 152, 299.
Greany, Ellen M., 2, 299.
Gruenberg, Benjamin C., 209, 299.

Hancock, Harris, 159, 299.
Haney, James Parton, 73, 299.
Hanus, Paul H., 59, 91, 99, 242, 299, 300.
Harper, Jane R., 243, 300.
Haynes, John, 72, 299.
Healy, William, 175, 300.
Heck, W. H., 162, 300.
Henderson, 91.
Hicks, Warren E., 194, 300.
Hill, David Spence, 133, 167, 300.
Hollingworth, H. L., 159, 300.
Hopkins, Ernest M., 209, 300.
Horton, D. W., 40, 108, 300.
Hoxie, Robert F., 202, 221, 260, 300.
Hyde, William DeWitt, 300.

Jacobs, Charles L., 44, 228, 300.
James, William, 159, 301.
Jennings, Irwin G., 270, 301.
Jevons, W. Stanley, 71, 301.
Johnson, George E., 57, 238, 301.
Judd, Charles H., 162, 301.

Kelley, Truman L., 171, 301.
Kelly, Roy Willmarth, 32, 292, 301.
Kennedy, Albert J., 182, 308.
Kitson, H. D., 127, 159, 171, 301.

Lapp, John A., 91, 301.
Laselle, Mary A., 301.
Lathrop, Julia C., 241, 301.
Leavitt, Frank M., 9, 49, 70, 85, 91, 124, 132, 302.
Lee, Joseph, 55, 302.
Lewis, Ervin E., 132.
Lord, Everett W., 183, 302.
Lough, James E., 157, 158, 302.
Lovejoy, Owen R., 302.
Lull, Herbert G., 302.
Lutz, R. R., 296.

MacCarthy, Jessie Howell, 246, 302.
MacKenzie, Henry, 21.
Maclaurin, R. C., 99.
Manly, Basil M., 215, 221, 262, 302.
Martin, Charles, 123, 302.
McCann, Mathew R., 91, 303.
Mead, A. D., 303.
Mead, George Herbert, 303.
Meumann, 147.
Miles, H. E., 89, 303.
Mitchell, John, 202, 221, 303.

Montgomery, Louise, 132.
Moore, Ernest C., 162, 227, 303.
Mote, Carl H., 91, 301.
Münsterberg, Hugo, 156, 303.
Myers, George E., 88, 133, 277, 303.

Nearing, Scott, 219, 304.

Odencrantz, Louise C., 6, 112, 304.
O'Leary, Iris P., 132, 296.
Overstreet, Harry, 304.

Parsons, Belle Ragnor, 59, 304.
Parsons, Frank, 20, 44, 85, 106, 132, 141, 162, 168, 171, 304.
Pascal, 21.
Peixotto, Sidney S., 82, 126.
Perkins, Frances, 132, 304.
Pillsbury, W. B., 162, 304.
Post, E. A., 236.
Pritchard, Myron T., 72, 274, 304.
Prosser, Charles A., 305.
Puffer, J. Adams, 153, 168, 305.
Purington, 172.

Rathmann, Carl G., 76, 305.
Redfield, William C., 201, 305.
Reed, Anna Y., 305.
Reilly, Philip J., 118.
Richards, Charles R., 130, 132, 139, 305.
Richards, Lysander S., 21, 305.
Righter, Leonard, 305.
Roman, Frederick W., 207, 305.

Schneider, Hermann, 10, 91, 92, 117, 132, 150, 151, 159, 197, 205, 220, 236, 249, 289, 291, 305.
Scott, Colin A., 238, 305.
Scott, Walter Dill, 161, 174, 306.
Sears, J. B., 10, 306.
Seashore, Carl Emile, 161, 306.
Segal, 147.
Shaw, Frank P., 132, 296.
Shaw, Pauline A., 23.
Shorey, Paul, 222, 306.
Snedden, David, 91, 197.
Spaulding, F. E., 123, 306.
Stevens, Bertha, 91, 132, 296, 298.
Stimson, R. W., 91, 139, 236, 306.

Talbert, E. L., 132.
Taylor, Frederick W., 200, 202, 306.

Thompson, Clarence B., 203, 306.
Thompson, Frank V., 34, 89, 91, 102, 114, 150, 160, 306.
Thorndike, Edward L., 126, 147, 162, 307.
Thum, William, 197, 198, 307.
Todd, Arthur J., 307.
Turkington, Grace, 274, 304.

Valentine, Robert G., 212.
Van Denburg, Joseph K., 179, 307.
Van Sickle, James H., 15, 307.
Veblen, Thorstein, 222, 307.

Ward, Lester F., 207, 307.
Weaver, E. W., 307.

Wells, Ralph G., 308.
Westgate, C. E., 136, 308.
Wheatley, William A., 44, 79, 132, 133, 152, 299, 308.
Wile, Ira S., 308.
Willits, Joseph H., 209, 216, 308.
Winch, W. H., 149, 308.
Wood, Arthur Evans, 217, 308.
Woods, Erville B., 77, 137, 207, 262, 308.
Woods, Robert A., 182, 308.
Woolley, Helen Thompson, 101, 108, 145, 148, 151, 159, 160, 180, 194, 308, 309.
Woolman, Mary Schenck, 132, 309.
Wright, F. W., 60, 309.

INDEX OF SUBJECTS

Activities of pupils, use of, in vocational guidance, 81, 232, 240, 263, 265, 275.
Advertisements, vocational, danger in, 5, 215.
Advisory committees, 50, 122, 123, 224, 229, 247, 249.
Age, for vocational choice, 125, 230, 234, 248; for compulsory schooling, 113, 286.
Agriculture, 48, 74, 263.
Aim, changes of, 2, 104, 123, 127.
Analysis, of personal qualities, 102–105, 144, 168.
Appointment agencies, 49.
Arithmetic, 69.
Association of pupils with each other, guidance through, 79.
Athletics, vocational value of, 80, 280.
Attempts to limit the field of vocational guidance, 5.

Beginnings in vocational guidance, 20–52.
Berkeley, 44.
Bicycle-balls test, 156.
Birmingham, England, voluntary committees in, 123, 224, 247.
Blind alley, 89, 148, 185, 196, 273, 277, 289.
Books on occupations, 269.
Boston Employment Managers' Association, 25, 120.
Boston Placement Bureau, 109, 114.
Boston plan for vocational guidance, 24–37, 61.
Boston Schools, Vocational-Guidance Department, 32, 33, 34, 65, 90, 124.
Boy Scouts, 80, 234.
Buffalo, vocational-guidance plan in, 43.

Bureau, Vocation, of Boston, 23, 24, 25, 31, 46, 241, 242; of Chicago, 42.
Bureau, of Education, U. S., 136, 244; of Occupations, Intercollegiate, 49; Vocation, of Boston, 23–25, 31, 46, 129, 241, 242; of Vocational Guidance, Harvard University, 32.

Camps, value for guidance, 47, 80, 237.
Career, opportunity for, 260, 262; child's interest in, 263.
Certificate, working, 175, 189, 252.
Character, 63, 64, 92–95, 164.
Chicago, plan for vocational guidance in, 42, 49.
Child labor, 178.
Choice of school, 2, 12, 273.
Choice of studies, 60, 231.
Choice, of vocations, 1, 246, 264; age for, 125, 230; alternative, 3, 127, 274; change of, 123; freedom, 10; investigation of, 266; tentative, 2, 274; time of, 11, 14, 125.
Cincinnati, 43, 101, 114.
Citizenship, relation to vocational guidance, 3.
Civics, guidance through, 70.
Civic Service House of Boston, 23, 125.
Civil Service Commission, U.S., 136.
Classification, of children, danger in, 11, 54, 150, 154, 155; of occupations, 137.
Cleveland, 91, 113, 133, 160.
Clubs, vocational-guidance work in, 48, 80–84, 275.
Colleges, courses in vocational guidance, 45, 281; placement in, 49; vocational guidance in, 236, 270.
Columbia Park Boys' Club, 82.

Commercial agencies for vocational counsel, dangers in, 172.

Commercial occupation, definition of, 289.

Commission on Industrial Relations, U.S., 216.

Competition, need for, 238.

Composition, written and oral, for guidance, 67, 267.

Continuation schools, 85, 88, 180, 187–189, 193, 195, 273, 277, 289; of Boston, 189, 257; of Wisconsin, 188.

Control, of schools by state, 229; of vocational guidance by other agencies, 144, 175.

Coöperation, for character training, 93; of children with each other, 105, 275; for choosing occupation, 246; for employment supervision, 253; for improving conditions of labor, 193, 254; for legislation, 255; for obtaining information, 245; for part-time work, 249; for placement, 250; for preparation for the vocation, 248; schools founded on, 193; for vocational guidance, 244–257, 284, 285.

Coöperative schooling, 289, see *Part-time plan.*

Coördinators, work of, 117, 250, 274; definition of, 289.

Correlation between mental and manual abilities, 148.

Counseling, at Boston Vocation Bureau, 26; erroneous methods of, 143–177; need for, 97; questions dealt with in, 99; requests for by mail, 28; special problems of, 122; through religious associations, 47.

Counselor, college courses for, 45, 281; equipment of, 141, 282; expert, 240; opportunities of, 214, 225, 236, 242, 278; teacher as, 141, 238.

Courses, for employment managers, 46, 121; for vocational counselors, 24, 26, 281; school, 77, 155, 283.

Dartmouth College, 46, 65, 121.

Dayton leaflets, 249.

DeKalb, Ill., plan for guidance, 43.

Democracy, in general high schools, 235; industrial, 255, 262, 284, 289.

Democratic management, 255, 262, 284, 289.

Dennison Manufacturing Company, 118, 217, 261.

Dexterity, 289.

Differentiation, in school studies and program, 59, 61, 285, 289.

Discharges from work, 119, 120, 187–192.

Discontent, constructive, uses of, 221.

Dramatization, 2, 55, 69, 75, 81, 238, 280.

Drawing, relation to vocational guidance, 68, 72.

Economics, guidance through, 70; necessity for, 71–72, 222.

Edinburgh, 41.

Education, desire for continued, 38, 54.

Educational guidance, 12, 14, 53, 265, 290.

Educational survey, 128.

Efficiency, 174, 200, 207.

Elementary schools, 58, 229, 267.

Elimination of pupils from school, 179–183, 239, 263.

Employee, problems of, 214.

Employer in relation to guidance, 110, 111, 116, 199–214, 246.

Employment, problems of, 199–226.

Employment agencies, 219, 286.

Employment manager, associations for, 25, 120; coöperation with school people, 121; courses for, 46; definition of, 290; extending the work of, 259; use of tests, 165; guidance through, 118.

Employment supervision, 114, 115, 117, 191, 194, 251, 253, 274, 284, 290.

Energizing jobs, 10.

England, plans used in, 122; see *Birmingham.*

English, use for guidance, 66, 67, 266, 267.

Environment, 153.

Examinations, 102; civil service, 136; physical, 210.

Experiments, on theory of types, 147.

Expert counselor, 240.

False methods of guidance, 4, 21, 143–177.

Farming, guidance in, 48, 263.

Field of vocational guidance, attempts to limit, 5.

Filene's Sons Company, Wm., 119, 210, 211, 225.

Flexibility in school organization, 62.

Follow-up work, 49, 114, 116, 129, 190, 290.

Foreign schools, guidance in, 50.

Foreigners in Boston, unguided, 36.

Forestry work, in summer camp, 47.

Formal discipline, theory of, 162.

Funds for vocational guidance, 286.

Gardening, 74.

Gary plan, 44, 65.

General shop, 233.

Geography, 70.

Germany, 277.

Glossary, 289–291.

Grand Rapids, 37–40, 39, 61, 67, 79, 103, 124.

Guidance, in association of students with each other, 79; educational, 12, 14, 53, 265, 290; through employment manager, 118; in entering upon work, 275; false methods of, 143–177; through governmental projects, 47; methods of, 263; through newspapers, 172; not for classifying children, 11; not merely practical or idealistic, 8; not prescriptive, 11; not a temporary act, 7; through other agencies, 46; through placement, 108; in preparing for a vocation, 272; problems in school, 15; in progress and promotion, 276; by religious organizations, 46; in surveying opportunities, 265.

Habits, formation of good, 157, 158.

Harvard University, 32, 233.

Health advice, 210.

Henry Street Settlement, 48, 192.

Heredity, 107, 108.

High Schools, 35, 60, 103, 235, 237, 270.

History, as a school study, 70; of vocational guidance, see *Beginnings*.

Homestead Commission of Massachusetts, 48.

Hood and Sons, H. P., 119.

"Idea-thinkers," 144.

Improvibility, measuring, 158, 284.

Indiana Survey, 128, 224.

Individual differences, 155.

Industrial education, 290; see *Vocational education*.

Industrial occupation, definition of, 290.

Industrial survey, 290.

Information about occupations, classifying, 137; collecting, 128–140, 245; uses of, 140, 244; for vocational choices, 266.

Intermediate school, 44, 59, 230, 234, 265, 290.

Investigations, in college courses, 281; of elimination from school, 239; in Iowa, 181; of labor turnover, 208; of types, 146; of vocation bureau of Boston, 25.

Janitor work, for pupils, 81.

Job, blind alley, 89, 185, 196; changing, 191, 209; clean-collar, 271; definition of, 290; mapping or writing specifications of, 118, 190, 260, 264, 277.

Junior high school, 44, 59, 230, 234, 265, 290.

Kindergarten, 55, 58, 229, 280.

Labor, improving conditions of, 254, 257; organizations, 220; problems of, 221.

Land, opportunity to use, 262.

Larkin Company, 211.

Leadership, 153, 275.

Leaving school, reasons for, 179.

Legislation, 198, 213, 225, 252, 255, 256, 285, 286.

Libraries, 48.

Life-career, definition of, 290.

Life-career class, 44, 77–79, 98, 139, 230, 231, 239, 246, 247, 248, 263, 266–270, 280, 281, 283, 285.
Life-career motive, 2, 9, 58.
London, messenger boys in, 261.
Long Beach, 44.
Los Angeles, 44, 59, 74, 225, 234.
Loyalties, use of, 94.

Manly Report, 215, 224.
Manual arts, 73, 74, 86, 232, 265.
Massachusetts, Institute of Technology, 122.
Mathematics, 73.
Mental antagonisms, 148.
Mental types, see *Types*.
Methods of teaching, 57.
Methods of vocational guidance, 54, 57, 263, 279.
Milwaukee, 43.
Minimum essentials of guidance, 36.
Minneapolis survey, 79, 86, 91, 128, 129, 179, 186, 197, 224, 245, 276.
Minnesota, University of, 45; school age in, 181.
Mishawaka, plan in, 40, 61, 116.
Morals and vocation, 3, 64, 174; see *Character*.
Motorman, test, 156.
"Motor-minded type," 146.
Museums, 76, 237, 268.
Music, 280.

National Association of Manufacturers, 89, 183, 188.
National Conference on Vocational Guidance, 24.
National Vocation Guidance Association, 44, 100.
Need for vocational guidance, 4, 20, 21, 50, 97.
Newton, plan in, 43.
New York City, 40.
Next steps in vocational guidance, 285.
Normal schools, classes in vocational guidance, 46, 279, 286.

Oakland, plan in, 44.
Occupational information, see *Information*.

Occupational survey, 291.
Occupations, books on, 269; Bureau of, 49; careers in, 260; center of interest, 2; choosing, 246; classes in, 50, 62, 77–79, 139, 230, 231, 239, 246, 247, 263, 265, 266, 283, 285; classification of, 137; constant, for girls and for boys, 195; definition of, 290; dramatization of, 55; industrial, 290; preparation for, 90; skilled, 291; teaching, 268.
Oral English, 67, 267.
Organization, of counselors, 286; of workers, 220; of schools and school studies, 58, 60, 62, 63, 65, 228, 283.
Over-guidance, 124, 170.

Parents, 122, 123, 195, 237, 240, 247, 249, 277, 283.
Parliamentary law, 69.
Part-time plans, 36, 117, 193, 197, 234, 239, 249, 257, 273, 291.
Philadelphia, 43.
Phrenology, 22, 155, 167.
Physical characteristics, 143, 154, 165.
Physical examinations, 210.
Placement, advantages of, 108; in business organizations, 49; co-operation in, 250–253; definition of, 291; disadvantages of, 109, 250, 275; efficiency of, 112; guidance through, 114, 108; only one step, 5; a problem for the counselor, 183, 194; in school departments, 48; unsatisfactory, 275.
Plans for vocational guidance, 20–52, 195.
Play, 2, 55, 80, 229, 237.
Portland Survey, 128.
Prevocational work, 14, 85, 193, 265.
Principal, work in guidance, 239, 240.
Problems, of vocational guidance, 1, 15, 17; of employment, 199–226.
Professions, 291.
Program for vocational guidance, 227–287; next steps in, 285.
Program of studies, 291; see *Studies*.
Project method, 234.
Promotion, in school and jobs, 260, 264; guidance in securing, 276.

Prophecy, to be avoided, 11, 124, 170.
Psychology, use of in guidance, 12, 22, 99, 143, 154, 156, 159.
Pseudo-guidance, 21–22, 143–177.

Readjustments, 264.
Records, cards for, 105, 161, 201, 239, 266, 270, 284.
Recreation League of San Francisco, 47.
Reed College, 45.
Richmond Survey, 79, 91, 128, 179, 183, 186, 224, 245, 277.
Rochester, 44, 249.

Salesmanship, 161, 174.
San Jose, 44.
Scholarships, 113, 196, 242.
Science, school study of, 72.
Scout activities, 80, 234.
Scientific management, 199–208, 260.
Scrap books, 267.
Self-analysis, 104, 168, 170.
Self-government among pupils, 81, 93, 234.
Service, ideal of, 94, 253.
Settlements, vocational guidance in, 48.
Signs of improvement in industry, 223.
Skilled occupation, 291.
Social perspective, necessity for, 144, 172, 175.
Social sciences, 70.
Somerville, 42.
Specialization, 92, 233, 235, 236.
Steadying employment, 208, 217.
Student activities, 81, 225, 240, 263, 265, 275.
Studies of school program, 66, 231.
Success, habit of, 62, 105, 164, 173; records of, 266.
Suggestion, misuse of, 174.
Summer camps, 80, 237.
Superintendent of schools, 243, 284.
Supervision of employment, see Employment supervision.
Surveys, educational, 128; industrial, 179, 290; occupational, 291; of occupational opportunities, 264, 265; vocational, 128–140, 291.

Taxation, 71, 262.
Teacher, work of, 141, 237, 254, 285.
Technical school, 291.
Telephone operator test, 156.
Tests, 14; limitations of, 143; overestimation of, 156; standardized, 161; use of, 99, 164.
"Thing-thinkers," 144.
Thrift, 63, 72, 274.
Trade school, 291.
Training for vocational guidance, 279, 284.
Transfer of mental qualities, 161, 162.
Trial courses, 233.
Troy, 44.
Turnover of employees, 208.
Types, of children, 54; of minds, 12, 87, 143–155; of schools needed, 228, 235; of thinking, 12.
Typewriter test, 156.

Unemployment, 215.

Versatility, need for, 233.
Vocation, definition of, 291.
Vocational counseling, 97–142.
Vocational education and training, 14, 15, 90, 92, 272, 291.
Vocational guidance, central bureau for, 241, 242; classes for study of, 45, 279, 291; definition of, 1, 228, 291; relation to other aims, 3; relation to other departments, 241; survey for, 291.
Vocational guidance through educational guidance, 53–96.
Vocational survey, 291; see Surveys.
"Vocophy," 21.

Wages, 186, 189, 201, 219.
Washington State College, 45.
Welfare work, 211.
Will power, misuse of, 172–175.
Wisconsin, 44, 89, 115, 187, 192.
Women's Educational and Industrial Union, Boston, 45, 50.
Worcester Polytechnic Institute, 45.
Work, betterment of, 193; as center of interest, 2; entering upon, 264, 275; guidance in obtaining, 214; how obtained by children, 182; kinds

of, open to young workers, 183; opportunities offered by, 187.

Work certificates, 175, 189, 252.

Worker, the young, 178–198; equipment of, 199; problems of, 214; rights of, 205, 220.

Working experience, during school time, 63; see *Part-time plan*.

Young Men's Christian Associations, 46.

Young Worker, see *Worker*.

Printed in the United States of America.

www.ingramcontent.com/pod-product-compliance
Lightning Source LLC
Chambersburg PA
CBHW031459270326
41930CB00006B/160